ON THE RUN

ON THE RUN

Al Browning

RUTLEDGE HILL PRESS
Nashville, Tennessee

Published in Nashville, Tennessee, by Rutledge Hill Press, Inc., 513 Third Avenue South, Nashville, Tennessee 37210

Typography by Bailey Typography, Inc., Nashville, Tennessee

Library of Congress Cataloging-in-Publication Data

Browning, Al.
   On the run / Al Browning.
     p. cm.
   ISBN 1-55853-007-X
   1. Allen, William Garrin. 2. Criminals—United States—Biography.
3. Fugitives from justice—United States—Biography. 4. Police murders—Tennessee—Nashville—Case studies. I. Title.
HV6245.A45B76   1989   89-24075
364.1′523′0976855—dc20   CIP

Printed in the United States of America
1 2 3 4 5 6 7—94 93 92 91 90 89

To Sissie

You never complained about
the time apart or the money we spent

In memory of

Ralph Canady,
one of many who have died
because of the disease of racism

Police officers everywhere,
who have died while performing
the most difficult, thankless job of all

ACKNOWLEDGEMENTS

I am grateful for the many people who helped me as I researched this story. I have benefited from the aid of many who went out of their way to be helpful, even when they were skeptical. To the following I want to express my heartfelt thanks:

For my mother and father, who taught me to support what is right and to challenge what is wrong; for Mark Maddox, who gave me a needed push; for three very special friends in Nashville (they know who they are); for the Federal Bureau of Investigation and agents like Bill Fallin, Joe Bonner, Joe O'Hara, Al Archer, and Rai Patton; for Metro Nashville Police Department officers who took the time to discuss a case they dislike, particularly Joe Casey and Robert Titsworth; for defense lawyer Sumter Camp, who opened his door and others for a stranger who became a friend; for defense lawyer Lionel Barrett and his office staff; for Ron Pitkin, an editor who asked the questions that slipped my mind; for newly found friends at the Davidson County Courthouse, who provided a tired writer space to catch his breath; for Jim Hayes, Jocko Potts, and Wayne Gillis, who saw a man in need of work and provided it; for the guidance that comes from prayer; for Billy Joe Linticum, who opened my eyes to the fact convicted men have loving hearts; for Ann Allen, whose faith is unshakable; and for all those other smiling faces encountered along the way, enough to make this thank you list a volume itself.

PROLOGUE

I was sports editor and sports columnist at the Knoxville *News-Sentinel* when I went to Brushy Mountain State Penitentiary in Petros, Tennessee, to gather material for a column or two. I planned to be locked up for two days—the last day of 1986 and the first in 1987—and do on-the-scene interviews with a couple of convicted murderers. We would watch football bowl games on television, then I would write about their lifestyles behind the wall.

The theme of my project was obvious: the dawning of a new year behind bars. Or so I thought.

As an assistant warden took me on a tour of the prison, we encountered a convict wearing blue jeans with Tennessee Department of Corrections written in white down both legs and a nice burgundy sweater over a pale blue shirt. When I first saw him, the convict was carrying several legal briefs and notepads. His face looked familiar.

"Who was that guy?" I asked after we got out of hearing range.

"That's Bill Allen."

"I've seen that face."

"Probably so," the assistant warden said. "He was on the FBI Most Wanted list twelve years, until he was captured last June in Jacksonville."

"That's it," I agreed. "He made the national news. Dan Rather. I remember. He was a model citizen and a convicted murderer."

"That's him."

"Well, I'd like to visit with him while I'm here."

"He'll be on Walk A with you for the next two days."

During dinner in the prison cafeteria, I sat and chatted with my cellmates, Billy Joe Linticum and Charles Tiller, in an effort to become better acquainted. As we conversed, I saw Allen seated by himself across the room. I asked Linticum and Tiller to excuse me so I could visit with him.

"Do you mind if I join you?" I asked upon approaching Allen.

"No, be my guest. Have a seat."

"I'm a sports editor from Knoxville. Al Browning."

"I know who you are," Allen answered with a smile. "The guys have been expecting you all day."

"And you're Bill Allen?"

"Right. How'd you know?"

"I recognized your face."

"So you know who I am?"

"Well, yeah, and I sort of feel like I'm sitting with an Untouchable from the other side."

Allen smiled, then broke into laughter. He extended a hand and said, "I'm glad to meet you."

I was surprised to discover such a congenial person. While we chatted for about ten minutes, Allen said the key to staying on the run so long was his ability to blend in with society, "to live a normal, productive life." I found myself liking him.

"I'd like to visit with you more while I'm here," I said when the guards indicated it was time to return to Walk A.

"For real," Allen replied. "Just stop by my cell whenever you get a chance."

That opportunity came the next morning when I excused myself from a conversation with Linticum and Tiller and strolled along Walk A. As I stood in front of Allen's cell, he waved at me, offered an infectious smile, and said, "Happy new year, Al."

"The same to you, Bill," I answered, while wondering how a man incarcerated for six months after spending more than twelve years free on escape from the Tennessee State Penitentiary in Nashville could be so friendly.

Eventually, Allen invited me to sit in his cell and asked if I wanted to see pictures of his family. I agreed. We visited for more than an hour, with much of the time spent in a lively discussion about his wife and two sons.

"You know, this is sort of a sad day," he said after proudly displaying pictures of Ann Allen, his wife, and Sekou Williams and Sulaiman Thomas, his sons who had carried fabricated names since their births. "I spent last night thinking about what we were doing last year, sitting at home in Houston and loving each other as a family."

I simply nodded. I had been warned about the conning ways of convicts and wondered if that was what was going on. But the more I listened to Allen, the more I became convinced I was in the presence of an unusual convict, a man with high intelligence and enviable manners.

"So do you have any children?" he asked. I told him no, that I was still waiting and hoping. "Well, man, they're wonderful. They're the greatest things in the world, my boys, plus my sweet lady." He talked with pride.

Bill Allen talked about happiness. He exhibited optimism. He was a positive individual in a very negative setting.

At some point, the conversation turned to civil rights for blacks, specifically how the struggle had been hard and progress had been slow. Allen, who is black, appeared somewhat surprised to learn that I had been reared in Alabama. He appeared more comfortable upon learning that I had fond memories of two high school classmates, Edward Sims and Marva Gillam, both black, whom I counted as friends as they made their ways in 1968 toward becoming the first of their race to graduate from T.R. Miller High School in Brewton, Alabama.

"Like Lynyrd Skynyrd said in their song," I said with a smile, "there are good people in Alabama. There are a multitude more of them, Bill, than there are bad ones. In fact, it's not a bad place for blacks to live now."

Bill Allen smiled. He said, "Yeah, and maybe it's better in most places now. I'll admit I've seen more harmony in recent years among blacks and whites."

Later Bill Allen went to the library to work on legal briefs. He had filed for executive clemency from his sentence on the grounds of exemplary behavior while on escape, an unusual statute, but a Tennessee law nonetheless. Supporting his case was a character reference petition that featured the signatures of more than three thousand people who had known him, including fellow workers and neighbors in Houston, where he had lived from the spring of 1977 until the spring of 1986.

I was impressed by that. I returned to my office and began reading filed articles about William Garrin Allen II. The more I read about the shooting in January 1968 that resulted in the death of two Nashville, Tennessee, police officers, the more I became interested in the life and times of my new acquaintance.

Likewise, I found every revelation about Bill Allen to be staggering. I talked to people who had known him and came to the same conclusions most of them had, that the forty-two-year-old man had experienced one bad night in his life. It was an opinion shared by Metropolitan Nashville Police Department Chief Joe Casey, who in 1968 was a patrolling police officer in North Nashville, where the shooting took place.

"From what I understand, he's from a fine family," Casey said about Allen when I interviewed him during the summer of 1987. "We didn't know anything about him until that night, which means he hadn't been in any trouble with the law."

"But he had an arrest for a sit-in demonstration, plus one for possession of marijuana," I replied.

"Yeah, but everybody was into that type thing back then," Casey said. "That's nothing."

I was surprised to hear the police chief—known nationally for his strong stance on crime—say that. It heightened my interest in discovering all I could about Bill Allen.

Bill Allen had been a gifted student at Haynes High School near his home in Old Hickory. He had starred on the football field as a running back and safety and had been elected team captain. He had done well at Tennessee State University for three years as a chemistry major, and he had worked peacefully for the civil rights cause. He had been influenced at age ten by a picture he saw in *Jet* magazine of a black civil rights demonstrator who had been slain in Mississippi. He had been arrested, but not charged, at age sixteen during a sit-in at a cafeteria in Nashville, and he had been arrested and charged with unlawful assembly, resisting arrest, and assault on a police officer during a sit-in in Cincinnati at age twenty-two. His one-year jail sentence had been revoked on appeal.

As a child, Bill Allen had lived with his grandparents on a farm so his mother and father could both work. He had been an industrious youngster. At age six he sold farm produce from a red wagon to motorists who passed his house; at age ten he cleared land while driving a bulldozer; and at age twelve he shined shoes for country music stars in Nashville.

People who had known Allen contended his life had been laudable, if not enviable, until one fateful evening. Then it became unraveled, so to speak, because of an unsightly incident in North Nashville.

There had been five young men in the white 1967 Plymouth two police officers stopped that January 16 night: Bill Allen, Charles Lee Herron, Ralph Canady, Steve Parker, and John Alexander, all between twenty-two and thirty years old. Supposedly, only two people other than the five black men and the two police officers had gotten glimpses of what had happened on Fourteenth Avenue, a dead end road, as gunfire erupted. They were Johnny Brown and Larry Wade, black high school students who in 1968 testified in court that they had seen more than they actually did. Almost two decades later, in November 1987, Brown contended in a signed affidavit that the two youths had been coaxed into offering such testimony through threats made by Nashville police officers. Wade disputed that claim, but his fresh account of the shooting differed drastically from his previous testimony.

Obviously, the police officers were dead when jurors were seated on Thanksgiving Day 1968 for the murder trial of Allen, Canady, and Parker. Officer Pete Johnson had been declared dead on arrival at Baptist Hospital. Officer Wayne Thomasson had died sixty-one days later, on March 17, having developed an infection after appearing to be safe from complications. Parker had run from the scene at the first sound of gunfire, as had Charles Lee Herron and John Alexander, which left Bill Allen and Canady as the only people alive who knew for sure what had transpired that Tuesday night.

That is, unless Thomasson had told police officers and/or interrogators for Davidson County district attorney Thomas Shriver what had taken place when he was strong enough to think clearly and to talk fluently. It had been reported at least three times in the Nashville *Tennessean* that both police officers had fired their revolvers that night, with two reports having Thomasson as the source of the information. Later that information had been denied publicly time and again by police officers, with some making such disclaimers on the witness stand.

Then in November 1987, as I continued to probe, Captain Tom Cathey, a Nashville police officer who had been a homicide detective in 1968, told me he had interviewed Thomasson at General Hospital three days after the shooting incident. "Yes," said the seriously wounded police officer, who was alert enough that afternoon to talk about bowling, "I got off four rounds."

Nobody seemed to know what happened to the Smith and Wesson 38 Special revolvers the police officers had with them. In November 1987 it was learned they are encased at the Nashville Police Academy, as is the norm with weapons used by slain police officers, so incoming rookies can see proof of the hazards associated with the profession. But the guns seem to have been lost in the shuffle just after the shooting incident. Also, several other related questions about the revolvers remained unanswered.

I read the court transcript, which consisted of more than three thousand pages, and found in the testimony presented to an all-white jury an absence of conclusive evidence about who shot the police officers with a 30-30 rifle and, perhaps, a 22-caliber rifle. That heightened my interest in the case because Allen, Canady, and Parker had received ninety-nine-year sentences for the death of Thomasson.

I found it interesting that the defendants had been tried for the death of a white police officer, when Johnson, a black police officer, had died sixty-one days earlier. Also, Canady and Parker had been allowed to remain free on five-thousand-dollar bond until the white officer, Thomasson, died, at which time they were locked up without bail.

I found it intriguing that the district attorney had advanced an ambush theory in court. He claimed Johnson was killed with premeditation just after he stopped the Plymouth because he thought it was occupied by men who had been involved in the cashing of stolen money orders, while Thomasson was killed by an angry mob, in essence, when he drove onto the scene a minute or two later to assist a fellow police officer. Police department radio transcripts, as well as interviews with Casey and other police officers, indicated the police officers had arrived on the scene simultaneously. Court testimony pointed out that the Plymouth had been stopped under a large security light on the side of a warehouse, when there were darker spots further along the road. Also, all of the five men, except Herron, were attired in dress pants, dress shirts, blazers, and dress shoes, hardly the type clothing a person would wear if he was aware he would need to flee.

I found it perplexing that Bill Allen had been indicted for murder in the death of Johnson more than nineteen years after the shooting, after he had spent six years in custody, had escaped from the Tennessee State Penitentiary, had been recaptured in Jacksonville, Florida, and had filed for executive clemency, a plea that was routinely rejected by a clemency board administered by outgoing Tennessee governor Lamar Alexander. By the end of July 1987 some interesting arrests had been made and some stunning, if not grossly inequitable, sentences had been meted out. John Alexander had been caught in 1971 and sentenced to two years after voluntary manslaughter pleas. Charles Lee Herron had been caught in 1986 and sentenced to two years after voluntary manslaughter pleas, then indicted for interstate flight. Canady had been caught on escape in 1986 and was found hanging in a Maryland jail cell before his extradition to Tennessee. Parker had been caught on escape in 1987, extradited to Tennessee, and indicted for murder in the death of Johnson.

Three men had received what amounted to life sentences in 1968; two men had received relative handslaps; two of the men previously sentenced were awaiting another trial for first-degree murder.

So I digested a lot of conjecture about what happened on that winter night in 1968—from the profoundly ruthless to the seemingly accidental—and stayed in contact with Bill Allen as he awaited the result of appeals filed to avoid another murder trial. As time passed, we conversed more openly, to the extent the convict eventually told me exactly what transpired on the dead-end road the evening the police officers were killed.

"I'll check that out and judge it beside the other theories," I said to myself after a staggering revelation had been given to me. I did. I discovered the theory advanced by Bill Allen, who admitted being the only person who shot the police officers that night, but with provocation, was more supported by the evidence than the many other propositions that had been offered.

In June 1988, at the FBI office in Memphis, Tennessee, I learned that special agent Joe Bonner had become suspicious of the Nashville police department a long time before me. In charge of the manhunt involving Allen, Parker, Herron, and Canady from 1977 until 1983, when the case was transferred for a brief time to the Nashville office, he quickly noticed several incongruous things about the reports provided him by law enforcement personnel.

"After only a brief period on the case, it became obvious to me that we had been sold a bill of goods by the folks in Nashville," Bonner said. "That's obvious. I got into the case and discovered it had been hyped up by both the police department and the district attorney's office.

"Black militants. Bullshit. Where did that come from? Where's the evidence of that?

"But while I found many of the things coming out of Nashville to be interesting, it wasn't the role of the FBI to question what local authorities said or did in such cases. There's a law on the books now that gives us investigative jurisdiction in cases involving the death of a police officer. At that time, it was our responsibility to find the fugitives and return them to Tennessee."

Bonner was equally unimpressed with the argument that the convicts had ambushed the police officers. "It's just a perception, nothing more, but my initial reaction was that those were rifles a country boy would have to go hunting rabbits and deer," he said in June 1988. "I'm certain it wasn't unusual for them to have rifles with them. I can take you out right now in Memphis, Tennessee, turn on the siren and stop a car, and find guns of that nature in the trunk or back seat. It's not an unusual thing for people to have guns or rifles in their cars. These weren't the type weapons somebody would rob a store with. Too large. Not the type they would use to defend themselves. They're either for pawning or hunting."

On one visit at the Tennessee State Penitentiary, I was accompanied by Ann Allen, Sekou Williams, and Sulaiman Thomas. An outsider with the family, I listened a lot. I heard how the oldest son was having trouble at school with a bully who abused him almost daily. I heard the father tell the son, "Ku, remember what we've always told you. Love people. Don't fight them."

I left the prison that day with tears in my eyes. I thought to myself: *I'm not sure about everything that happened when those police officers were killed. I don't guess anybody can be. But I'm sure Bill Allen isn't the type person who needs to be in prison the remainder of his life. Instead, he should be allowed to be productive. He's a husband and a father who should be living with his wife and children. As for Parker, well, he didn't commit a criminal act. The criminal justice system is at fault this time."*

As I drove home, I thought more about the amazing story that featured a convicted murderer who used his time on escape to get married, to father two sons, to become a businessman on the brink of unbelievable success, and to become a respected member of a free society. In summary, one question rang clearly in my head: *God, how can this be?*

It was a tragedy no matter how I looked at it. I thought about the dead police officers, about the three children Thomasson had left behind, and how his widow had committed suicide about a year after the trial in 1968. I saw several pictures taken of him just after his death and became nauseated by the sight of a body riddled by gunfire and sliced by the knives of surgeons.

I thought about the turbulent 1960s. I wondered if Bill Allen and his friends had been too forceful while advancing the cause of civil rights. I considered the tensions that existed between blacks and police officers. I listened attentively to Metro Nashville police officer Bob Hill, a black captain, who in November 1987 told me Bill Allen and the other four black men had been "totally radical" while advancing the civil rights cause, that they frequently read controversial printed material about it. Also, he told me Thomasson had been a good man who lacked any bad feelings about blacks.

I wondered if I had been conned.

So I kept asking questions and prayed for guidance.

Frankly, after eleven months of investigating the incident, I realized I was getting too emotional about it. I'd turn one way, then I'd turn the other. I'd get angry at society for what it did to five men, then I'd think about the two who were killed and become nauseous. Then I'd realize that all seven men have been victims of their times.

It wasn't until I met Robert Titsworth, a Metro Nashville Police Department major—the former commanding officer for Johnson and Thomasson—that I began to feel more comfortable with the position taking form in my mind. I encountered this honest man, age 62, on Pearl Harbor Day 1987, when in his office I asked him what he remembered.

It wasn't so much what Titsworth recalled about the incident that struck me, but the questions he asked without prompting, as well as his willingness to admit how much his views of blacks had changed during the last twenty years. "I could've lined up all five of them and shot them that night, could've killed them on the spot, and considered it doing my duty," he said. "But that's not the case now. I'm sort of ashamed to admit I ever felt that way. I've mellowed. We all have."

Titsworth was clinging to a softened version of the one advanced by his fellow police officers, that Johnson and Thomasson were caught by surprise when they were shot by black men who were guilty of cashing stolen money orders. He gave several reasons why those men could have been frightened, said he could understand why they were armed, and presented numerous questions in his mind that challenged the validity of court testimony presented by the prosecution in November and December 1968.

"We warned our police officers every day at roll call to beware of armed people, blacks and whites," Titsworth said. "It was a tense period all over Nashville. And as I recall, we'd had a racial incident on the Tennessee State campus that caused a lot of unrest not more than two weeks before the night of the shooting. I'm not sure the public ever knew much about it; but it added a lot to the mistrust that existed between the campus community, really a large sector of the black community, and the police department. It had everybody on edge, as I recall.

"Police officers were still carrying the riot gear we had used the summer before. So, no, I wasn't surprised to hear that those five black men were armed with loaded weapons."

As for Johnson and Thomasson trailing the Plymouth occupied by the five young men that night, Titsworth said, "The light-colored car [the Plymouth] was just there. It appeared out of nowhere, and they followed it. They were watching another car, a Ford. I knew that much because I had heard it on the radio.

"I've heard there was supposed to have been a high-speed chase that night. But I don't see how there could've been because of a dip in the road on Herman Street. It isn't there now, but it used to be, and a car going real fast would've bounced out of control, especially with the weather like it was, with snow and ice on the streets. I'm not saying Wayne and Pete didn't think those men were trying to get away from them. I'm just saying nobody could've been going real fast."

Titsworth, who was driving police cruiser number 10 that night, arrived quickly on the scene of the shooting. He had been at a foundry "about ten blocks away" answering a burglary alarm. "I noticed two wounded officers, Wayne and Pete, and attempted to give them medical aid," he said. "I remember steam rising from their blood because it was so cold."

Titsworth remembers handling the revolver carried by Johnson that night. "But I can't tell you if it was fired," he said, "because the homicide division unloaded it and was supposed to file the report on that." He said he recalled digesting information that both police officers fired their revolvers. But he added, "Maybe I just read it in the newspaper, too."

Titsworth had other questions:

"Why did those men park that Plymouth right under that big [security] light? It was bright down there.

"Did Officer Johnson get shot as he approached the Plymouth? Did they shoot Wayne [Thomasson] as soon as he opened his door? I remember seeing a large puddle of his blood several feet to the left of his car. It led me to believe he was away from his car, maybe going to assist Officer Johnson. Or maybe he was approaching the Plymouth. He might've left his car and then crawled back to it.

"Why didn't Pete and Wayne use shotguns instead of revolvers? A police officer is trained to exit his car with a shotgun if he encounters an armed suspect, especially multiple suspects. It's easier to hit somebody with a shotgun than it is with a pistol. But their shotguns remained in the racks. That leads me to believe it was an instantaneous thing."

In conclusion, Titsworth said, "I don't guess we'll ever really know everything that happened."

He was correct, for sure, and I wondered if perhaps he knew a lot more than he was willing to tell me. After all, it was unusual that numerous police officers had testified for the prosecution during the trial in 1968, while Titsworth was not summoned to the witness stand although he was the commanding officer for Johnson and Thomasson and had been among the first police officers to arrive at the scene of the shooting. He had taken a far-too-passive role in the investigation because he was forced to, I thought.

There were numerous questions to be asked. So I gathered the facts available and came to a conclusion that is advanced on the following pages, replete with contrary opinions offered by others.

From what I have heard, both Thomasson and Johnson were good police officers. But neither of them used good judgment that fateful night. To the contrary, they were good law enforcement representatives acting foolishly. They forced frightened men into frantic behavior by backing them into a corner and set off an explosion that could have been avoided had they not been so aggressive.

From what I have learned, as well as what I have witnessed up close, Bill Allen and his companions on that dreadful night were not the hardened criminals the majority of citizenry in Nashville think they were. Yes, they were insistent when it came to equal rights for people of all races. What is at issue is that in what they perceived to be the defense of their lives three had the good sense to run, one found cover, and one fought.

It could have been avoided.

The officers did not have a solid reason for stopping the Plymouth that night. Nashville police said the five black men inside it were wanted for cashing fraudulent money orders, but there are no records to support that statement. Instead, there is reason to believe that Johnson, who was estranged from his wife, pursued the automobile because he thought another man, who had secured the affections of a coed with whom he had found romantic favor, was in it.

"The police officers stopped a car they thought was being used for the commission of a crime," Chancellor Robert Brandt said in March 1988, more than twenty years after he, as a twenty-seven-year-old assistant district attorney, began putting together the legal case against three defendants. "There's nothing wrong with that."

I reminded Brandt that a pick-up order was not issued for the Plymouth, that there had been no mention of the automobile until Johnson chose to pursue it. "Yeah," he said in agreement.

It was suggested to Brandt that neither Johnson nor Thomasson knew who was occupying the Plymouth. "Yeah," he agreed.

"Probable cause wasn't used much back then. Things are a lot different in the 1980s than they were in the 1960s."

Still, Brandt pointed toward blank money orders and an ink blotter found in the trunk of the Plymouth that night as proof the five black men were involved in the cashing of fraudulent money orders. "What were they, stamp collectors?"

It was suggested to Brandt that, at most, only two of the five men were involved in cashing fraudulent money orders, as were numerous others who frequented dwellings in North Nashville, and that at least three of them had not known of the scheme. "That might be true in the case of Alexander," he said. "He was just along for the ride that night, literally hitching a ride to Cincinnati."

However, while testifying in the interstate flight trial for Herron during the summer of 1987, Alexander admitted that he and Canady had cashed fraudulent money orders, but that he had no knowledge of Allen, Parker, and Herron doing so. When told that, Brandt said, "It was a poorly investigated case. While putting together the evidence, I never could determine who from the police department was in charge. If there was any organization, I didn't see it."

Still, Brandt stuck with the theory advanced by the prosecution in the case, although he admitted he never thought the police officers were ambushed. "They drove to the end of a dark street," he said, choosing to overlook the fact the Plymouth could have been driven much farther along Fourteenth Avenue to a darker spot. "They didn't know where they were going. They were going to kill the cops or be killed. So they killed them."

Brandt said it does not matter if the police officers fired their revolvers that night, not even if one of them shot first. "Show me the evidence if you think either of them did," he said.

The chancellor was told that a report filed by Tom Cathey, who had interviewed Thomasson three days after the shooting, stated that the officer fired his gun four times, a fact that was never brought to light during the trial. It was suggested to him that such a disclosure would be important in a capital case in which a jury determines whether defendants live or die, especially if that fact might have caused jurors not to give a death sentence. "That's hearsay evidence," Brandt replied. "Besides, if I knew it and forgot it at the time, it doesn't matter. It's immaterial. It wasn't significant. It'd be wrong for a district attorney to present a known false fact to a jury, but if it's not relevant—not admissible in court—as a lawyer I'm not gonna pay attention to it."

Cathey agreed with that logic in March 1987. It was suggested to him that almost everybody involved with the investigation knew the police officers fired their guns, while such information was never revealed by the district attorney or defense lawyers in court. "Why hell, yes," he said. "But it doesn't make any difference one way or the other. I would have been in hopes that they got off all twelve rounds and reloaded if necessary." The police department captain was told there is a theory, supported by a lot of evidence, that indicates Thomasson fired the first shot that night. "He could very well have shot first," he said. "But Wayne was shot to pieces. I think court testimony indicated he was shot five or six times."

Yes.

But the ballistics report filed by police department homicide detective Bill Nichols indicates otherwise. He discovered two empty 30-30 casings and one empty 22-caliber casing at the scene of the shooting. Four days later, he took possession of a 30-30 rifle and a 22-caliber rifle, the weapons used, and noted an abundance of live rounds in them. After the rifles were fired during testing, the 30-30 twice and the 22-caliber once, the numbers did not add up properly in support of the theory that either police officer was shot as many times as the prosecution said.

"I never did think Wayne was shot more than twice," Cathey said after hearing this.

The discrepancy of whether or not the officers fired their guns remained intact when Thomasson died at 4:09 P.M. on March 17, 1968. The debate was ended then because of hearsay evidence laws, meaning that defense lawyers would not be able to ask Cathey in court what Thomasson said during their interview.

It seems inexcusable, however, that nobody in the police department was able to tell me the location of the police officers' revolvers when I asked about them.

"Maybe they gave them to their families," answered John Hollins, an assistant district attorney who ranked as the most powerful figure in the first-degree murder trial for Allen, Parker, and Canady, in 1968. He was speaking in his law office in Nashville during the summer of 1987.

That was not the case, unless they had them for a short time, because the revolvers ultimately were encased in the Nashville Police Academy.

"Please check and see how many of the shells were spent in the revolvers officers Thomasson and Johnson used," detective Bill Nichols asked by telephone in November of 1987. There was a pause, then Nichols said, "OK. I see," a perplexed expression on his face. "Thank you."

Normally, said Nichols, who filed the ballistics report after the shooting, the hulls from a revolver used by a slain police officer are encased with the weapon, "which makes it easy to determine how many rounds were spent. Apparently they didn't do it in this case."

With that revelation comes more evidence that members of the Metropolitan Nashville Police Department fabricated much of its case against the five black men stopped that night on a dead-end avenue. Likewise, a statement made by Titsworth in 1988 indicates that something was wrong with the way the evidence against the suspects was gathered and arranged for court purposes. During our second interview, he said, "You're asking all the right questions about this case."

During the fall of 1987, after conducting his hard-nosed plea bargain negotiations with Parker, Shriver was appointed to a judgeship, meaning new district attorney Torry Johnson would handle the case.

Torry Johnson continued to deal with Parker, who continued to reject a voluntary manslaughter plea because he wanted to prove once and for all that he was innocent of all wrongdoing. Nobody was offering Bill Allen any deals, basically because Shriver was convinced he was "the obvious trigger man." That was fine with Allen because he wanted to go back to trial—even if it meant doing so alone—to tell what had happened in 1968.

All told, it was a terrible thing that happened in January 1968, obviously, and not just because two men died and five men had their lives turned upside down. It was a painful happening that points out how tragic life can become, or can end, when cool heads do not prevail and errors in judgment are made by individuals armed with guns.

FBI Agent Bonner put it more emphatically: "The entire thing got out of hand, from the stopping of the car all the way to the building of the case. We call it a 'goat-rope,' the building of a case when nobody knows what happened. It was just a screw-up, that's all."

The tragedy that presented itself on a cold night in North Nashville has reared its ugly head for more than twenty-one years, from the time of the death of two police officers, through the years as a once-perplexed FBI ended a compelling manhunt by apprehending four fugitives, and until Bill Allen returned to a courtroom to explain what really happened during the shooting.

I had concluded by then that the jury should side with him, leading to much-deserved executive clemency. Others disagreed.

And a statement Cathey made in November 1987 came to mind: "It is better to be tried by twelve than carried by six."

The answers to my questions were slow to come, but they eventually pointed out how emotions can sometimes overrule the quest for justice, how disregard for the truth can create hell on earth for the victims of lies, and, most of all, how mistrust can lead good men to a level of deceit that destroys others.

Those answers, which are the result of more than two and one-half years of research and study, are included in this book. Included is the legal maneuvering that took place over two decades, what transpired just before, during, and after the shooting, the bold escape from prison, the lengthy period in flight from the FBI, the apprehensions after eighteen, thirteen, twelve, and twelve years on the run, the social trends that prompted such a tale of woe, and, ultimately, a resolution that triggered the emotions of a city with a long memory.

ON
THE
RUN

"There is no hunting like the hunting of man, and those who have hunted armed men long enough and like it, never care for anything else thereafter."

—Ernest Hemingway

ONE

It was a miserable night, more suited for sitting in front of a roaring fireplace than for driving on icy city streets.

The air was cold and dismal, and the relentless sleet mixed with fog so thick that Nashville looked like a giant prop for a 1950s black-and-white science-fiction movie. The white 1967 Plymouth moved gingerly over ice-covered Hermosa Street, its windshield frosted over and the driver peering anxiously through a small crack created by rolling down the iced left window.

It was 9:38 P.M., Tuesday, January 16, 1968.

Inside the car, however, the atmosphere was festive. After much delay, the five young men were finally on their way. Four of them were returning home to Cincinnati, the fifth, William Allen, to his parents' house in nearby Old Hickory. Two of the four from Ohio had been in Nashville several months, while the other two had arrived five days earlier for a weekend of good times with friends and, for Steve Parker, a bit of romance.

"Say, Bitsey, my man," Ralph Canady teased, "I guess you're in love, man."

"Drop dead, Slim," Parker retorted with some disdain. "You're dreaming if you think you'll ever know."

From his position in the right rear seat, Canady chuckled, then extended his hand to John Alexander seated just to his left. Each gave the other a soulful slap.

"Right on, Slim," said Alexander.

"What's this hitting my foot?" Parker asked as he took a hand from the steering wheel and reached toward the floorboard.

"It's a gun, man," said Allen. "A new 30-30."

"Well, move it, Doc. I can't drive with it there."

3

From his position in the front passenger seat, Bill Allen reached for the rifle, pulled it toward himself, and stuck it under the front seat. The barrel pointed out from between his legs. The butt extended toward Canady in the back seat.

"So this must be the 22?" Alexander inquired while looking at the rifle stretched across the back floorboard.

"That's it," said Allen.

As they neared a wooded area where Hermosa dead ended and turned toward Herman Street, a car with its bright lights shining suddenly darted at them. Squinting at the sudden glare through the iced-over window, Parker turned sharply to the right, almost spinning the Plymouth out of control.

"Damn good move, Bitsey," Allen laughed. "He almost put us in the ditch over here."

"Yeah, but who was it?" Parker asked.

"Probably a drunk, Blood. Tuesday night is as good as any for a drunk."

Parker turned right onto Eighteenth Avenue for a short way, then left onto Herman, where project apartments were on the right and left sides. As they approached Fourteenth Avenue, he noticed a flashing red light reflecting on the brick buildings and snow-covered ground and trees in front of them. "We're being stopped. What'd I do to cause this?"

In the back seat, Canady turned around, wiped the fog from the rear window, and saw one patrol car in the left lane obviously intending to pass them. Another was less than a block behind them, its red lights also flashing.

"He's on your ass, Bitsey, and he's coming 'round," he said in a panicky voice. "There's two of them, man. Another coming up behind us."

"Be cool," said Charles Lee Herron from the back left seat. "We haven't done anything. They're probably gonna warn us about driving in this weather."

"Maybe they want us to get out of the way," Parker said. He pulled to the extreme right side of the street.

Parker gazed through the slightly opened window at the officer on his left. He had pulled to a position partially in front of Parker, with his right fender preventing forward motion. The officer, Pete Johnson, motioned him to turn right and proceed down Fourteenth Avenue.

Herron wiped the fog off the rear side window, allowing all three men in the back seat to see the officer.

"Is it Car 16?" Canaday asked.

"I didn't catch it," Parker answered. "But I'm going to do whatever he says."

Turning onto Fourteenth Avenue, which headed slightly downhill at this point, Parker traveled alongside the Phillips and Buttorff warehouse that stretched some seventy-five yards on the left. "Why the hell does he want us down here?" Parker complained. "I don't like it." He stopped the car under a large security light at a level spot near the end of the warehouse.

Both police cruisers followed, slipping and sliding en route.

"Be cool, Blood," Herron cautioned. "Like I said, man, it's nothing to be alarmed about."

"Well, I'm going to talk to them," Parker said as he opened the left door and stepped onto the icy street. "It's my place to meet them back there."

From the back seat, Canady surveyed Officer Johnson, who was out of his car, his revolver in hand. "Watch out," he warned. "The cop's got his gun out."

By now Parker had taken a couple of steps in Officer Johnson's direction. "Stop it right there!" he screamed. "And get your hands up. On top of the car with 'em."

Unable to see because of the bright lights, Parker squinted toward the glare, saw the outline of a man, and put his hands on top of the car, leaning forward on the left rear door.

As Johnson made his next command, the second policeman, Officer Wayne Thomasson, was getting out of his police cruiser. "Out of the car, all you boys!"

"Let's do what he says," Herron said as he attempted to open the left rear door, hitting Parker with it.

"You, the driver, against the wall," Johnson commanded after seeing that Parker was blocking Herron's exit.

As Parker hurried toward the warehouse, slipping at every step, the remaining three doors were opened. Herron walked toward the wall. Behind him, Alexander crouched with his right hand on Herron's back.

Suddenly Alexander muttered, "Go, Lee. Haul ass," and pushed Herron, who almost fell to the ground. Both darted toward the corner of the warehouse, about six feet away.

In rapid succession, Officer Thomasson fired two shots at Herron and Alexander, who were turning the corner and running toward the railroad tracks as the trigger was pulled.

As the guns fired, Parker ran, too, at first slipping on the ice. As he turned toward darkness, two more shots whistled past him. "Damn," he thought. "What the hell is going on?"

Johnson had fired twice.

Meanwhile, Canady had reached the right rear bumper of the Plymouth when Officer Thomasson opened fire, igniting the madness. Without a word, Canady dived to the pavement between the Plymouth and the patrol car. He stayed there on his stomach, silent and not moving, with his face pressed against the snow and ice.

He was in that position when Johnson fired.

Allen had stood still, frozen by the sight of the officers' drawn weapons. When he saw Canady tumble forward, he began screaming, thinking his friend had been hit. "Dammit, no! Don't shoot him!"

So when Johnson fired at the fleeing Parker, Allen dived toward the open door and reached into the Plymouth, where he grabbed the 30-30 rifle. Looking up with the gun in hand, the terrified Allen saw the obviously shaken Thomasson's revolver pointed at him.

Although Thomasson got off two rounds, he was a second late. Allen had fired first, and his bullet hit the door frame, sending fragments of lead and steel tearing through Thomasson's upper body, from upper abdomen to groin.

By this time Officer Johnson was in a panicked state. He shot twice more over the top of the Plymouth, wildly, but he was firing at a small target and Allen had ducked his head to avoid being hit.

Allen also was in total panic. His body trembling in fear, he jumped up, wheeled to his right, hastily aimed the 30-30 at Johnson, and pulled the trigger. Johnson was hit squarely in the chest and fell to the ground, landing flat on his back. He was dead almost instantly.

Officer Thomasson was attempting to find cover behind the door of his cruiser. As Allen looked his way just after shooting Johnson, he saw movement from the ground near Thomasson's door and fired again. His emotions had taken total control of his mind.

"Shit!" he screamed. "Shit! Shit! Shit!"

Then after perhaps ten seconds of horror, the street was silent, except for the voice of the woman dispatcher trying to make contact with Johnson: "16. Car 16. Car 16. 1–6."

Johnson and Thomasson remained still, but Canady was crawling on his belly like a snake back to the open right rear door he had exited. Despite feeling relief at seeing Canady, Allen reacted as if he was seeing a ghost. "Damn, Slim," Allen screamed, his eyes wide and cold sweat rolling down his face. "I thought you were dead. What the hell have we done?"

Allen paused as Canady pulled himself from the ground, then told his friend, "Get the other gun, and let's get the hell out of here."

As the silent Canady grabbed the 22, pulling it quickly from the back floorboard, the rifle went off in his hands. He dropped it as the bullet flew skyward, then picked it up, saw Allen running from the scene, and gave chase.

Their footsteps broke prints in the snow on the darkened night as the dispatcher tried again. "Car 16?"

Thomasson, slumped beside his car, had his back turned toward them as he clutched the transmitter in his left hand.

"Car 45. They shot us all to pieces down here."

TWO

Although the weather outside was a chilly seventeen degrees, inside the apartment it was warm. The gas heater radiated its comforting heat as three friends—Bill Allen, Ralph Canady, and Charles Lee Herron—sat in the kitchen talking about sports.

The partment at 1910 Hermosa Street, which Allen leased with Ernest Cowan, was known as a gathering place for Tennessee State University and Fisk University students, as well as acquaintances who arrived in Nashville for visits. The setting epitomized the 1960s; an open door policy prevailed, and almost any young man or woman who needed a place to stay could find room on the floor.

The same could be said about the apartment leased by Rick Hughes and William Bostic at 1906 Hermosa Street. It, too, was known as a haven for friends and strangers alike.

Allen, Herron, and Canady were not surprised when the back door opened and seven friends who had been visiting their friend Herbert Munford at nearby Hubbard Hospital walked in from the cold, discarded coats sprinkled with sleet and snow, and proceeded to the living room where a rhythm and blues record was playing on an old phonograph.

A biting breeze ripped through the kitchen again a few minutes later when John Alexander, who had picked up some fried chicken at a nearby fast food restaurant, opened the door and stepped inside.

"Are we still rolling?" he asked.

"For real," answered Herron. The clock indicated it was 8:20 P.M.

"Yeah, man. Cincinnati at last," said Canady.

8

It had been a glorious weekend, an almost continuous series of parties, for some even hot romance in the still of winter. All of them, however, were feeling a little defeated. Not even the jive offered by the talkative Canady, the most hip among them, or the banter about baseball and football could diminish the tensions that existed between blacks and police officers in a neighborhood characterized by project apartments.

Allen, Canady, and Herron had been working for two years registering black voters in Ohio and Tennessee for the 1968 presidential election. Herron, age thirty, was the most influential among them; he was an Air Force veteran with strong allegiance to the Student Non-Violent Coordinating Committee, whose literature he collected. But Allen, age twenty-two, an honor student getting ready for his senior year at Tennessee State, and Canady, age twenty-six, a Bowling Green University graduate who had done postgraduate work, also had been resolute when working for civil rights.

Allen, who was from Old Hickory, near Nashville, had flown home the previous Thursday from Newark, New Jersey, where he had been visting Jackie Wade. He had met her in Cincinnati during the summer of 1967 when he worked as a youth counselor and in the quality control department of a dairy owned by Kroger, the giant grocery chain.

Herron, who had been active in civil rights activities in Alabama and Mississippi, and Canady, who had left a managerial position at a Cincinnati department store to work for the same cause, had been in Tennessee a few months. They had accompanied Allen to a voter registration rally in downtown Nashville three days earlier. It had been an eventful occasion because it nurtured the ill feelings between blacks and police officers.

While handing leaflets to two blacks, Allen had been knocked to the ground by a police officer, who pinned him to a sidewalk and, with a revolver pointed at his head, lectured him in no uncertain terms.

"One move, you fucking nigger, and I'll blow out your scrambled brains," the police officer had said. "You're scum, nigger, black trash."

Parker, age twenty-three, of Cincinnati, had been in Nashville five days. He had flown to the city to take a long weekend break from work while he considered opening a bookstore on the Tennessee State campus. He had been sympathetic toward the civil rights cause, having met Allen six months earlier when they worked for the Citizens Committee for Youths in Ohio, but he had not been as active as his companions.

Alexander, age twenty-four, of Cincinnati, had been in Nashville off and on for four months. He had returned to Cincinnati for Christmas, then had returned to Tennessee with Parker five days earlier. They had known each other several years and had run into each other at a party in Ohio about two weeks previously. Alexander had talked him into visiting Nashville, a decision that had been made on the spur of the moment.

It was a jovial group, except when the subject was civil rights, the concern that linked them all together. Their only serious debate was about what to do with Alexander. He seemed more interested in a good time than in the cause and liked the action provided by the four other men, who were smooth in their dealings with women. But he was not as vocal as they were about racial issues. It had taken a strong objection from Allen to stop a move by the others to disassociate from him.

So on this night the eight men and three women ate chicken and agonized over the memory of the riots that had taken place in the neighborhood during the spring and summer of 1967, even as singer Marvin Gaye filled the room with lyrical hope for better days in future years. They fretted over the few blacks who had registered to vote in the upcoming election.

"We still don't have the hundred acres and a mule they promised," Allen said in frustration as the song ended.

"For real, Blood, and it's not getting any better," Herron chimed in with equal burden. "They're saying we're free, but we're still in chains."

"Well, we're about to take a break from all this," said Canady. "It'll be good to be back home."

Allen nodded as he walked to a kitchen window and wiped moisture from a pane so he could see the wintry scene outside. "We can't fight them, not with force," he said. "That's never been our way. We've got to do it at the polls and with peaceful demonstrations."

"I heard that," said an intrusive female voice. "But what I saw this afternoon tells me all that love and harmony bunk doesn't make sense."

In unison they turned to watch Parker and a young woman enter the kitchen holding hands. They had pulled on their heavy coats.

"So what's going on?" Canady asked.

"I saw a cop with a brother pinned to the side of a car," she said, her voice showing signs of disgust. "He had his revolver in his hand. He was yelling, 'nigger' this and 'nigger' that, and pushing and shoving. It was harassment, pure and simple."

Herron pounded a fist into an open palm. "Damn them," he

said, his voice near rage. "Why don't they leave us alone? It doesn't have to be like that."

"Well, fellas, we're going out back for a talk," Parker said as he and the woman moved toward the door. "If we're leaving tonight, I'm gonna visit some more with the lady."

"Be quick about it," said Canady. "It's getting late. We need to be in Ohio by dawn."

Allen, Herron, and Canady laughed as the door closed behind the couple, who proceeded to a secluded place between two buildings. Parker was a little nervous because the weather had caused his flight to be canceled, and he already was two days past the deadline his father had given him for returning to work. The woman was glad the snow and ice had delayed his departure.

"He's a Romeo, man," Canady laughed as they continued their conversation in the kitchen. "He has a way with all the ladies."

"Yeah, he's a lover, for sure," Allen answered as the friends not planning to leave town walked toward the back door.

"We're out of here," they said. "We're going over to 1906 and listen to some more music."

"Well, I guess we'll see you in a while," Alexander said. "We're rolling tonight. It's Cincy or bust."

What had been happening in the cold outside was proof that what was being said in the warmth inside was prophetic. Four Metro Nashville Police Department officers—G. L. Lilley in Car 40, Pete Johnson in Car 16, Raymond Black in Car 42, and Wayne Thomasson in Car 45—were coordinating with each other and a woman police radio dispatcher to establish surveillance of a 1966 red Ford owned by Rick Hughes and parked curbside in front of the apartments on Hermosa Street. At 9:16 P.M. the dispatcher had responded to Lilley's transmission of a minute earlier.

"10–4, Sergeant Lilley," said the radio dispatcher. "Attention all cars and stations. All cars. Be on the look out for two male coloreds. They're driving a car with Michigan license number 2893C–Charles L–Lincoln. 2893C–Charles L–Lincoln. Don't know the color or the make of the car. This car has in their possession some stolen American Express money orders. Just cashed a money order at the liquor store at 1218 Jefferson. Pick up and hold for Car 40."

"Car 40 to Car 42," Lilley said to Black.

"42," Black said to Lilley.

"Are you close to Fourteenth and Jefferson, Black?" Lilley asked.

"That's 10–4," Black said to Lilley. "I'm on Seventeenth Avenue

North. I saw a car with Michigan license on it about an hour and a half ago."

"Signal 8 with me in front of this whiskey store before you go up there on the street," Lilley answered.

"That's 10–4," Black responded.

Then Johnson entered the conversation. "16. What kind of car was that?"

"42," said the police radio dispatcher to Black.

"42," Black answered.

"42, Car 16," said the police radio dispatcher, connecting Black to Johnson.

"This is Car 40," said Lilley. "He has asked for the make of the car. I do not have a make of the car. The man didn't have time to get it. The only thing he got was the license number 2893C, like in Charles, L like in Lincoln, Michigan. Two male coloreds. Both of them have long hair. Believes it hangs around their collar jacket or somewhere."

Hughes and Kenny Bridges were listening to music inside the apartment at 1906 Hermosa Street, unaware that they had been described by the owner of the Val-Dot Liquor Store.

Another officer informed Lilley that a car with a Michigan license plate had been seen earlier parked on Hermosa Street. So Lilley, who knew Johnson had been frequenting that area while on patrol, contacted him on the police radio.

"You know where he's talking about, don't you, Brother Johnson?" Lilley said to Johnson.

"10–4, Sergeant," Johnson answered.

"Are you going to check it for me?" Lilley said to Johnson.

"10–4," Johnson said to Lilley.

Johnson received those orders from Lilley at 9:20 P.M. Four minutes later, Thomasson, who was parked on Hermosa Street about two blocks west of the apartments, got on his police radio and asked for and received the license plate number.

Two minutes later, Johnson radioed Lilley that he had located the automobile. "That car is here. A 1966 red Ford. You got the car you were looking for in that apartment."

Johnson was sitting curbside about a block west of the apartments on Twenty-first Avenue where he could see both in front of the apartments and behind, where a white Plymouth was parked under a tree behind Bill Allen's apartment. Johnson was joined by Black in Car 42. They discussed approaching the apartment occupied by Hughes and Bridges, and at 9:29 P.M., Johnson tried to radio the location to Lilley.

"They're in the bottom," Johnson said to Lilley, explaining how

the apartments on Hermosa Street sat in a valley between two relatively steep inclines.

Inside Allen walked into his living room, turned over the record,
then pulled back the window curtain and glanced outside to check
the weather. He shook his head in disgust and walked back into the
kitchen.

"Hey, Doc, what do you think about the UCLA-Houston game?"
Canady asked. "Who do you like?"

"I'm going with the Bruins," said Allen.

"But Houston has Big E," said Alexander.

"UCLA is UCLA," said Allen.

"It'll be a show, for sure," said Canady.

"Forget basketball for now," said Herron. "Let's get ready to roll
toward Cincinnati."

A silence prevailed in the room, except for the record playing on
the phonograph. Allen glanced at Canady to check his reaction.
Alexander glanced at his watch. "It's after 9:30, fellas, and I'm
ready to roll," he said.

"So you're really going, even in this weather?" Allen said with
some surprise. "Maybe it'd be better to wait."

"No way, man," Alexander said. "The ride is gassed."

"Then I want a ride to Old Hickory," Allen said. "My folks will
still be up. I'm anxious to let my dad see his rifles. He and Uncle
Lonnie might . . ."

"What rifles?" Alexander asked as he interrupted Allen and
reached into a box for a last piece of chicken.

"A 30-30 and a 22. Dad collects them and works on them. It's a
hobby from his service years. He'll love the 30-30. It's perfect for
hunting deer. I imagine he and Uncle Lonnie are in the woods a lot
these days."

"Where'd they come from?" Herron said, his tone indicating he
suspected something illegal.

"I got a deal," Allen said. "They're like new. The 30-30 still has
the instruction tag on it."

Allen told the group how he had bought the rifles a day earlier for
sixty dollars from a neighbor who had worked at a sporting goods
store. He told them how the rifles were loaded when he bought
them, that the seller was prepared to show him they worked, that he
declined to shoot them because they still had tags on them, which
proved they were new.

"Well, let's have a look at them," Canady said.

"They're in the car," Allen said. "I'm not about to go out in the
cold and drag them in here."

"Then let's roll," Herron said. "I'm loaded in the trunk."

"For real," said Canady.

As the men inside the apartment grabbed their coats, Johnson and Black sat in their cruisers with motors running, steam rising from the slush under them. Thomasson was in his cruiser about the same distance from the apartments on Hermosa Street, only on the other side.

Herron, Alexander, and Canady were already seated in the back of the Plymouth when Allen came out the rear of the apartment. Parker and his girlfriend were kissing while standing on the back porch of the apartment at 1906 Hermosa Street.

"I don't mean to bust up the love nest," Allen said to Parker, who quickly pulled back from the embrace, "but it's time to get out of here."

"So soon?" Parker said as he stepped backward off the porch, tumbling into the snow. "We could wait for better weather, you know."

"For real, Bitsey," Allen said as he pointed toward the automobile. "But the debate is over. The other fellas, they're on go."

Parker smiled at his girlfriend and walked toward the automobile.

"And it's yours to drive," Allen said as he pitched the car keys to Parker.

"Right," Parker said. "That's cool. At least I'm saving air fare. I'd just as soon ride as fly in this mess."

Before getting into the automobile, Parker waved goodbye and scraped some of the thick ice off the windshield with his glove. It created a small hole through which he could see until the defroster did its work. Attired nicely in dress slacks, a dress shirt, a blazer, and dress shoes, as were all of the men except Herron, who was dressed in blue jeans and an army fatigue jacket, Parker brushed snow off his clothes, got into the car, and started the engine.

It was 9:37 P.M.

Meanwhile, Johnson and Black had been watching the activity near the Plymouth from their vantage points on Twenty-first Avenue. Johnson made a surprising declaration to the dispatcher.

"16," Johnson said. "I'm going to check out this car that is parked behind this apartment. I'm going to stop this other car and see who's in it."

Johnson was not acting on a whim. He had seen something disturbing to him several minutes earlier, a female from Fisk walking across the yard leading to the apartment buildings, a familiar twenty-year-old woman taking a shortcut between the dwellings to the back door at 1910 Hermosa Street. The sight made him seethe and determined to stop the Plymouth.

THREE

As Officer Pete Johnson completed his transmission, Steve Parker steered the white 1967 Plymouth Fury along a dirt driveway running alongside the apartment complex. Driving precariously, he plowed through the snow and slush, then turned left onto Hermosa Street.

Meanwhile officers G. L. Lilley, Raymond Black, and Wayne Thomasson remained in place. Because of the fog and the ice on the windshield, nobody in the Plymouth could see any of the officers' cruisers parked in the neighborhood. In reality, Parker's view was so distorted by the frost and fog that as he drove he had to strain to avoid hitting cars parked on the street. The coat of ice on the rear window was even thicker than it was on the windshield, so no one inside the Fury could know that Johnson had started to roll Car 16 behind them.

Parker leaned forward, straining for a better view of the road. Then he cracked open the window to his left to see better. "Damn, what a mess!" he exclaimed. "I hope the interstate is better than this."

Johnson was saying nothing as he drove along Hermosa Street behind the Plymouth.

Parker continued to struggle while trying to drive, the rear end of his car fish tailing right and left as he steered it. Allen fiddled with the radio dial from his position in the front seat until he heard a clear voice, "The time, 9:38 on WLAC, Nashville, Tennessee. John R way down south in Dixie."

As the Plymouth began moving slowly up a steep incline about two blocks along Hermosa Street, Johnson was a little more than one block behind it. Black was not so fortunate in Car 42. His car was stuck in the ice about one block west of the triplex apartment.

15

"There's a car at the top of the hill, and I'm gonna try and stop it," Johnson radioed.

"There's another car at the top of the hill," Black replied. "Why don't you see if he can stop it?"

Thomasson, who was in that car, heard what Black said to Johnson. He also saw approaching headlights as the Plymouth moved toward him.

Meanwhile, Johnson tersely responded, "I want this."

At the top of the incline, less than a block in front of the Plymouth, Thomasson turned on his headlights. Although he was facing the sedan, because of the ice on their windows and the lingering fog, the five men could barely see his lights as they approached him.

At this point there was no sign of urgency, no mention that any of the men in the Plymouth were wanted by anybody for anything.

As the car approached him, Thomasson turned on his bright headlights and moved his car slightly in front of the sedan. As Parker avoided the oncoming vehicle, Thomasson moved back into his lane, then continued in the opposite direction along Hermosa Street, meeting Johnson in Car 16, before turning around. Not a word was spoken by either officer.

In the meantime, two high school juniors, Larry Wade and Johnny Brown, were walking along the curb on Herman Street in the same direction the Plymouth was traveling. They were on their way to Brown's home from Watkins Park Community Center several blocks away, with Wade carrying a basketball.

As the Plymouth approached, both Wade and Brown stepped into the grass on the side of the street to give it a clear path, the moisture from the weeds wetting their shoes and chilling their feet. As they continued toward Brown's home less than a block away, their eyes widened.

"Uh oh, somebody has trouble," Wade said.

"Yeah," Brown replied. "It's two cop cars."

"Let's hide and watch."

"No way," Brown answered. "I'm getting outa here. Let's go home."

So that is what the two high school students did, finding the warmth of the project apartment at about the time Johnson and Thomasson closed in on the Plymouth.

Johnson, in Car 16, was back on the police radio.

"16," he told the dispatcher. I'm at Sixteenth and Herman. He's trying to get away from us."

"Where's he going?" Thomasson asked.

"All cars stand by," the dispatcher radioed.

"Car 45," Thomasson transmitted. "Had car stopped and they tried to run over me."

[Note: At that moment, the taped recording of the police radio transmission later played in court contained a blaring siren. It was clear, as if it were in the courtroom, while many of the verbal exchanges heard on the tape were filled with static.]

After getting close enough to the Plymouth for his headlights to illuminate the tag, about a block short of Fourteenth Avenue, Officer Johnson was afforded his first view of Ohio license plate number 4716CJ, and he turned on the emergency flashing lights.

When the Plymouth stopped at the intersection of Hermosa and Fourteenth Avenue, Johnson pulled in front of it slightly, motioning to the driver to turn down Fourteenth Avenue. As he followed the Plymouth, he radioed, "I'm going to a dead end. I'm going down toward . . . traveling south on Fourteenth at the railroad."

"Do you want me to stay down here, Sergeant, or help T.J.?" an officer asked over the police radio.

"45," Thomasson answered. "Put me out with him."

The dispatcher reacted, "45."

Then Lilley, in Car 40, radioed the dispatcher. "This is Car 40. I'm at 1908 Hermosa Street. I need another car out here. I've got a car parked here. I can't leave. These other cars are chasing the other one. This one is 2893CL Michigan. I need another car to stand by here so I can go to that other car and catch that one. Get me another car over here, please."

"10-4, Sergeant," the dispatcher replied. "Give me your 10-20 again."

"That's 1908 Hermosa," Lilley responded as he and Black watched Rick Hughes and Kenny Bridges walk toward the red Ford they had under surveillance, get into it, and drive away.

"10-4."

[Note: Actually, Lilley was at 1906 Hermosa Street, where the red Ford was under surveillance. Also, his mention of "these other cars are chasing the other one" is surprising because he could not see the police cruisers and the Plymouth to determine a chase was in progress. This is the only time such terminology was used until court, when the prosecution advanced a chase-ambush theory. It also is intriguing that he would use such terminology when describing police cruisers occupied by officers who patrolled the area and knew the surroundings, but were trailing an automobile down a dead-end avenue.]

FOUR

The heavy battery of gunfire created a stir in the neighborhood. Among those who walked outside to see what the shooting was about were Johnny Brown, his mother, Pearlie Brown, and Larry Wade. They stood on a stoop behind their project apartment and gazed toward the emergency flashing lights reflecting off buildings and bushes more than two blocks away. Their view was obstructed by the church in the spacious field that adjoined the project.

Larry Wade and Johnny Brown were shaking as they strained to see what was happening beside the warehouse.

"I can't see what's going on," Wade said. "It's too dark. Who's down there?"

"I don't know," Brown answered. "But it's probably the cops and that car they were following."

Parker, Herron, and Alexander were wondering much the same as they ran along the railroad tracks.

Short of breath, Herron stopped and urged the other two to continue without him. Parker and Alexander grabbed him under his arms, hoisted him, and dragged him along with them. The trio stopped when a security guard who thought he had heard gunfire stepped onto the loading dock of the Carrigan Iron Works building.

"It's terrible out tonight," the guard commented.

"Cold, man, real cold," replied Parker.

"Yeah, that's why I'm getting back inside."

At the scene of the shooting, Canady ran between the Plymouth and Car 16, intending to run east along the railroad tracks, toward

18

downtown. Instead, he stopped and stared at Johnson, who was lying dead on the street, glanced toward Thomasson, who was almost unconscious, and ran a circle around the sedan, following Allen.

"Well, there goes somebody," Wade said in a whisper as he pointed toward the railroad tracks about twenty-five yards from them. "It's a guy running with a gun over his head."

Wade, Johnny Brown, and Pearlie Brown watched Allen, who appeared to them as a tall and lanky shadow in motion, as he ran along the railroad tracks. They saw him duck behind a bush to let a car pass.

With the sound of sirens ringing in his ears, Allen reached into a coat pocket and pulled out two 30-30 shells that had been given to him by the neighbor who had sold him the gun. Frantically, he attempted to put them into the weapon, only to jam the second. The gun could no longer be used.

Then he continued his run.

"Here comes another one," said Johnny Brown.

They watched Canady running behind Allen.

Meanwhile, as Allen and Canady sprinted, the dispatcher was shaken and confused about the whereabouts of the shot police officers.

"210. Get an ambulance on the way," radioed an officer. "He said he was shot all to pieces. Get an ambulance on the way."

"I'm going to send it, but I've got to get his 10–20 on Sixteenth Avenue North," the dispatcher answered. She paused, then attempted to make contact with the wounded Thomasson: "45. 4–5."

"262. I'm headed that way," said another officer. "What have you got?"

"262. Got a car that's been shot, Sixteenth Avenue North," answered the dispatcher.

Thomasson began talking with the dispatcher while slumped on the ice and snow beside Car 45. His head was resting on the front seat and his radio cord stretched so the speaker could reach his mouth. His cap and his revolver were lying on the pavement beside him.

"10–4. 10–4," Thomasson radioed.

"10–4. We're on our way to you," said the dispatcher.

"10–4. Hit bad," Thomasson replied. "Hit bad," he said again, his voice now more urgent.

"Tell all cars in that section to get over there," called an officer. "Get every car you've got over to that section."

The problem was in determining exactly where Thomasson was. Previous radio transmissions had been inaccurate, and officers were looking in the wrong places.

"Clear the air," police officer G. L. Lilley transmitted in Car 40. "See if you can clear the air and raise that car and find out where he's at."

The dispatcher tried to reach Thomasson, "45. 4–5."

Thomasson responded, again erroneously, "45. Fifteenth just off of . . . of Herman, I believe."

"Fifteenth near Herman?"

"Herman, Herman," Thomasson answered.

"That's Fifteenth and Herman?"

"10–4. South of Herman and Fifteenth."

Lilley responded, telling everybody about the dead-end avenue.

"Three fellas jumped out and ran," Thomasson reported. "They're armed with sawed-off shotguns. Tell them to hurry. I'm hit bad."

"Attention all cars," called the dispatcher. "These subjects are armed with shotguns."

There was a pause. Then Thomasson radioed, "Shot me three times. Tell them to come on."

[Note: Thomasson was confused, with good reason, and his mind was clouded at that desperate moment. His body was stinging in several places because of the numerous fragments that had entered it, causing him to think he had been hit by pellets fired from a shotgun. In his brain was the echo of gunfire, which contributed to his thinking he had been shot three times when only two 30-30 casings and one 22-caliber casing were lying on the ground beside the open doors of the Plymouth.]

As officers rushed toward the scene, they were asking for a description of the men involved and the car they were driving.

"They're not in a car," Thomasson radioed. "They're on foot. They left running east on the railroad."

That was the case with Parker, Herron, and Alexander, who heard sirens blaring and wondered what had happened on Fourteenth Avenue.

But Allen and Canady were running west, with Allen fully aware of what had taken place, while Canady was too frightened to think about it.

In the yards of the project apartments nearby, people stood, wondering what had happened and asking questions of one another. No one had seen the incident, and little did those who had been watching "Gunsmoke" on television realize that outside their homes a drama had been taking place that would cost two police officers their lives and would continue to haunt many others for years to come.

FIVE

Bill Allen and Ralph Canady could see the flashing emergency lights at Fourteenth Avenue and Herman Street as they ran along the railroad tracks. Sirens were screaming, cutting through the still of the night, and the sound quickened their pace. Their minds were active—indeed they swirled with thoughts—and their feet were becoming soaked by the slush under them.

"Little Doc, wait up," Canady called to Allen, who was running about twenty yards in front of him. "Let me catch up with you."

Allen stopped and waited for his friend as residents of the project apartments they were passing assembled in their yards to see what was causing such a commotion. The two young men looked behind them three blocks, where the red lights reflecting off trees and buildings made the area they had left appear to be the hub of a disaster area.

"Damn, Slim, this didn't have to happen," Allen gasped to Canady before they resumed their run, which had become a trot since the excitement had left them winded. "I never dreamed this'd happen to us. It sounded like Vietnam."

"Let's get rid of these guns," answered Canady.

So they did, placing the rifles in shallow bushes beside a two-foot concrete wall that separated the front yards of two houses in the 1800 block of Herman Street. From there they ran three blocks to Fisk University, where they stood in front of the student union building and let the shock of the evening subside a bit.

"I thought they had shot you," Allen told Canady.

"That's why I hit the ground," Canady replied. "I thought the brother was shooting at us. I felt the bullet go past."

They paused as three students, two women and a man, walked

21

beside them on the sidewalk and started up the steps of the building.

"I'm cold and scared, Doc," Canady said.

"Me too, Slim," Allen answered. "I've got to make a telephone call and get us out of here."

At the scene of the shooting, five police cruisers had arrived. The first two Metro Nashville Police Department officers to arrive were Jack Burnett and Robert White, who were quickly joined by others in uniform and dozens of gawkers. Burnett immediately went to Car 16 and looked at police officer Pete Johnson. He knelt beside his slain comrade, felt for a pulse, and thought for a second that he had detected one.

White went to Car 45, where he found police officer Wayne Thomasson sitting with his back to the 1967 white Plymouth with blood streaming down the front of his coat.

"I've been shot bad," Thomasson told White, whose coat he grabbed as he attempted to get up. "They've shot my legs off. Help me get up."

"Just sit still until the ambulance gets here," White told him. "It's on the way. Just calm down, Wayne, and relax until we get some help down here."

Police officer Bob Hill, who worked in the intelligence division, was also on the scene. He watched fellow officer Jim Ball attempt to revive Johnson, to no avail, then walked to Thomasson for a look at the seriously wounded man.

"They tried to shoot his balls off," Hill told a fellow officer after noticing a tear in the crotch area of Thomasson's pants. He moved around frantically with the other police officers on the scene as energy overwhelmed logic. They were desperately searching, both for clues and for a plan.

Two ambulances arrived on the scene. Medics put Thomasson on a stretcher and hustled him into one ambulance. He was breathing and talking. When they placed Johnson into the back of the other, they knew the effort was pointless.

Two officers, G. L. Lilley and Robert Titsworth, both sergeants, were looking for evidence, with the motors on all cars still running. White walked to Lilley, reached into his coat pocket, and handed him the revolver he had found a few inches from Thomasson. Then White walked to Titsworth and handed him the revolver Burnett had found less than a foot from Johnson. "I think you'll want to hold on to this," he said. The sergeants put the revolvers in their coat pockets and continued their searches.

Homicide detective Bill Nichols, age thirty-two, arrived as

Thomasson was being placed into an ambulance. He began combing the area for evidence, discovering two empty 30-30 casings below the right front floorboard of the Plymouth and a 30-30 slug in a puddle of blood where Johnson had been found on the ground. He also discovered a spent 38-caliber bullet, the type used by police officers.

Slowly, the curious onlookers disbursed to return to their apartments with a tale of horror. Just after 10:00 P.M., the motor on the Plymouth was turned off, and police officer Charlie Stoner began a long walk. Noticing two sets of footprints in the snow alongside the railroad tracks going west, he followed them for several blocks until he came to a house and noticed that the trampled snow ended at a street. He looked around, then returned to the scene of the shootout.

About ten blocks away, Steve Parker, Charles Lee Herron, and John Alexander were seated at a table in a crowded cocktail lounge on Jefferson Street, trying to catch their breaths after a run from Fourteenth Avenue. It felt good to be inside a heated building filled with revelers.

"I'll get us a pitcher of beer," Parker said as he stood and started toward the bar.

"Man, I can't drink anything," Herron answered. "My stomach hurts, and my chest is caving in. I can't breathe."

"Go get it, Bitsey," Alexander replied. "It'll help calm our nerves." He paused. "And I'll keep an eye on the door, just in case."

As Parker returned to the table with a pitcher of beer and three glasses, he heard Herron say to Alexander, "There were so many shots. I'm afraid somebody got hurt."

"I'm not sure what happened, but it has to be bad," Herron whispered to Alexander. "I'm afraid for Doc and Slim. They could be dead."

"We've got to get out of here, find some place to think this out," Parker said. "I'm gonna call a cab, a wildcat, to get us away from the crowd."

Herron and Alexander finished the beer while Parker was on the telephone. They waited until the taxi stopped in front of the bar, then got in it and rode about two blocks.

"Hey, man, you know I've only got a fifty-dollar bill!" Parker told the driver.

"Then you've got to get out," the driver responded. "I don't have change for that."

So Parker, Herron, and Alexander were back on the streets as police cruisers began combing the neighborhood. They set out toward Brookside Apartments, but stopped at a vacant house that had been gutted. After they were inside, they sat for several minutes. Herron became sick and vomited.

"I'm sorry, Blood," Herron apologized after relieving his upset stomach. "It's just too much."

"It's OK," Parker replied. "But remember, Lee, we're really not a part of this. We've just got to get somewhere safe until people figure that out. What you say we truck it on to the Brookside Apartments and try to get in touch with [John] Walker? We've got to find out what went down."

"That's cool," Alexander agreed.

At police headquarters downtown, homicide detectives were scrambling to determine who had been in the Plymouth.

With sweat on their foreheads in spite of the bitter cold evening, Allen and Canady knocked on the door of the house at 1508 Cecilia Street, where they had walked after talking over the situation on the Fisk campus. They smiled when Tyler McCormick Smith answered their summons.

"Hello, Tyler," Allen said.

"So what's happening, Bill?" Smith answered. They had known each other for several years.

"Well, man, I was wondering if I could use your telephone to hitch a ride. My car is down again. We're trying to get across town."

Smith looked at the pair standing in front of him wearing soaked clothes. He glanced over his shoulder to see if his wife was watching. Betty Joyce Smith was in a bedroom watching television and attending their small son.

"Well, uh, Bill, there's one you could use down at the shopping center."

"Right," Allen agreed. "We'll do that."

Betty Joyce Smith had not heard the knock on the door, nor did she hear the next one, when Allen and Canady returned to the house a few minutes later. Their telephone call had been unsuccessful.

"Tyler, we're in need of a ride," Allen said upon their return. "How's your car running?"

"It's not. The transmission is shot."

"Well, could we come in and use your telephone?"

"Right. Come on."

Allen, Canady, and Tyler Smith were seated in the kitchen with Austin Smith, Tyler's father, when Betty Joyce Smith walked into the room from the bedroom. The two visitors had their shoes off and were holding wet socks in front of an open oven door. Tyler Smith had noticed that Allen had been pacing a lot, rubbing the back of his neck while walking from his chair to the window, looking outside, and returning to his seat. He had heard Canady say, "Ease up, Doc, and relax," and had noticed that Allen was smoking more than usual.

"They said on the news that a policeman got killed over in the Valley," Betty said. "They said another one got shot, too."

"Who did it?" Canady asked.

"They don't know," Betty answered. "But they think it was some brothers, maybe students."

In back of the house an automobile engine could be heard racing loudly. Tyler Smith looked out the kitchen door and said, "It's Herman Harlan and some guy. It might be Harold Bentley with him."

"Good," Allen answered. "Maybe they can take us over to Twenty-sixth and Heiman. That's where [William] Huff lives. We can throw down there."

Thirty minutes later at General Hospital, Thomasson was hovering near death as surgeons began repairing the holes in his body left by fragments from a 30-30 slug and a shattered police cruiser door. His wife, the former Judy Milligan, was asking questions in the waiting area outside the emergency room. She had learned about the wounding of her husband while watching television at their home in Hermitage, just outside Nashville. As soon as the news bulletin was flashed, she had arranged for a sitter for their three children—Bunny Ann, age nine, Kerstan, age three, and Patty, age two—and had hurried to the hospital.

A bookkeeper at Jaccard's jewelry store, she had been married to Thomasson for about four years, since just after he joined the police department. Her oldest child was from a previous marriage.

"Who did this to him?" she asked a homicide detective in the waiting area.

"We think some coloreds," the detective replied. "They've killed Pete Johnson. Wayne has what could be a tough fight on his hands."

Mrs. Thomasson burst into tears. "That's what I thought. Wayne feared that. He said they feared that. He said the tension had become too much."

Later, with Titsworth at her side, Mrs. Thomasson felt more comfortable. The police department shift commander, who had sent her husband into duty that evening with a we-all-must-be-careful lecture at roll call, had a comforting effect on the troubled wife.

"I told him . . . I told him . . . I told him . . . ," she said many times as Titsworth comforted her.

As they sat at the Brookside Apartments, waiting to see if a friend had been able to find John Walker, Parker asked Herron and Alexander, "Do you guess we should go to police headquarters and tell them what went down? I mean, we can get the matter worked out and. . . ."

"I'm not going down there, man," Herron answered, interrupting Parker. "That's suicide tonight."

"I'm with Lee on that one," Alexander agreed. "We've got to get our asses out of Tennessee."

"That's for sure," Herron said. "Man, you've got to remember who we are and who was down there on that road with us tonight. It isn't like . . ."

Herron was stopped in mid-sentence as John Walker and the man they had sent to find him entered the apartment. "What in the hell is going on?" Walker asked as he entered the room. "The Valley is being ripped apart. I haven't seen so many cops on Jefferson Street since the riots last summer."

"That's what we're wondering," Herron replied. "That's why we want to get out of this town." He paused. "What about going home? What about a ride? Like now, or as quickly as possible."

Herron's friends looked at each other as if they suspected the obvious, then looked at Parker and Alexander, who nodded in agreement.

"Where's Doc and Slim?" Walker asked.

"We don't know," Parker replied.

Walker looked at each of the three as he paused. He looked at his friend and asked, "Are you free to ride?"

"I've got my Chevy. It's running right."

"Then let's get it rolling," said Walker. "Let's get moving toward Ohio."

By this time youthful newspaper reporter Keel Hunt had completed dictating information about the shooting to the city desk at *The Tennessean*. A student at Middle Tennessee State University, he had been on the weeknight police beat only twice, but now he was working on the most exciting story of his newspaper career.

He had talked at General Hospital with assistant police chief Donald Barton, who told him, "Wayne Thomasson and T. [Thomas] Johnson have been shot." He also was told that Johnson had fired his revolver four times, a statement that was published and never disputed.

That was about all that Hunt or any other reporter would learn about the case for several days. After he left General Hospital, he went to police headquarters, where he was told a "blackout" had been put into effect. The news media would not be given any more information.

During this time several police department representatives gathered in the office of Mickey McDaniel, the leader of the criminal investigation division, assisted for the most part by Nichols and Cathey. Together they mapped out a plan. Several ranking police officers, including Titsworth, the commanding officer for both Thomasson and Johnson, were not included in the meeting for reasons they never understood. Nor were they ever asked what they thought about the case, which was equally perplexing to them.

Nevertheless, a panic of sorts set in, a "Chinese fire drill, like it is so many times when a police officer is hit" is how Cathey described it. The frayed emotions led to a bizarre, if not ruthless, evening in North Nashville.

Adding to the confusion were off-duty police officers who arrived at headquarters in cars and pickup trucks, wearing civilian clothes and carrying shotguns and other weapons.

SIX

Soon after midnight, Charles Lee Herron, John Alexander, and Steve Parker were headed out of Nashville in a 1962 blue Chevrolet driven by John Walker's friend. Chicago was their ultimate destination, although they intended a brief pause in Cincinnati.

By then, the police had set up numerous roadblocks on the main thoroughfares of Nashville. They did not have anybody in mind, but they were looking for anybody suspicious, anybody who looked like he or she was in a hurry to leave the area.

"Well, that didn't take long," Alexander observed as he discovered they were moving toward a roadblock at a busy intersection.

"Let's stay cool. Act like nothing has happened," Herron cautioned as they drew closer to two police cruisers whose emergency lights were flashing.

"He's waving some people past without stopping them," Walker commented as he saw one of the officers with a flashlight in hand.

"But he's checking out some cars," Parker noticed.

The driver began waving at the police officer as soon as they got close enough for him to see them. The police officer smiled, returned the wave, and motioned them through.

"Damn," Alexander exclaimed. "He didn't even think twice about us."

"Maybe it isn't as bad as we thought," commented Parker, remembering the battery of gunfire they had heard on Fourteenth Avenue.

Information being gathered at police headquarters was equally nonconclusive. Homicide detectives and police officers were huddled in an effort to determine who they were looking for. The frequency of visitors to the project apartments on Hermosa Street had them perplexed because they could not put a finger on who had spent time there and who was unaccounted for. Nor were they having luck tracing the origin of the 1967 white Plymouth with Ohio license plates.

"We'll just have to knock down some doors and get to the bottom of this," a homicide detective declared.

"I know who lives over there and who doesn't," said Joe Casey, a police officer who at the time was on patrol in the area while beginning a lengthy climb to the position of police chief. "I referee basketball games at TSU. I know the faces and some of the names."

"Good. Then let's get a plan together. We've got to put our hands on those nigger cop-killers. We've already got men in the neighborhood."

Less than an hour later there were more than two dozen police cruisers lined up in the 1900 block of Hermosa Street. Their flashing lights illuminated the sleet that continued to fall on the city, and the exhaust from their tailpipes cut holes in the ice on the pavement. The activity outside did not cause undue alarm among many of the residents; some were asleep, and others had seen this kind of thing before, only on a smaller scale and with far less emotion. When the *Nashville Banner* published pictures the next afternoon, the Valley looked like a wartime scene.

"We're about ready to wake up the neighborhood," an officer bragged over his radio as he stood with a homicide detective beside his cruiser. "We're in place. We're ready to move."

"10–4," said the dispatcher. "You've got a go. Proceed as planned."

William Bostic, a senior at Tennessee State who was teaching civics at a junior high school, was asleep inside his apartment at 1906 Hermosa Street. He had missed the excitement of the evening, having been working at a part-time job when the shooting took place. He had been home about an hour and had gone to bed after discovering that his roommate, Rick Hughes, was not in the apartment.

Bostic was wearing his pajamas when he heard a loud knock at his door, as well as shouting, "Police officers. Open up." One of the four officers at his door bolted into the apartment and rushed through a quick search. Two of the other three were carrying high-powered rifles.

"Where are those cop-killer brothers?" asked an officer who stayed near the door of the apartment.

"Where are who?" Bostic asked.

"Don't play dumb with me, nigger, because you know who did it and where they are. Where is Amos Bridges and Ralph Canady? Where are all those guys who've been cashing stolen money orders at the liquor store?"

"This must be a bad dream, officer," Bostic answered. "I don't have any idea what you're talking about."

Another officer walked into the living room. "There's a gun in the bedroom, but it's not a 30-30 or a 22," he said. "There's nothing else in there."

"Well, let's make some more rounds."

Bostic returned to bed. In another of the triplex apartments at 1906 Hermosa Street, Bobby Meeks was routed from his bedroom by about ten police officers. He answered similar questions and returned to sleep. The same thing was happening all through a neighborhood that had seen more than its share of unrest during racial riots less than eight months earlier.

Several blocks away in William Huff's home at Twenty-sixth Avenue and Heiman Street, Bill Allen and Ralph Canady were wide awake and conversing with their host. They explained to him that they needed to get out of town in the next day or two and that it would be helpful if they had false identification with them. Huff came up with the obvious conclusion about the evening and provided Allen with his driver's license.

More tension was developing at Rolling Mill Hill, the city garage. According to his testimony in court in April 1989, sometime after midnight homicide detective Tom Cathey, age thirty-seven, was exploring the trunk of the Plymouth that had been towed there. He discovered a black brief case on which a Student Non-Violent Coordinating Committee decal had been pasted. Inside, he found a newspaper article titled "Dynamite" that had been written by civil rights leaders Stokely Carmichael and Charles Hamilton, four books—*The Rebel, The World in Africa, The Betrayal of the Negro,* and *American Negro Slave Revolts*—a notebook, a pair of size 32 undershorts, a size 36-38 undershirt, a pair of blue socks, and a used tube of Colgate toothpaste.

"Well, they're activists," Cathey said to himself, drawing a popular conclusion for the time.

Then Cathey struck gold, at least as far as the police were concerned. According to a report he filed, in the trunk of the Plymouth he discovered blank money orders and an ink blotter that could be used to forge them, evidence that somebody in the car knew about a criminal act. In the trunk was a briefcase with the initials AKB

(Amos Bridges) on it, which had obviously been used in the deceitful scheme in North Nashville, although the owner was not in the car when it stopped on Fourteenth Avenue.

The Chevrolet carrying Parker, Herron, and Alexander to Cincinnati had skirted another roadblock, with the driver taking a detour around it. They were traveling along a snowy highway toward the Tennessee-Kentucky border. Then came what they would remember as a sickening sound, evidence that their good fortune was reversing itself on a cold and lonely road.

"Damn, a flat tire," muttered the driver. "And the spare isn't very good."

"It'll work, won't it?" asked Parker.

"We don't have much choice. It's all we've got to work with."

They changed the tire, as the frost became more biting, and continued their ride.

At General Hospital, Dr. William Alford continued surgery on Thomasson that had started at 11:00 P.M. He had given the police officer five pints of blood and was to give him ten more before finishing at 6:00 A.M. The doctor had discovered wounds in ribs on the left side, with intestines protruding, the left forearm, and the left leg. He had removed numerous fragments from a 30-30 slug, several pieces of metal from the door of the Plymouth, and bone chips from a broken hip.

Meanwhile, Parker, Herron, Alexander, Walker, and the owner of the automobile were huddled in a small room beside a rural highway in Kentucky. They had experienced a second flat tire and had seen a light in the distance. They had driven on the rim for about a mile to the front of a service station, where they had found a young man watching television and drinking coffee. They persuaded him to repair the tire.

"I was just about to call it a night," the attendant commented. "There's not many people out in this weather. I was headed for bed."

"Well, we appreciate you doing this for us," Herron responded. "We would've been in for a long night."

As the attendant labored, the five listened to a radio bulletin: "We have a news bulletin from Nashville, Tennessee. Two police officers have been shot in a predominantly black neighborhood of that city. Investigators are working to determine the identity and location of the assailants."

Parker looked through the side doorway of the service station to check the attendant's reaction. He saw nothing more than a man at work. "It's cool," he said.

"But not that cool, man," answered Alexander. "It's as bad as I thought it could possibly be."

"Let's keep it quiet in here," Herron cautioned.

By about 5:00 A.M., the pieces of the puzzle were beginning to fit together. Witnesses who had seen Allen, Canady, Parker, Herron, and Alexander together the previous afternoon told officers about the Plymouth they had been using, and another raid was made on Hermosa Street. This time numerous people were arrested, a few on legitimate, but unrelated, charges, and some for no reason.

By then Parker, Herron, and Alexander were rolling nearer to Cincinnati without further problems. They were attempting to nap but found sleep elusive. Allen and Canady were dozing off and on at the William Huff residence. Mrs. Thomasson was awake at General Hospital.

The Tennessean was being distributed on the streets with a sickening headline story about the shooting, in which assistant police chief Donald Barton told reporter Keel Hunt that police officer Pete Johnson fired his revolver four times.

By the time citizens were reading over breakfast about the death of Johnson and the wounding of Thomasson, police headquarters was crowded with blacks who had been taken from their beds in North Nashville and arrested. Among them were Bostic, Meeks, Hughes, and Amos Bridges.

Bostic had encountered ten police officers at his door not long before dawn. He had been handcuffed and placed in a police cruiser by an officer who, in a car parked behind the state capitol building, threatened, "Nigger, we're gonna find out what you know one way or the other."

Bostic claimed to know nothing, so he said nothing. He remained silent at headquarters while being questioned. In a police brutality lawsuit filed later, Bostic said he was knocked from his chair in the interrogation room, then kicked and struck on an ear with a cupped hand while on a stalled elevator, rendering him deaf in that ear for life. Also, he claimed he was taken into a bathroom to be "questioned" by two other police officers.

"You'll agree it's lonely in here, huh, nigger?" an officer said as he handcuffed Bostic to the plumbing at the rear of a toilet.

Bostic nodded.

The other officer pulled a metal coathanger from a coat pocket and spanked Bostic on his posterior. "Now maybe you'd like to tell us where the killers are," he threatened.

"I don't know who they are," answered Bostic, who later became a high-ranking official in the Pennsylvania state government.

"Well, maybe a little fire down below will help your memory, nigger."

Bostic was told to spread his legs over the toilet seat. His pants were unbuckled and dropped to below his knees. A sanitary napkin was placed in his mouth, and a flaming cigarette lighter was placed under his testicles.

[Note: Such claims by Bostic were denied by the Metro Nashville Police Department. A lawsuit was dismissed after an internal probe found no evidence that the police department was any more guilty of using excessive force than others like it in the nation. But in 1987 Major Robert Titsworth of the Metro Nashville Police Department made statements related to the incident. "I couldn't condone some of the things that happened that night," he said. He was asked for examples. "Like the bathroom episode at headquarters," he said. "You've heard about that one, haven't you?"]

While such things were allegedly happening to Bostic in a secluded restroom stall, the third floor of police headquarters was the scene of high tension. Here were housed the offices of homicide detectives, as well as their superior officer, Mickey McDaniel, a captain. The restrooms were located near his office, at the end of a long hallway of smaller offices. A lineup room was adjacent, two steps up, opposite the restrooms, as was the entrance to an elevator. A reception area was one floor below, containing a lobby of sorts; the booking room was two floors below.

The surroundings were remembered vividly by the black men in custody, particularly Bridges, who at 5:00 A.M. had been discovered hiding in an attic at 1906 Hermosa Street. He was found by police officer Bob Hill, who stepped on some insulation and felt a body under it. The police officer also uncovered a sawed-off shotgun.

Not long after dawn, Bostic, Meeks, Hughes, and Bridges were loaded onto the elevator at police headquarters for a trip to the booking room.

Suddenly, the elevator stopped between floors.

"We've got a problem on the elevator," a Davidson County sheriff department deputy alerted homicide detective Tom Cathey and assistant police chief Barton, who were waiting in the booking room.

They began running toward the stairway but were stopped. "Everything is under control," they were told.

The suspects did not think so, particularly Bostic, whose "ear was ringing," and Meeks, whose face was swelling quickly and badly. The mug shot taken of Meeks supported his claim that he was slugged in the side of his face by a police officer after being charged with unlawful possession of marijuana. Bridges had a scrape over his left eye. Hughes showed no signs of having been physically abused.

"This one appears to have a toothache," a police officer said when positioning Meeks for his booking picture. Meeks did not reply. Instead, he surveyed a scene in which more than two dozen blacks were being escorted to and from interrogation rooms.

Meeks remained in custody for four days before the drug possession charges were dropped. He was treated for his injuries at General Hospital.

Faye Weaver was not arrested. She simply watched and listened to what was happening from one of the triplex apartments at 1906 Hermosa Street. She saw Hughes being arrested beside his automobile, the 1966 red Ford, with a police officer pointing a rifle at his head and saying, "You killed one of our brothers." Hughes was handcuffed and forced into a police cruiser.

Sunrise was greeted with open arms by everybody concerned with the shooting; its glow had a subduing effect on fear. But Allen and Canady found that another day brought more reason for concern. As they looked out a window at William Huff's residence at about 7:30 A.M., they saw police officers armed with M-16 rifles entering apartments across the street.

"Oh, shit," Canady exclaimed. "What now?"

"We're gonna borrow some textbooks and start walking to class," Allen replied.

Filled with anxiety, Allen and Canady said goodbye to Huff, put textbooks under their arms, and walked past a dozen police officers on their way to the Tennessee State campus. Once there, they went to the gymnasium. Allen telephoned his uncle, Lonnie Pinkston, in Donelson.

"You got your good ride?" Allen asked his uncle.

"No," Pinkston answered. "The old wheels."

"Well, Lonnie, you've got to come get us. This isn't the place to be after the shooting last night."

"I'll be there in a little while," declared Pinkston, who did not press his nephew about why he was so anxious to leave North Nashville.

Pinkston also agreed to telephone his sister, Ellariz King Allen, who was working in the cafeteria at Vanderbilt Hospital. He told her that Canady and her son wanted to ride with her that morning to Louisville. She agreed and decided to visit her grandmother, who lived there.

It would seem that Bill Allen and Canady made their exit from

Huff's apartment in the nick of time. At 8:00 A.M., police officers swarmed into neighborhood apartments, including one rented by Tom Stephens, a former Washington, D.C., police officer who would later become a court officer during an important trial in the case.

"Man, you're looking in a clothes hamper?" Stephens asked an officer, although he wanted to say more about the procedure. "You can't come in here like this and—"

The glare offered by the officer caused Stephens to stop in mid-sentence.

Meanwhile, Bridges was questioned at headquarters. During his interrogation, he was sprayed in the face with some kind of fluid and gave a statement that provided the names of the suspects: Steve Parker ("Bitsey"), John Alexander ("Skin"), William Allen ("Doc"), Charles Lee Herron ("Lee"), and Ralph Canady ("Slim").

Bridges said much more, too, at the urging of "one guy who was acting tough and one guy who was acting like he wanted to be my buddy," according to notes transcribed that morning. Later he declared that it was fiction, that it was forced.

> At 7:00 P.M., I left the apartment at 1910 Hermosa Street and went to the Val-Dot Liquor Store with Steve Parker, John Walker, and Rick Hughes. We had money orders made out to Ralph Canady.
>
> At 9:15 P.M., we returned to the apartment and I shot a pistol into the air, a 22-caliber Browning. Inside the apartment I noticed my briefcase with AKB written on it.
>
> At 9:30 P.M., the five left in a 1967 Plymouth Fury. They took my briefcase. They said they were going to leave town, possibly to New York, with the rest of the money orders. Bill Allen had a 30-30. Ralph Canady had a 22.
>
> I went back to my house at 9:45 P.M. Broom [William Bostic] was there with Rick Hughes. I noticed a police car in front of the house. Hughes went outside and talked to the police officers.
>
> Bobby Meeks came in at 10:15 P.M. He said the police were coming.
>
> I went into the attic and sat awhile on a foot locker. Broom closed the attic for me.
>
> I hid under some insulation. A whole lot of police officers came. An hour or two went by. They searched the attic but missed me.
>
> The police found me at about 6:00 A.M.

[Note: In November 1987 Cathey admitted such statements are

sometimes "cleaned up," that the actual phraseology is changed when tapes are transcribed. But the police officers had the names of the five black men they were to hunt.

Still, in May 1989 Bridges contended that almost all of the statement was fabricated. He said he was making love in a bedroom at the apartment when the Plymouth left the apartment complex and that he did not shoot any kind of gun that night—"I didn't have one, so what did I use, my finger?" He said he did *not* say that anybody had taken his briefcase with him. "I don't know exactly where it was, but I assume it was in the apartment some place. It was like my lady. It was with me in the apartment, then it was gone. I don't know if the police took it or what." He said that none of the men who left in the Plymouth ever mentioned the money orders, much less taking them anywhere. "That's ridiculous because they weren't trying to get away after commiting any crime, definitely weren't out to kill any police officers. I wanted to go with them to Cincinnati, only the car was full." He said he did not see any guns—"How could I when I was in the bedroom with a lady?" He said Meeks did not appear at the apartment that night, not once, that the first time he saw him was at police headquarters after he had been beaten up. "In fact, they tried to burn my nuts with a cigarette lighter in Rick Hughes's bedroom before taking me to police headquarters." He said he did give the names of individuals who had frequented the apartment complex.]

Suspecting that the five fugitives had already left Tennessee, police, in conjunction with Davidson County district attorney Tom Shriver, began seeking assistance from the Federal Bureau of Investigation. The process set in motion the longest manhunt in history for a fugitive on the Most Wanted list.

"They can't be around here," McDaniel told Shriver by telephone.

"Then we've got unlawful flight to avoid prosecution for murder," Shriver answered. "It's a case for the feds. I'll get it rolling."

So five warrants were issued after the U.S. attorney in Nashville approved a petition for them and forwarded it to a United States magistrate for acceptance. This action prompted a battery of teletypes and telephone calls between the FBI offices in Washington, Nashville, and Memphis, with the latter taking principal jurisdiction in the case.

"OK, Bob, you've heard what's going on over this way," a representative from the U.S. attorney's office in Nashville said by telephone to Bob Jensen, the FBI special agent in charge of the Memphis office.

"Yeah," Jensen said. "It's looking like an 88, a violent thing. But what I've got on it is sketchy."

"It's like this. One policeman is dead. Another is critical. Black militants with high-powered rifles. Rebellious types. Maybe tied to the Black Panthers."

"I see," Jensen answered. "I'm sure it's something we want to check out. It's the type thing headquarters wants to get on quickly. So what else can you tell me?"

"Not much. We've got descriptions and unconfirmed names. For now, the warrants are for five John Does, but I'm betting those are your men."

"I see," Jensen answered as if he thought the FBI would be whistling in the dark for a while.

"We've got to be sure on this."

"That's 10–4," Jensen agreed. "We'll start with that. We'll get a data bank under way."

Jensen wasted little time getting in touch with FBI headquarters in Washington. Nor did it take long for him to receive more information from Nashville, including copies of newspaper reports about the incident. He forwarded the materials to Claude Curtis, an FBI agent in his office, and made him the first of twenty-three men who would be placed in charge of the case during the next two decades.

Pinkston was almost as bewildered as newspaper readers in Nashville when he learned his nephew was not still in New Jersey, where he had visited friends earlier in the month. Without asking questions, he drove a 1951 Chevrolet that was missing a window through the bitter cold to pick up Allen and Canady. Then they stopped in downtown Nashville with intentions of pawning a wrist-watch—parking within a block of police headquarters—received an unacceptable twenty-dollar offer, and continued their twenty-minute ride to Donelson.

At 11:00 A.M., Ellariz King Allen walked into the Pinkston home. She discovered her son and Canady sitting at a table in the kitchen eating bacon and eggs and conversing with Pinkston.

"Why the sudden trip to Louisville?" she asked.

"It's an important day up there," Allen answered. "There's a demonstration Slim and I need to be at."

"Well, I'd be careful, Bill, because bad news spreads quickly. The folks in Louisville probably already know about the shooting last night in the Valley."

Bill Allen nodded.

"Honestly," she said, "I just don't know when people are gonna put down those guns and start loving each other like we should."

Canady looked at Allen, who showed concern, then said, "Mama, I'm probably gonna be gone for a while."

"Gone where?"

"I don't know. I think I'm going back to New York."

"What about your schooling, Bill? You know that's the most important thing right now. You're close to graduation. You're almost a chemist."

The mother was suspicious, as was her brother, but neither of them asked him about his involvement in the shooting, not then and not during the ride to Louisville.

SEVEN

I t was a nervous, if not frantic, Steve Parker who paced back
and forth as Charles Lee Herron and John Alexander took naps
off and on. They were holed up in an apartment in Cincinnati the
morning after the shooting, and every telephone call Parker placed
to friends in Nashville brought worse news. So did the afternoon
newspaper in Cincinnati, which told the story of one Nashville police officer who was dead and another who was in critical condition.

"There isn't much more to report than that," Parker said after
Herron and Alexander read the newspaper report. "There's no
word about Doc [Bill Allen] or Candy Man [Ralph Canady]. But
the folks down there are saying the police are looking for all five of
us."

"They're naming us?" Alexander asked.

"That's right."

"Then being at home isn't as safe as we thought," answered Herron. "If they're talking about us in Nashville, they'll be talking
about us in Cincinnati."

"Exactly," Alexander agreed.

"Then let's go to Chicago," Herron declared.

"I'm with you," Parker said.

So after making a call to arrange transportation, the three got into
a green 1966 Chevrolet of a friend from Chicago and moved on to
the Windy City. Once there, they found that the shooting in Tennessee was not in the news.

Parker kept thinking about their innocence and initiated a debate. "I think we ought to go back down there and get this worked
out."

"I'm staying where I am," Herron replied.

39

"I'm with Lee," Alexander agreed.

Meanwhile, Bill Allen and Ralph Canady were preparing to board a bus in Louisville.

In Nashville, the police department was relatively empty because most of its officers were in the streets looking for the suspects and anybody who might have seen what transpired on the dead-end avenue. The key figures in the investigation, homicide detective chief Mickey McDaniel and homicide detectives Clarence Huffman, Bill Nichols, and Tom Cathey, were huddled in an office.

"The DA wants to know what we've got," McDaniel declared.

"What did you tell him?" Cathey asked.

"Not much," McDaniel responded as a few other police officers entered the room. "Just some names."

"And a dead police officer," Huffman reminded him.

"Where are the 38s [Pete] Johnson and [Wayne] Thomasson had?" an officer asked.

"So they were cashing bad paper?" McDaniel asked before answering the question.

"I don't know if anybody actually saw that," Cathey answered. "It was [Amos] Bridges and [Rick] Hughes, for sure. The ones in the red Ford."

"I'll go by the liquor store and see what I can come up with," another officer said.

"I'll find a witness at the shooting site," volunteered another.

"There's a woman, Pearlie Brown, on Herman Street who said she, her son, and another high school boy heard the gunfire, then saw two men running in the dark," Huffman commented. "Said they were on the railroad tracks going west."

"Let's talk with them some more," McDaniel suggested. "Let's see if they can help."

"That's right," Cathey agreed. "But I'd imagine they're as scared as everybody else in the Valley."

One frightened person was the mother of John Walker. She looked out of a window at her home and saw police officers armed with powerful rifles in the yard. They were looking for her son, who was out of the city with Parker, Herron, and Alexander.

Then there was a knock at the door.

"Where's John Walker?" an officer asked as he looked inside the house.

"I haven't seen him in a few days," she answered.

"Get out of the way, lady, and let us have a look for ourselves," another officer ordered.

Then they rushed past her.

She was afraid, with good reason, and began crying. Others in North Nashville were fearful, too. The Nashville newspapers, *The Tennessean* and the *Nashville Banner*, were contributing to the feeling of panic by the way they presented the information furnished by the police department. Articles were run praising the bravery of officers Johnson and Thomasson and labeling the five men black militants.

Even knowing that all this was happening, Parker decided to return to Cincinnati. He wanted to confer with his father, Correlus Parker, a lawyer who ran a cocktail lounge and restaurant. "I think I've got to tell the truth and let the chips fall," he said as the debate raged in Chicago. He convinced the friend who had driven them to Chicago to accompany him on the return trip to Cincinnati. He had no way of knowing it at the time, but Canady was having the same thoughts. He, too, was moving toward his home in Cincinnati.

In Middletown, Ohio, less than one hour from Cincinnati, Parker had a memorable meeting.

"Damn, we're about out of gas," the driver exclaimed as he looked at the gas gauge.

"We don't have much further," Parker responded.

"But we've got zero gas."

"And zero money."

But Parker saw hope in the strangest of places. A police cruiser was parked alongside the road in downtown Middletown, and he instructed the driver to pull in behind it.

"Hello, men," Parker said after tapping on the window of the cruiser and awakening two white officers who were snoozing away the cold night.

"Could we help you?" one of the officers asked.

"I hope so," Parker answered. "We're students trying to get home to Cincinnati, but we're out of gas and money. I was wondering if you could loan us a couple of bucks."

"Well, I don't know if . . . ," the officer said before Parker interrupted him and showed him a torn piece of paper and a pen.

"Sir, if you'll give us two bucks and put your name and address on this paper, I'll gladly send you the money as soon as we get home."

The other police officer reached into his pocket and brought forth three dollars. He handed the money to Parker and shook his head as he attempted to hand him the paper and pen.

"That's OK. You can have the money. I just want you to do one thing."

"What's that?"

"When they talk about police brutality, I want you to tell them about this."

With a sigh of relief, Parker thanked the officers and returned to the Chevrolet, thinking to himself that he would find the men again and repay them after he cleared his name.

But the Nashville police department was one step ahead of Parker while building its case against the five black men involved in the shooting. That became apparent the next morning when Pearlie Brown, her son Johnny Brown, and Larry Wade were interviewed in their apartment.

"Like I told you, Larry and I saw the police cars and that other car," Johnny Brown told the investigating officers. "Then we went inside to get warm, heard a lot of shooting, and came back out."

"I think you saw it, didn't you?" asked an officer. "I mean, you saw them shoot the policemen and take off running."

"No sir," Johnny Brown answered. "Just heard it."

"Don't you hang out at the barbershop with those troublemakers, that gang of thieves we're watching?" one of the officers asked.

"I'm there sometimes. But I don't know nothing about thieves."

"Well, we might be able to put together information tying you to them, those barbershop boys," one of the officers countered. "That's if you don't tell us what you saw down there on Fourteenth."

"I didn't see nothing."

"Come on, son," coaxed another officer. "You don't want the trouble that comes with protecting those killers. We think it happened like this. We think you and Larry Wade saw . . ."

Officers approached Wade in a similar way at school that day. After they had what they wanted, they hurried back to headquarters with their reports.

"What's happening upstairs?" Officer Robert Titsworth asked a fellow worker after noticing the door leading to McDaniel's office had been closed for a long time.

"They're working on the Johnson-Thomasson case."

"Well, why don't they talk to me? Hell, I'm the commanding officer. I've got some thoughts that might be helpful."

"They don't need our help."

"Don't need it or don't want it?" Titsworth retorted in anger. "Hell, from what I'm hearing about it, which isn't much, there are some questions that should be asked. Damn, I've got a bunch of them."

"So how's Thomasson doing?"

"He's coming around," Titsworth replied. "Pretty good, actually. I think he'll make it all the way back."

In downtown Nashville, meanwhile, four black men, three from Birmingham and one from New York City, were being surrounded by police officers who had noticed they were driving a car with Ohio license plates. They had exchanged currency for a roll of dimes at a bank.

"What's this about?" Preston Williams asked officers who had guns trained on him and the other three men. "I don't understand."

"Shut your fucking mouth," swore an officer who pushed him against the car. "We're asking the questions, not you cop-hating niggers."

Eventually the four men were questioned and cleared of any wrongdoing in regard to the shooting. But they were arrested on vagrancy charges, with Williams also being charged with reckless driving, unlawful use of an auto registration, and improper registration.

"If I were you, I'd get out of town with those Ohio license plates on your car," an officer advised Williams at police headquarters.

With both newspapers competing with each other to tie the five fugitives to the "black power" movement—calling them militants—representatives from the local chapter of the Student Non-Violent Coordinating Committee announced that none of the men were members of that group.

EIGHT

As the police department continued its hunt for the fugitives, two old bowling buddies got together at General Hospital to have an important conversation. Homicide detective Tom Cathey visited officer Wayne Thomasson on January 19, less than three full days after the shooting.

Cathey went armed with mug shots in search of conclusive identifications, bringing photographs of Bill Allen and Charles Lee Herron from their arrests in Cincinnati in connection with previous civil rights activities. As they met in the intensive care unit, Cathey was pleased to see his longtime friend so alert.

When Cathey asked him if he felt like talking or looking at some mug shots, Thomasson said yes.

"Did you see officer Johnson shot?" Cathey asked.

"No," Thomasson answered. "I heard the gunfire, but I didn't see the actual shooting. I stepped out of the police car, and they started shooting." This agreed with the theory later advanced in court by Davidson County district attorney Thomas Shriver. "They ambushed me. It seemed like they were all around me."

"How many shots did you fire?" Cathey then inquired.

"I got off four rounds. But I don't know if I hit one of them or not."

Thomasson continued. "They shot me in the gut. I went down, and he shot me again. I could not tell how many subjects there were in the car because the glass was fogged up, but there were definitely more than one. In fact, one of them called another by name, something like Jesse."

Interestingly, Thomasson gave a vivid description of the man who "did most of the shooting," to use his phrase. "He was a male

44

colored, six feet or taller, with a slender build and wearing brown pants, a gray sportcoat, and a green pullover sweater. He had a shotgun or a rifle. I think it had a short barrel. The first shot felt like it hit me in the stomach. The second felt like it hit me in the ass."

Cathey showed Thomasson mug shots of Allen and Herron. As soon as he saw the picture of Allen, he stated that this subject looked very much like the one who had shot him. "I'm sorry I can't help you any more," he apologized after looking at all the photographs.

The rest of their conversation had to do with bowling. "You might have to spot me a few frames the next time out," Thomasson joked with his friend as their conversation ended.

Leroy Dunn, Jr., a first grader at Pearl Elementary School, was on an errand to borrow a cup of sugar from a neighbor for his mother on January 20, when he found what Nashville police had been looking for.

"Wow, this looks like a real gun," he said to himself when he saw a Winchester 22-caliber rifle in the bushes. Reaching for the butt of the rifle, he struggled with it as he began dragging it across the yard.

Leroy Dunn, Sr., was working in the back yard when he looked up and saw his son dragging a rifle toward him. "Look, Daddy, it's a gun," the boy said in an excited tone. Then he pointed the rifle at his father, who stopped, backed up a step, and stood frozen.

"Put it down, Leroy," he said.

His son laughed, looked overhead, and noticed birds flying over his house.

"Put the damn thing down!" yelled the father.

His son yanked up the rifle with a struggle and pulled the trigger. *Boom!*

The father ran toward his son, knocked the rifle from his hands, and tackled him. Observing the alarming action from inside the house, his wife ran to the back porch. Although he told her, "Honey, go call the police," he went inside and placed the call himself.

Lieutenant Bob Hill, who was working in intelligence, answered Dunn's frantic call. When he arrived at the house alone, Leroy Dunn, Jr., took him to the bushes in front of the house, where he combed through the weeds, which were still wet from the snow that had blanketed the city most of the week, and stared wide-eyed at the Glenfield Model 30-30 leaning against the concrete wall, adjacent to where the 22-caliber rifle had been found.

Hill hurried back to his cruiser and radioed headquarters. Informing his commanding officer, James Gossett, about what he had found, he explained, "I think we've got the weapon used to kill Officer Johnson, plus the 22 used in the shoot-out." Within moments a police lab photo crew and a backup cruiser were on the scene.

Gossett, a sergeant in charge of identification, examined the rifles at police headquarters, then gave them to homicide detective Bill Nichols.

Eventually, the rifles were examined by Robert C. Goodwin, a firearms examiner for the Tennessee Bureau of Investigation, who confirmed that the 30-30 and 22 casings found on Fourteenth Avenue could be matched with the weapons. He also matched the slug that had been discovered under slain police officer Pete Johnson with the 30-30.

Included in the discovery file prepared after police officers found the guns was a notation that the book *Quotes From Chairman Mao* was found alongside the 30-30 rifle. Interestingly, the picture taken of the book showed it to be in immaculate condition, none the worse for wear. Later, defense lawyers ironically noted that the inclement weather did not damage the book although the snow had washed fingerprints from the already rusting rifles that were found beside it. They alleged the publication was put there by police officers who were attempting to make the suspects appear to be black militants, perhaps Black Panthers.

Meanwhile, that evening Steve Parker and Ralph Canady were considering turning themselves in at the Cincinnati police department, although neither knew of the other's activities.

Canady had arrived in Cincinnati on January 18, two days after the shooting. Bill Allen and he had stayed one night in Louisville, lodging in a six-dollar motel room near the Greyhound Bus Terminal. The next afternoon they caught a bus for New York City through Columbus, Ohio.

"I think I'd rather go home," Canady told Allen when they were within thirty miles of Columbus.

"No, go with me," Allen pleaded. "It's a big city. It will be easy to get lost in the crowd."

"I think I'd rather be with the home folks," Canady answered, solidifying his decision.

So Canady got off the bus in Columbus and caught the first one available to Cincinnati. Allen stayed on the bus to New York City.

Steve Parker had arrived in Cincinnati by automobile—thanks to an assist from a generous police officer—and had hurried to visit with his father. They met over a cup of coffee on Friday morning.

"Dad, that's the way it went down," he explained. "I was there for a few minutes, then I was gone. Then I heard the shots being fired."

"There's nothing more?" his father asked.

"Nothing. So what now?"

There was a long pause before his father answered. "It's sticky, son. You're black, and there's a white policeman involved in this. And, by all means, let's don't forget that we're talking about Tennessee."

"I know," Steve answered. "I know. Believe me, Dad, I know."

"But all that considered, I think you should turn yourself in to the police department here and start getting this mess straightened out," his father counseled.

There was another pause.

"But for now, son, get some sleep. You'll need to be rested."

At 8:05 P.M. on January 20, Steve Parker and his father walked into the Cincinnati Police Department. "Hello, sir," he said to the desk sergeant.

"Yes, can I help you?"

"Yes sir, I'm Steve Parker," he answered as his father stood beside him. "I believe I'm wanted by the police in connection with a shooting in Tennessee."

"Just stand over there and wait," the sergeant replied. "I'll be with you in a minute."

The son and his father stood for more than ten minutes before the desk sergeant picked up a telephone speaker and announced, "Hey, I've got a guy down here named Parker who says he's wanted in Tennessee."

It did not take nearly that long for the lobby to be filled with detectives, many of whom shook hands with the wanted man and reminded him that they had played high school football against him. Parker took comfort in his fame, but knew it was only a matter of time until things would be much more uncomfortable.

Ultimately, when Steve Parker was interviewed, he told his side of the story. When, however, he read the statement placed in front of him at 11:30 P.M., he refused to sign it.

"Man, you've got a lot of personal stuff in here to make all the other stuff look believable, like I've spilled my guts. You embellished the whole thing, sir, and I'm not going to sign it."

"How so?" asked an officer who was standing nearby.

"For one, you've got me saying things about those rifles that I didn't say. No way. I'm here trying to tell the truth, and you won't let me."

But whether or not he liked the statement, Parker was under

arrest, and law enforcement personnel in Nashville were in the process of extraditing him.

In talking with Cincinnati officials, Correlus Parker gave some wise advice. "I think Nashville needs some time to cool off before my son goes back down there to clear this up."

Steve Parker did not realize it, but Ralph Canady was also in custody in Cincinnati. He also was interviewed by Officer William Dunn. Arriving at police headquarters at 10:30 P.M., Canady told his story and signed a statement at 11:55 P.M.

Just before Parker was taken to jail for a ten-day stay in Cincinnati, his father told him, "Ralph turned himself in, too. He called me. I advised him to come forward, to tell the truth."

The stories Steve Parker and Canady related were strikingly similar, although they were erroneous in spots. Parker's information was more truthful than Canady's. Both said they ran from the scene when the shooting started and rode buses to Cincinnati from Nashville.

Whether the stories told by Parker and Canady were true or not did not appear to matter much to chief homicide detective Mickey McDaniel and some of his associates in the Nashville police department. All they seemed to care about was that two of the five black men were under arrest and would be returned to Tennessee for prosecution.

"Yep, that's correct," McDaniel said during a telephone conversation with an FBI agent in Nashville. "You can tell your friends in Memphis that it's two John Does down and three more murderers with real names to go, that it's definitely William Allen, Charles Lee Herron, and John Alexander we're looking for."

"Where'd you get the info?" the agent asked.

"From the Cincinnati PD," McDaniel answered. "From the interrogators who talked to Parker and Canady."

"We'll act on that when we get their reports," the agent responded.

Two days later, after extensive correspondence between FBI offices in Nashville, Memphis, Cincinnati, and Washington, Allen and Herron were placed on the FBI Most Wanted list and Alexander was placed on the FBI Identification Order list. Agent Claude Curtis of the Memphis office, the man in charge of returning the three remaining fugitives to Tennessee, was suddenly working on the case of his life.

"What have you done the last couple of days?" an agent in Washington asked Curtis by telephone after the case was made such a high priority.

"We're building a data bank," Curtis answered. "We're locating family and friends."

"What's the progress?"

"Just names and addresses for now. They're unknowns without rap sheets. Demonstrations and stuff like that. Nothing big. They're different than most 88s we've seen."

"Well, dammit, they're known now," Washington replied. "Hell, Nashville says they're militants who've killed a police officer. And, Claude, that means you've got to get your ass in gear. The top brass in headquarters wants those fugitives returned to Tennessee. We're gonna put pressure on you. It's a priority."

"Right," Curtis replied. "We're almost around the clock."

"Good. It has to be solved. It's one of those social time bombs, another racial unrest case. The general public is sick of hearing things like that."

Four days after his surrender in Cincinnati, Canady was on his way to Nashville in a police cruiser. He chose not to fight extradition after being advised to take that course of action by his court-appointed lawyer, James Havron, who thought the first man back on the scene stood the best chance of defending himself. He remained talkative during the six-hour trip.

Parker chose to delay extradition, stating that "Nashville needs a period of time to cool off." But he was in Tennessee ten days after his surrender.

Upon their arrivals in Tennessee, both Canady and Parker were charged with first-degree murder in the death of Johnson. Both had hoped that their stories would be believed when they read a story in *The Tennessean* the morning after they surrendered in Cincinnati. The article said, "Thomasson told investigating officers [in fact, homicide detective Tom Cathey] he was shot in the stomach. Thomasson said he fired 'four quick shots' and believed he 'got one of them' because he saw one of the men bend over."

Those statements, which corresponded with similar ones Thomasson made in the hospital that week to his wife, Judy, and in an interview with Cathey, were relayed to the newspaper by his brother, Mort Thomasson, Jr. They were published the same day Johnson was buried after an emotional funeral service at Friendship Baptist Church.

Still, Parker and Canady were having trouble convincing interrogators that Johnson and Thomasson shot at them that night on Fourteenth Avenue.

"I'm telling you, sir, there was a lot of shooting going on as I ran from the scene, down the railroad tracks," Steve Parker told them.

"I haven't talked to anybody else who was there about what happened, but it's impossible for one or two guys to do that much shooting."

That was the last time anybody other than a defense lawyer publicly mentioned, or even hinted, that one or both of the officers fired their revolvers the night of the shooting.

That is, until Allen was apprehended and had the opportunity to tell his side of the story.

NINE

Bill Allen had no idea he was providing lethal evidence against himself when he wrote a letter while he was holed up in the Hotel Grampion in New York City. Since his childhood, he had believed in social equality for blacks and in honest justice, and he was attempting to help Steve Parker and Ralph Canady, as well as his other friends in Nashville who were being treated roughly by police interrogators.

Allen's uncle, Lonnie Pinkston, who was more like an older brother, had told him by telephone that Parker and Canady had received rough treatment since arriving in Nashville. This troubled him, for he considered them brothers, almost literally. He felt the same way about his neighbors and friends who had been stunned and mistreated during the police dragnet in North Nashville.

So with pen in a left hand scarred from a cut sustained years earlier in an automobile fan and with the hope of calming a ferocious storm, Allen wrote:

January 23, 1968

To whom it may concern:

I am the only one who did any shooting in the incident with the police. Steve Parker, Ralph Canady, and the other fellas had nothing to do with it. By the time you get this letter, I will be out of the country. Also, here are some prints to prove who I am.
Sincerely
William G. Allen.

Allen read the words written on a stenographer pad and addressed an envelope to John Walker. Using the pen to put ink on his
right thumb, he pressed it against the paper. He was, in essence,
making a confession.

Allen had no plans to leave the country. He was young and troubled and did not think like a fugitive. But he was smart enough not
to give away too much about his whereabouts. Catching a ride to
Long Island, he mailed the letter.

When John Walker received Allen's letter, he turned it over to public defender James Havron, who had been appointed to represent
Canady. Bound by law, he turned the letter over to the police department, which gave it to Davidson County district attorney
Thomas Shriver.

Shriver and police officers were pleased with the words the letter
contained, and they immediately leaked the letter to *The Ten-
nesseean* and the *Nashville Banner.* When the letter was published,
both newspapers touted it as a confession of guilt. The FBI, which
already had placed Allen on its Most Wanted list, was delighted,
too. Agents had been searching for him in Ohio, and only recently
had they found reason to think he was in New York, as the
postmark indicated.

Allen had been staying alone in a cheap hotel. As he read the
newspaper accounts, he saw that journalists writing about the
shooting had a lot of things wrong. He also realized that people had
not grasped the fear that was gripping blacks in North Nashville,
and probably never would, and that it was going to be difficult for
him to return to his home city.

The atmosphere in North Nashville was frightening. Officers continued to move through the neighborhood at a frantic pace, interrogating people in their apartments during daylight hours and
combing through bars and nightclubs after dark. While they believed that the suspects had left the city, as was proved in the cases
of Parker and Canady, they wanted to be sure.

Meanwhile, Shriver and his associates were building a case
against the suspects. They formulated a theory that the officers had
been ambushed, but witnesses were needed and few, if any, were to
be found.

The people who lived near the shooting were the best prospects.
Therefore Pearlie Brown, Johnny Brown, and Larry Wade—who
had come out of the Brown apartment at the sound of gunfire—
became the objects of intense interrogation. Later they would become star witnesses for the prosecution, by the admission of

Shriver, because "they saw the shooting and saw the trigger men running from the scene with rifles."

[Note: In November 1987 there arose a reason to dispute the total truth of Shriver's claim. That is when Johnny Brown produced a signed affidavit stating he was coerced into testifying that Wade and he had crouched in bushes behind a church and observed the shooting.

Johnny Brown said he lied on the witness stand because police interrogators threatened to link him to a robbery staged by a group of troublemakers he called the "Barber Shop Boys." He said that police officers vowed to arrest him in connection with one of the robberies if he did not testify that he and Wade saw the shooting.

His vow that he lied in court was supported by Pearlie Brown, who said that her son was in their apartment when the shooting took place. She also acknowledged that police officers searched their dwelling after the shooting and later returned to question Johnny Brown. She was not present when the interrogation of her son took place.

But no sooner had Johnny Brown claimed that Wade and he had been in his apartment during the shooting, than Wade claimed that his testimony in 1968 had been accurate. He said they had watched from the spacious field and that they had heard "a lot of rapid gunfire" and "saw fire coming from the barrels." He said it was impossible to tell who had fired weapons or who had run from the scene of the shooting. And while Brown said there was not a chase in progress before the Plymouth was stopped, Wade said there was one. Wade also said the shooting incident was over in a flash, in less than a minute.]

Allen spent his first two days in the New York area with Jackie Wade and her parents in Newark, New Jersey, but friends who telephoned from Cincinnati warned them that he was wanted for murder. They gently suggested that he find another place to stay.

After he had been at the Hotel Grampion for a few days, Allen recalled another friend he had met in Cincinnati. He smiled when Brenda Shivley answered his knock at the door of her apartment in Brooklyn. During the three weeks he stayed there, he sold jewelry from cardboard tables on New York City streets.

On one Saturday morning, acquaintances from Cincinnati arrived to visit Shivley. When they left, Paul and Edna Williams invited him to stay with them in a brownstone apartment in Brooklyn.

During the next several weeks, Allen stayed in contact by telephone with his uncle in Nashville. Every conversation brought worse news. He learned that he was being described as a ruthless murderer. When he began to see his picture in New York newspapers, he knew he was more than a man without a country. He needed to find a new country, and quickly.

"You've got to come back and defend your name," Pinkston pleaded as Allen stood in a telephone booth in Manhattan.

"There's no defense for a black man in Nashville, Uncle Lonnie. You know it's true. They won't believe anything I say."

"Well, that letter won't help you," Pinkston answered.

Nor did going to a party on March 17, after which he was arrested on a marijuana possession charge. He had caught a ride with four other men, but the car had been stopped and marijuana had been found. He had convinced police officers that he was merely in the wrong place at the wrong time, therefore avoiding being booked. He had been fingerprinted already, however, and when the results came back, the FBI soon knew that a fugitive on its Most Wanted list was in the New York area.

Allen did not know that the FBI was tracking him, but he was uneasy because he had been fingerprinted. So he continued to move about the city while waiting for an opportunity to leave the country.

Hope of further escape evaporated about dawn on Saturday, March 23, when the FBI office on Lexington Avenue in Brooklyn received a telephone call from an informant.

"I think that Paul Williams fellow, the one you said might be hanging out with that guy from Tennessee, the one in the picture you folks have, well, I think he's staying in an apartment on Park Place," said a male caller who had been questioned by the FBI.

"How would you know that?" asked the agent.

"I've seen them around, you know, just hanging out. I'd say the guy you want is one of them."

Within minutes, calls were placed to four off-duty FBI agents, including Billy Bob Williams, age thirty-four, and Don Bullard, age forty, and they were summoned to that FBI office.

"Billy Bob, we've got a good lead on a Top Ten," Williams was informed at his house fifty miles away in Middle Town, New Jersey.

"Who's that?" he asked as he glanced toward his wife and their eight-year-old-son.

"William Allen, the guy who's wanted for killing two cops in Nashville."

"Come again?" Williams asked as he glanced again at his son. "Did you say William Allen? My son is named William Allen Williams."

"Well, we need you and Bullard as fast as possible," the agent replied. "We'll round up some help for you."

FBI agents assembled at a brief meeting discussed the possibility that a fugitive on its Most Wanted list was in a three-story, brownstone apartment building on Park Place, then hurried to the scene.

Four FBI agents in two cars pulled to the front of the apartment building, with numerous backup agents waiting to be summoned by radio. It was decided that Williams and Bullard would enter the building, with the others watching the rear.

"Sir, I'm with the FBI," Williams said as he showed his identification to a black man who stood in a hallway just inside the front door. "We're here on a serious matter and would appreciate your help."

After the man walked away, a black woman gazed at the card and badge, then turned toward the stairway without saying a word.

"We're looking for this man, whom we think is staying in this apartment, maybe using the name Paul Williams," Agent Williams said after he followed her up two flights of stairs.

"That's not Williams," she answered while looking at the flyer he was holding. "But he's in an apartment with him. They're probably asleep because I heard them up late last night."

When agent Don Bullard joined Williams on the third floor, he discovered his friend had drawn his 38-Special pistol.

"So we're going on in without backups?" Bullard asked. "Even with a Top Ten in there?"

"We can't risk missing this one," Williams answered in a whisper as he approached the door the woman had identified. "We're going in after him. We'll make the hit. But with caution, for sure."

Then he turned toward the startled black woman and said, "Ma'm, please go out back and tell those other two men what we're doing." He and Bullard watched her hurry down the stairs.

Then Bullard reached for the door knob, quickly turned it, and pushed it open. Williams and he rushed into the room, with Williams reaching for a light switch he did not find.

Once inside the apartment, the agents saw a man asleep on a double bed in the living room. Williams approached him cautiously, with his revolver trained, as Bullard walked toward a smaller bedroom, where he saw a man he thought was asleep in a single bed.

Billy Bob Williams stood over Paul Williams for a second, then gently nudged his nose with the barrel of his pistol. As the startled sleeper opened his eyes, the FBI agent motioned for him to remain quiet.

"I'm an FBI agent," he said in a whisper, "and we're going to sit still a minute. But I want to know who's here with you."

"Just me and him, another guy," Paul Williams said, speaking softly as advised. "My wife is at the store."

Allen had been faking sleep in the adjoining room. He had heard the chatter in the hallway but had stayed under the covers thinking about what he would say. He was not shocked when he opened his eyes and saw Bullard's pistol trained on his head.

Bullard pulled back the covers, looked at the foot of the bed and saw trousers lying across it, and glanced at a nearby chair where he saw a rifle.

"Are you William Garrin Allen?" he asked.

"No, I'm William Huff. I've got a lot of identification to prove that."

"Well, that's interesting," Bullard answered as he pulled the picture of Allen from his coat pocket. "You look like this man to me. I'd like for you to look at this and tell me who you are."

Allen glanced at the picture, nodded slightly, and admitted, "OK, that's me. I'm that man."

"That's what we thought," Bullard replied as a smile came over his face. "Then you won't mind coming down to headquarters with us for a chat, maybe telling us where your friends Herron and Alexander are these days."

For several minutes, all four men discussed the situation. Eventually, they moved to the FBI office on Lexington Avenue, where the questioning continued, mostly about the letter Allen had written almost two months earlier.

"Mr. Allen, give us your story about what happened that night in Nashville," an agent instructed. "You've got to help yourself all you can." Allen told the men he had nothing to say.

"Come on, son, you've got to cooperate," an agent answered politely.

"OK," Allen said. "Five of us were—"

Abruptly, Allen stopped talking after hearing two agents speaking in the doorway of the next room. One of them had commented, "That's the guy who made widows out of two wives in Nashville by killing two police officers."

Allen glanced toward the men, then at the interrogating agent. "I don't have anything else to say." he said. "You're all the same, you guys and them."

The questioning continued after Allen was moved to the West Street Federal Detention Center in New York. The Metropolitan Nashville Police Department already had dispatched three officers to transport him to Tennessee, and he remained quiet. He also refused to sign any of the many documents placed in front of him. He did not fight extradition; he was too inexperienced to understand the process, and he did not have a lawyer to assist him.

During the long automobile ride from New York to Tennessee, Allen repeated his story about why he had written his letter of confession. On the advice of a prisoner he met during his last two nights in New York, he said nothing about the shooting itself to Metro police officers Clarence Huffman, Harold Woods, and John Estes, who were transporting him.

Allen knew he would be facing murder charges in Tennessee. What he did not know at the time was that he would be tried for the death of a white police officer, Wayne Thomasson. Thomasson had died less than two weeks earlier, on the same day that Allen had been arrested on marijuana possession charges.

For obvious reasons, Allen was frightened during the automobile ride to Tennessee. It ended on Sunday night, when he was questioned by Nashville law enforcement personnel. His fear was heightened when he was questioned on Monday night by Nashville police officers and detectives.

The first round of interrogation spawned the fear for his life that kept him from telling the truth on the witness stand during his first trial.

"We want answers to all our questions, straight talk from your stinking black mouth," an investigative officer raged after cocking the trigger of a 45-caliber revolver. "We want to know what you've got to say about what happened out there that night."

Allen remained quiet.

"We're gonna get it out of you one way or another," he threatened. "So you might as well make it easy on yourself. We've talked to Canady and Parker. We want to hear it from you."

"OK, I'll tell you what happened," Allen said. "The dude [police officer Wayne Thomasson] started shooting. I feared for my life, and I shot back at them."

The officer slapped Allen across the mouth.

"You black-ass lyin' nigger," he swore. "You can't say that about one of our brothers. We're not gonna allow you or no other nigger to get on the witness stand and say something like that. We can blow your black ass away any time we want to, just by saying you tried to escape.

"If you go out there and say that, that's exactly what we'll do to you. We can come get you any time we want to. Do you understand that? If you tell somebody that story, we'll be back to get you."

Those words echoed for a long time, from that night in late March until the start of a murder trial in late November, and Allen took them to heart. He thought about telling his lawyer, Whitworth Stokes, about the threats, but decided against it because he thought the public would consider his revelation the pitiful cry of a criminal.

When Parker, Canady, and he were escorted to court by police officers armed with high-powered rifles, Allen became more determined to avoid telling the truth in court.

Coming clean seemed senseless to him, anyway. Press coverage of the case was downright cruel to the defendants, a sign of the time. The stage was set for a trial, yes, but public sentiment made it appear that it would be another round of *To Kill a Mockingbird*.

"Well, that's interesting," Bullard answered as he pulled the picture of Allen from his coat pocket. "You look like this man to me. I'd like for you to look at this and tell me who you are."

Allen glanced at the picture, nodded slightly, and admitted, "OK, that's me. I'm that man."

"That's what we thought," Bullard replied as a smile came over his face. "Then you won't mind coming down to headquarters with us for a chat, maybe telling us where your friends Herron and Alexander are these days."

For several minutes, all four men discussed the situation. Eventually, they moved to the FBI office on Lexington Avenue, where the questioning continued, mostly about the letter Allen had written almost two months earlier.

"Mr. Allen, give us your story about what happened that night in Nashville," an agent instructed. "You've got to help yourself all you can." Allen told the men he had nothing to say.

"Come on, son, you've got to cooperate," an agent answered politely.

"OK," Allen said. "Five of us were—"

Abruptly, Allen stopped talking after hearing two agents speaking in the doorway of the next room. One of them had commented, "That's the guy who made widows out of two wives in Nashville by killing two police officers."

Allen glanced toward the men, then at the interrogating agent. "I don't have anything else to say." he said. "You're all the same, you guys and them."

The questioning continued after Allen was moved to the West Street Federal Detention Center in New York. The Metropolitan Nashville Police Department already had dispatched three officers to transport him to Tennessee, and he remained quiet. He also refused to sign any of the many documents placed in front of him. He did not fight extradition; he was too inexperienced to understand the process, and he did not have a lawyer to assist him.

During the long automobile ride from New York to Tennessee, Allen repeated his story about why he had written his letter of confession. On the advice of a prisoner he met during his last two nights in New York, he said nothing about the shooting itself to Metro police officers Clarence Huffman, Harold Woods, and John Estes, who were transporting him.

Allen knew he would be facing murder charges in Tennessee. What he did not know at the time was that he would be tried for the death of a white police officer, Wayne Thomasson. Thomasson had died less than two weeks earlier, on the same day that Allen had been arrested on marijuana possession charges.

For obvious reasons, Allen was frightened during the automobile ride to Tennessee. It ended on Sunday night, when he was questioned by Nashville law enforcement personnel. His fear was heightened when he was questioned on Monday night by Nashville police officers and detectives.

The first round of interrogation spawned the fear for his life that kept him from telling the truth on the witness stand during his first trial.

"We want answers to all our questions, straight talk from your stinking black mouth," an investigative officer raged after cocking the trigger of a 45-caliber revolver. "We want to know what you've got to say about what happened out there that night."

Allen remained quiet.

"We're gonna get it out of you one way or another," he threatened. "So you might as well make it easy on yourself. We've talked to Canady and Parker. We want to hear it from you."

"OK, I'll tell you what happened," Allen said. "The dude [police officer Wayne Thomasson] started shooting. I feared for my life, and I shot back at them."

The officer slapped Allen across the mouth.

"You black-ass lyin' nigger," he swore. "You can't say that about one of our brothers. We're not gonna allow you or no other nigger to get on the witness stand and say something like that. We can blow your black ass away any time we want to, just by saying you tried to escape.

"If you go out there and say that, that's exactly what we'll do to you. We can come get you any time we want to. Do you understand that? If you tell somebody that story, we'll be back to get you."

Those words echoed for a long time, from that night in late March until the start of a murder trial in late November, and Allen took them to heart. He thought about telling his lawyer, Whitworth Stokes, about the threats, but decided against it because he thought the public would consider his revelation the pitiful cry of a criminal.

When Parker, Canady, and he were escorted to court by police officers armed with high-powered rifles, Allen became more determined to avoid telling the truth in court.

Coming clean seemed senseless to him, anyway. Press coverage of the case was downright cruel to the defendants, a sign of the time. The stage was set for a trial, yes, but public sentiment made it appear that it would be another round of *To Kill a Mockingbird*.

TEN

The 1960s were years of misunderstanding and polarization in the United States. A decade of drastic social change, it brought immense personal suffering to many who were at the forefront of the turmoil.

It would be wrong to attribute the deaths of officers Pete Johnson and Wayne Thomasson or the first-degree murder convictions of Bill Allen, Steve Parker, and Ralph Canady to the tensions growing out of civil rights conflicts. However, it is clear that the climate that existed in Tennessee at that time was a contributing factor.

The national plague was a matter of misunderstanding. Blacks did not understand whites; whites did not understand blacks. Blacks did not understand blacks; whites did not understand whites. It was as if everybody wanted harmony, a return to peace in the streets, but nobody knew how to bring it about.

Not even hippies singing about love and Vietnam protesters chanting about peace could detract from black-versus-white tensions in the United States.

Newspaper articles mirrored that tension as they reported the horrifying news of the decade. In Nashville, *The Tennessean* and the *Banner* magnified the tension with their reporting in the months leading to the trial, presenting civil rights leaders as communist inspired threats to the nation's security.

Interestingly, Allen, Parker, and Canady were tried for the death of a white police officer, Thomasson, when a black police officer, Johnson, died first after the shooting. District attorney Thomas Shriver said it was because the surviving family of Johnson, which included an estranged wife, did not want to prosecute in the case.

So it was black against white, again, a bitter sign of the times, and Allen, Parker, and Canady were victimized by rumors that tied them to the Black Power movement first advanced by Stokely Carmichael. Certainly "black power" was a term the citizenry of Nashville was familiar with and, in the majority of cases—blacks and whites included—disdained with a fervor.

On April 7, 1967, Carmichael brought his Black Power movement to Nashville as a part of a national tour of college campuses. He told a rally at Tennessee A&I (the former name of Tennessee State University), "Your universities are controlled by and for white people. And they happen to be against you, the black students."

At Fisk University that same day, Carmichael said, "If we don't get justice, we're going to tear this country apart." He spoke at a symposium at Vanderbilt University, a predominantly white private institution, and said, "Our Negro communities can become either concentration camps filled with miserable people who have only the power to destroy, or they can become organized communities that make a meaningful contribution to our nation."

The appearance in Nashville of Carmichael, then the chairman of the Student Non-Violent Coordinating Committee (SNCC), made an impact, to say the least.

On the evening of April 8, a black owner of a cafe on the Fisk campus called police to eject a black for drunkenness. The police officers who answered the summons became targets for rocks, bottles, and bricks. Shouts of "black power, black power, black power" were heard. The next night, the unrest moved a mile away to Tennessee State. Several hundred blacks were growing uneasy as they milled on that campus; gunfire, looting, and arson followed. One black student was wounded by a gunshot, ten police officers and seven students were injured by thrown objects, and fifty people, including two Carmichael associates, were arrested and charged with "inciting a riot."

"Beyond a doubt, black power is a deep-seated, cancerous conspiracy and its advocates put forth tremendous effort to have this dangerous disease permeate every phase of our university life," said W. S. Davis, then the president of Tennessee State.

Nashvillians remembered the alarming words offered by Carmichael and Davis. What seemed to be lost on them was the debate that raged among blacks and whites alike as to how to define the term *black power.*

When Willie Ricks, a twenty-three-year-old official with the Student Non-Violent Coordinating Committee, first advanced in 1966 the "black power" term in Yazoo City, Mississippi—citing that a "white backlash" had led to the defeat of the Civil Rights Bill in

Congress—it was denounced by many members of the black leadership.

The Reverend Martin Luther King continued to preach that peaceful demonstration was the way to secure racial equality. He fretted over the militant behavior of some blacks until his death in April 1968.

Charles Evers, field secretary of the National Association for the Advancement of Colored People (NAACP), called black power a dangerous thing.

"It doesn't mean that you take over the country," Carmichael said in defense. "Black power is the coming together of black people in the struggle for their liberation. Once they have a power base, they can lobby effectively for their own interests."

That said, King softened his objections, commenting, "I see it as an appeal to racial pride. [It is] an appeal to the Negro not to be ashamed of being black. [It is] the transfer of the powerlessness of the Negro into positive, constructive power."

Said Floyd McKissick, who had succeeded James Farmer as head of the Congress for Racial Equality (CORE), "Unless we can get around to unifying black power, we're going to be in bad shape."

So the entire nation, not just Nashville, was confused and upset with black power. The term had about as many definitions as there were people who contemplated it.

The basic connotation was something wicked, from blacks and whites in Mississippi, Alabama, and Tennessee to blacks and whites in Chicago, Illinois. It was in Chicago in 1966, as public schools integrated in the Deep South with relative peace, that King faced an unruly crowd during a speech. It was there that he said, "I have never seen such hate, not in Mississippi or Alabama, as I see here in Chicago."

The same misunderstanding had presented itself in 1962 when James Meredith enrolled at the University of Mississippi, breaking the color barrier, and in 1963, when Alabama governor George Wallace unsuccessfuly attempted to block integration at the University of Alabama by standing in the door leading to registration tables. It was still commonplace in the nation in 1968, when Allen, Parker, and Canady awaited their trial in Tennessee.

It was a most eventful year.

On April 4 in Memphis, Tennessee, Martin Luther King was shot and killed by James Earl Ray, a prison escapee from Missouri who supported segregation. On June 5 in Los Angeles, former U.S. attorney general Robert Kennedy, then a forty-two-year-old senator from New York with presidential aspirations, was shot and killed by Sirhan Sirhan.

George Wallace, the controversial Alabama governor, ran unsuccessfully for the presidency, advancing a states rights platform but rarely discussing segregation. The winner was Richard Nixon, who would later be forced from office because of the Watergate conspiracy.

And in a monumental accomplishment, Medgar Evers was elected mayor in Fayette, Mississippi. He was the first black to secure such a position in the Deep South.

Allen, Parker, and Canady watched from a jail cell in Nashville as most of these events transpired. Parker and Canady had been allowed to go free on bond until Thomasson—the white officer—died in March. Then they were locked up with Allen until their trial opened.

"Oh, my God," Parker exclaimed the afternoon he read that Thomasson had died. "It could get worse now."

"But you're innocent, son," Correlus Parker replied.

"I know that, and you know that. But this changes the entire picture."

Allen, Parker, and Canady knew what was being said on the streets of Nashville, as well as what was being written in the newspapers. They did not, however, have first-hand knowledge of the events that had taken place during the previous spring and summer after Carmichael had built a fire under Nashville blacks and sent many of them on emotional sprees in the streets. All three of them had been working in Cincinnati.

That raises a question that begs an answer. Was it fair, or honest, for Nashville leaders to tie the defendants to the fiery confrontations on the Fisk and Tennessee State campuses the previous spring when they were not even in Tennessee at the time?

ELEVEN

J ean Gourieux seated herself in front of the stenography machine and surveyed her surroundings. The cramped courtroom on the sixth floor of the Davidson County Courthouse in Nashville was more crowded than usual, with several police officers mixing with curious and concerned observers jammed into five rows of pews on both sides of the room. The court reporter felt tension in her legs and in her normally relaxed fingers as she prepared to record the proceedings in the highly publicized trial.

"Keep your eyes open, Miss Gourieux," a police officer warned. "And if the Black Panthers charge in here with guns blasting, get under the table with your face pressed to the floor."

"Surely we won't have anything like that," Gourieux answered in disbelief.

"I don't know," he commented. "We're hearing they're gonna come in here firing. But don't worry too much about it. We've got the place covered."

He then pointed toward the back of the courtroom, where officers were now lining the back wall with rifles in their hands. Shaking her head, she asked, "You're serious about this?"

"Yes, Ma'm," he replied. "And we're serious about bringing these men to justice."

From the outset it was obvious to Gourieux that the trial was going to be unusual, if not downright fiery. Her opinion was shared by Judge Raymond L. Leathers, who had to oversee proceedings against three black men charged with first-degree murder in the death of a white police officer.

The man on a seat almost as hot as those occupied by the defendants was Davidson County district attorney Thomas Shriver. He had a perfect case to try, and it appeared not so much a question of what the verdict would be, but what the sentences would be.

Leathers realized this. He had taken much care to ensure that the jury selection process was done properly, but the jury selected contained eleven white men and one white woman. Of the 324 prospective jurors questioned, only six were blacks; at the time Tennessee voter lists did not include many of that race. It was ironic that Bill Allen, Steve Parker, and Ralph Canady would have their futures resting in the hands of twelve whites because civil rights activists before them had failed to register enough black voters, something they had worked diligently to accomplish.

On Thanksgiving Day 1968, jurors were sworn in a trial that could have resulted in three deaths in the electric chair. That is the sentence Shriver and most of the public wanted, and he had been quoted several times in Nashville newspapers to that effect. He was young, in his thirties, eager, and, according to many observers, politically ambitious. He was supported, most ably, by assistant district attorney John Hollins, who was known for his skillful courtroom interrogations.

Since two police officers had been killed, Shriver and Hollins had public outcry on their side. Readers in Middle Tennessee had digested newspaper reports that labeled the defendants "cop-killers," "Black Panthers," "racial activists," and the like. During that time, those words were guaranteed to ignite the emotions of the masses, especially with the memory of civil unrest from the spring and summer of 1967 still lingering.

Whitworth Stokes, the thirty-one-year-old white lawyer for Allen, understood the situation facing him and his client. So he developed an almost casual plan of defense, advising his defendant to, in essence, keep quiet and hope for the best. His goal was clear: avoid the electric chair.

Allen was frightened. His fears had been heightened by a police officer the morning the trial opened. The officer told him that either the jury would punish him or somebody else would after the verdict had been rendered.

Canady was represented by Eugene Smith, a black lawyer from Cincinnati in his forties, who had replaced James Havron, who had been appointed by the court. Smith's strategy was to point the finger elsewhere. Smith and his secretary were booked at the ninth floor of the Hermitage Hotel. Nobody else was put on that floor, which was closely guarded. In fact, Smith was not permitted to come and go at will, either. His meals were brought to him and he was only permitted to leave the hotel when armed deputies escorted

him to the courthouse each day. In the meantime, his car was locked
away in the Davidson County garage and, according to him, he was
denied its use to secure information he needed to defend his client.
He would later become a story himself because of his constant objections and peculiar questions.

Parker was represented by two black lawyers, David Vincent and
Robert Lillard, both of whom seemed to have an easier case to defend. It was obvious that their client had driven the Plymouth to the
scene of the shooting but that he had been clear of the automobile
and any weapons when the gunfire erupted. That was their planned
case for the jurors, most of whom admitted having previous knowledge of the events leading to the trial.

Parker was also supported by his father, Correlus Parker, a lawyer.
So vocal during recesses was the elder Parker from his seat among
the observers that Stokes chose to put him on a list of prospective
witnesses, just to get him out of the way.

The prosecution was the favorite, no doubt, and the defense was
disarmed somewhat by Allen's unwillingness to advance a self-defense or in-fear-for-life explanation. Stokes, president of the state
chapter of the American Civil Liberties Union, had a scared client.

Shriver put together a strong case based on the theory that the
police officers had been ambushed by blacks who had been taught
to fight a prejudicial society with force. Also, he relied heavily on
the notion that the defendants had been involved in the cashing of
stolen money orders and that they were getting out of town to avoid
arrest. He presented fifty witnesses before court was adjourned on
December 9.

There were only five witnesses for the defense—not counting two
for the state who were declared hostile—before the closing arguments were presented on December 10 and 11. The three defendants took the witness stand on their behalfs, with a nervous and
tentative Allen being last and the least impressive. They were supported by testimony from Lonnie Pinkston, an uncle to Allen, and
Mrs. Ellariz Louise King Allen, mother of Allen.

Shriver wasted little time stabbing at the hearts of jurors. The
district attorney called as his first witness Mrs. Wayne Thomasson,
widow of the slain police officer.

Mrs. Thomasson, who sat through the entire trial at the prosecuting attorney's table, provided jurors with evidence that she had
been married to Wayne Thomasson and was the mother of three
children, ages two through nine. She told them she had learned
about the shooting through a news bulletin on television, had telephoned police department headquarters and discovered it was her
husband who had been wounded, had gone to General Hospital that

night to check on his condition, and had visited him almost daily until his death caused by totally unexpected infections. She was an attractive lady, who committed suicide less than a year after the trial ended, and her testimony coupled with her teary behavior provided more foundation for an already emotional case.

Vincent, who attended school with Johnson, noticed that the prosecution team and Judge Leathers had numerous conferences during the jury-selection process. Jury selection had become particularly tricky because of U.S. Supreme Court rulings on capital punishment and civil rights cases elsewhere, mostly in Illinois and Mississippi.

A snicker arose in the courtroom when a prospective juror, when asked if he had anything else to add, replied, "Yeah. I don't like niggers."

It was not a modern court case, to say the least, because woeful little investigation went into the preparation of the presentation heard by jurors. As Vincent put it, "It was trial by trick in those days. You waited for emotional moments and went for the kill. The judicial system at that time was so archaic that defense lawyers did not have access to such important documents as police reports, which included an overview of the ballistics tests, or a list of witnesses for the prosecution.

"An ideal jury for the defense in those days was twelve retired railroad or street car men. That has changed in these more sophisticated times. Now, it'd be good to have twelve college professors up there, individuals more capable of weighing the merits of complicated evidence."

As it was, the emotional factor was where Hollins shined for the prosecution. Opposing lawyers were humored by his approach to a murder trial: "Bird in the cage, rat in the trap, fish in the barrel; then they killed them," as Stokes described it.

No doubt, the prosecution had jurors capable of taking such a description at face value. At the time, most blacks were viewed with suspicion by much of the Nashville population, and few had a chance to be seated on the jury, a fact that became the source of debate among lawyers. The criminal court clerk summoned so many prospective jurors who were not accepted, that new candidates had to be found overnight. The defense argued that the state should use electric or telephone service subscription lists when tapping candidates, not voter lists. When that motion was denied by Judge Leathers, Stokes smiled; he was hoping to find procedural errors in the trial so he could appeal the case, which he was convinced he had no chance of winning in Nashville.

Stokes, who attended school with Thomasson, knew the prevailing passions did not favor the defendants. They were alive; the police officers were dead.

Nor was general public sentiment in their corner, at least in the white community. As for the black community, some of its citizens had sympathy for the defendants, but they were afraid to show it.

TWELVE

District Attorney Shriver knew he had to present a reason why officer Pete Johnson stopped the Plymouth driven by Steve Parker on the night of January 16. There had not been a pickup order for the automobile, so the state needed to provide an explanation why cars 16 and 45 followed and halted the vehicle, after forcing the defendants down a dead-end avenue.

So on the first day of the trial Shriver paraded private citizens and police officers to the witness stand in an effort to prove the accused men were involved in cashing fraudulent money orders. He elicited testimony from R. L. Mitchell, who worked at Val-Dot Liquor Store and indicated that Canady and John Alexander were in the store the day before the incident to cash American Express money orders. Mitchell's testimony was supported by Matt Willard, who worked at the St. Charles Liquor Store, and Nashville police officers Jesse Patterson, William St. John, James Byrd, and G. L. Lilley.

But there was no mention of Allen, Parker, or Charles Lee Herron knowing about the scheme or being involved in it.

The witnesses also testified that Kenny Bridges and Rick Hughes were involved in cashing fraudulent money orders. Bridges and Hughes lived in the 1900 block of Hermosa Street, from which the five young men had left the night of the shooting. It also was testified a red 1966 Ford owned by Hughes was used in the money order scheme, as on occasion was a light-colored sedan presumed by prosecutors to be the Plymouth.

That contention was supported a couple of days later by detective Edward Beach. He was called to the witness stand after it became evident that an undisputable link between the Plymouth and the cashing of fraudulent money orders had not been established. He testified that an employee at Val-Dot Liquor Store told him "male coloreds in a white Plymouth with Ohio license plates" had been seen on the premises. That was the last testimony relating the Plymouth to the money orders, even if it was hearsay.

Future testimony indicated that while no arrest warrants had been issued with regard to the fraudulent money orders, the police department had been zeroing in on suspects. Officers were looking for the Ford with Michigan license plates 2893CL. On the witness stand Lilley stated he answered a summons to the Val-Dot Liquor Store on the night of January 16, the date of the shooting, after receiving a police radio transmission from Patterson. Through another police radio transmission he learned that Johnson had located the Ford in front of the triplex apartments at 1906 Hermosa Street, but he did not testify the Plymouth with Ohio license plates 4716CJ was under surveillance. To the contrary, under cross-examination by the defense, he confirmed there had not been any mention of the automobile Johnson and Thomasson stopped.

The testimony by Lilley, a sergeant, was supported by St. John, an assistant police chief with province over communications, and Byrd, a sergeant in charge of the radio room that night.

Lilley, who was driving police cruiser 40, testified he had conferred with Johnson and police officer Raymond Black in the 2100 block of Hermosa Street. He said they had discussed searching the triplex apartments at 1906 Hermosa Street and that he had arrived there after answering the call to Val-Dot Liquor Store. Johnson and Black were seated in their police cruisers in front of the apartments, and Thomasson was in his parked cruiser three blocks east of the apartments.

Lilley testified that Johnson, Black, and he were preparing to go to the triplex apartments at 1906 Hermosa Street when they spotted the Plymouth turning onto the street from a driveway running alongside the buildings. Johnson then decided to follow the departing automobile.

When asked specifically why Johnson and Thomasson followed the Plymouth, Lilley answered,. "They did that at their own will." He also said, "There was no connection [between the Plymouth] to the money orders or the Ford."

So *why* remained the key word to consider.

[Note: During the fall of 1987, as North Nashville residents began talking more about an old case, a likely reason reappeared. Many North Nashvillians said Johnson had become romantically interested in a woman who attended Fisk University, that he had been having problems at home, and was estranged from his wife,

and that he had become miffed when one of the men who frequented the triplex apartments had secured the affections of the
woman he was pursuing. There was plenty of conjecture that he had
followed the sedan that night with the thought that the man he was
angry at was in it.]

Surprisingly, the next witness called by the prosecution was a
Knoxville College student who had visited two of the triplex apartments on Hermosa Street that night. Beverly Amelia Howard, who
in 1968 had been a student at Fisk University, confirmed that Allen,
Canady, Parker, Alexander, and Herron had left 1910 Hermosa
Street in the Plymouth. She confirmed seeing a rifle leaning against
a wall in the apartment, seeing luggage being packed in the trunk of
the car, and hearing the men say they were going to Old Hickory
and on to Cincinnati.

The prosecution declared Howard a hostile witness when her testimony contradicted a statement she had given police officers early
on the morning after the shooting. She had said all of the five men
in the Plymouth had knowledge of the fraudulent money order
scheme, also that she had seen them put rifles into the car that
night. In court she said the statement had been forced from her by
police department interrogators who coerced her and frightened her
by their aggressive behavior. In support of her change in testimony,
she detailed how numerous residents of the 1900 block of Hermosa
Street had been roused from sleep and treated rudely by police officers after the incident.

On cross-examination, defense attorneys used the next witness,
U.S. marshal W. W. Batey, to advance the thought of police department brutality. The middle district chief deputy confirmed he had
requested police radio transmission tapes from between midnight
and 9 A.M. on January 17 to investigate a claim against officer
Thomas Smith. He testified he learned later that the man who had
identified himself as police chief Herbert Kemp had told him those
tapes had been reused, even though tapes of the police radio transmission from the hours just before and just after the shooting had
been preserved and transcribed.

That testimony added suspense to substantial legal squabbling on
the part of attorneys. The prosecution wanted the jury to hear the
tapes of radio transmission just before, during, and just after the
shooting, and the defense objected to such evidence being used in
court.

Judge Leathers, who heard arguments in the absence of the jury,
ruled in favor of the prosecution. The tapes were played and became a matter of record, with the frantic words of a wounded
Thomasson the most moving, and with Lilley testifying as to what

was happening among police officers as the radio transmissions were being made.

This precedent-setting decision by Judge Leathers marked the first time that taped recordings were permitted as evidence in court.

A transcript of the tapes lacked several minutes, when court testimony said the tape recorder used that night automatically labeled police radio transmission at minute intervals. That created a questionable lapse in time; the transcript indicated only four minutes passed from the time the Plymouth and Car 16 left the triplex until Thomasson announced that both police officers had been shot. Following a transmission recorded at 9:33 P.M., there were no further recorded conversations until 9:37 P.M. The ride covered several city blocks on icy and snowy streets, with two significant inclines to be negotiated and two stops to be made. Officer Robert White testified that speed in excess of twenty miles-per-hour was all but impossible under such conditions.

Later, when portions of the taped recordings were played in the presence of the jury, it was pointed out by Eugene Smith that a woman police radio dispatcher had been replaced by a man police radio dispatcher during the alleged high-speed chase. The prosecution said he had merely spelled the woman, without further explanation, and at 9:38 P.M. said, "All cars stand by," which was his first statement. This was just after Thomasson had asked, "Where's he going?" This confusion heightened suspicions among the defense that the taped recordings had been tampered with.

Twenty years later, in January 1988, it was learned that the police department and the district attorney had used a large reel of tape to pull off portions of the police radio transmissions that were "pertinent to the case." Also, the district attorney had a typed transcription of the police radio transmissions at its disposal in the event the taped recordings were not allowed in court. That transcription was made on January 17, the morning after the shooting, and was somewhat different from the taped recordings heard in court in that various statements were lumped together and various statements were attributed to people different from those named by Lilley on the witness stand.

Sandra McMurty Corbin of the police department services division testified it took her three hours to type a transcript of the taped recordings of about an hour of the police radio transmissions. She said that police officers and she had to listen to much of it several times before they could definitely determine what was said and who said it. She affirmed the accuracy of the transcript she completed.

Still, there seemed to be a glaring recorded mistake and a revealing recorded statement made by Johnson as he followed the

Plymouth, stopped the automobile, and met his terrible death. He stated he was pulling over the automobile at the intersection of Herman Street and Fifteenth Avenue, which reached a dead end at Herman Street, which did not appear on the transcript. Lilley also had testified that Johnson had said, "I want this" when he decided to pursue the Plymouth, but that comment did not show up on the typed transcript, either.

The defense did not advance the love triangle conjecture during the trial, although many North Nashville residents claim it was known at the time.

[Note: In July 1988, Bill Nichols, a lieutenant on the Metro police force who in 1968 served as a homicide detective, said archaic police radio equipment could have caused the suspicious lapses on the taped recordings from that night. "Our transmitters weren't too good in 1968," he said. "For instance, the statement made by Johnson to Lilley ('I want this') could've been heard by Lilley because he was near Johnson, but not heard by the radio dispatcher at headquarters. That's a possible reason it didn't show up on the taped recording."]

Nor did the defense question two recorded statements made by Thomasson just before and just after the shooting. The introduction of both statements as evidence would have damaged the credibility of the contention by the prosecution that Johnson was killed as soon as he stopped the automobile and that Thomasson was killed when he arrived a minute or two later. After Johnson said he was stopping the Plymouth, Thomasson said, "Put me out with him," police department banter that indicates both police cruisers were on the scene. After the shooting took place, Thomasson told how the men jumped out with "sawed-off shotguns" and ran around the warehouse "on foot." Thus, the question: If Thomasson was not on the scene and if he was ambushed a minute or two later, as the prosecution claimed, how did he see any of the men exit the automobile with weapons or see any of the men flee on foot?

[Note: Although during the summer and fall of 1987, several Nashville police officers said there had never been any question about when Johnson and Thomasson arrived on the scene, Shriver painted another picture. The police officers contend that authorities knew all along that Johnson and Thomasson had arrived at the scene simultaneously.

In March 1988, after defense lawyer Sumter Camp was provided a cassette tape of the police radio transmissions by the district attorney, another interesting omission came to light. On the transcript of the transmissions provided by Nashville police in 1968, Thomasson was quoted as saying, "Three fellas jumped out.

They're armed with sawed-off shotguns." On the tape provided twenty years later, he said, "Three fellas jumped out (and ran). They're armed with sawed-off shotguns." The "and ran" was left out. Three men running from police officers, as Parker, Herron and Alexander did, and being shot at is much different from all five of the men waiting to ambush somebody.

If the taped recording was somewhat accurate, if not totally, it filled in some of the gaps in time for those who studied the shooting. For instance, only fifty-five seconds passed from the time Johnson said he was going to stop "this other car at the top of the hill" until he said the car was trying to get away from him at least four blocks away. And only one minute and forty seconds passed from the time Thomasson asked "where's he going" on the police radio until he returned to the police radio and said he and the other police officer had been shot. In other words, the entire ordeal happened fairly fast—with three vehicles being stopped on a slick street, with a police officer getting out of his police cruiser, with one man exiting another automobile, putting his hands on top of it and walking to a warehouse wall, with another police officer getting out of his police cruiser, with four men being flushed from an automobile, with two men leaving the automobile and running, with enough gunfire being exchanged to kill one police officer and seriously wound another, and with the wounded officer collecting his senses, getting back to his cruiser, and telling a police radio dispatcher what had happened—too quickly to support the theory that an ambush had taken place.

During the trial, another interesting picture was painted in the minds of jurors when it was stated that a "stamp machine" had been found in the trunk of the Plymouth. In reality, the "stamp machine" was an ink blotter that had been used to put dates on the fraudulent money orders cashed by several of the men who frequented the triplex apartments on Hermosa Street. The term *stamp machine* conjures a picture of something more elaborate, such as a machine!

But painting pictures was the responsibility of the prosecution team in this case. Its members did so vividly, employing deception at times, whether intentional or not.]

THIRTEEN

The testimony district attorney Thomas Shriver elicited from Johnny Brown, Larry Wade, and Pearlie Brown was invaluable. Other than the defendants, they were the only alleged eyewitnesses who could tell the jury what transpired at the scene of the shooting.

Johnny Brown and Wade had been walking home from a basketball game at a nearby recreation center when they saw the police following the defendants. According to a notorized affidavit signed by Johnny Brown in November 1987, they had been told what to say in court by police officers.

Pearlie Brown had braved frigid temperatures when she saw two men running along the railroad tracks within twenty-five yards of her back stoop. She had come out of her apartment at 1601 Herman Street after hearing gunfire.

In court Johnny Brown and Wade testified that they had seen emergency flashing lights on Fourteenth Avenue and had seen unidentifiable males running to and fro and they had heard gunfire. They testified that they had witnessed the shooting while crouched behind bushes at a nearby church. They said they had seen three men running from the scene, heading east along railroad tracks, moving toward downtown.

All three also testified they had seen two men, one taller than the other and both slim, running west along railroad tracks, each carrying a rifle.

Shriver concluded that the two men they saw with the rifles were Bill Allen and Ralph Canady, which led him to portray them as the trigger men. As for the other defendant, Steve Parker, Shriver portrayed him as being on the scene and, therefore, part of what he perceived was a plan to kill the police officers.

But there were so many contradictions in the testimony of the three key witnesses that it seemed logical to conclude that only the man (or men) who shot the officers could tell what had actually transpired on the dead-end avenue.

Johnny Brown and Wade differed in their testimonies under direct examination and cross-examination as to whether both police cruisers were trailing the Plymouth when they first saw the vehicles, whether the emergency flashing lights were on when they first saw the police cruisers, whether the sirens were on when they first saw the police cruisers, and whether the men they saw running from the scene, going east down the railroad tracks, started fleeing before or after the first shots were fired.

The defense did a good job of using the weather to discredit their testimonies, citing the fog and sleet as reasons they could not have seen well enough to offer conclusive accounts of what had happened.

Pearlie Brown was more vague in her testimony. She could not recall how many shots she had heard, other than "a lot of shooting," which left the state's theory that Johnson and Thomasson never fired their revolvers and the newspaper reports that both police officers had fired their revolvers at a stalemate of sorts.

However, the state had the police department ballistics report working in its favor, in that regard; there was later testimony that neither of the revolvers used by Johnson and Thomasson was fired. However, there was, and remains, considerable question as to who handled the police department revolvers after the incident, as well as to where they were kept during the ten months leading to the trial. And then there had been those reports in Nashville's newspapers that quoted Thomasson as saying he had fired "four times" and thought "he hit one of them."

At about 6:00 P.M. one day early in the trial, Judge Leathers called an adjournment after jurors heard gripping testimony from Officer Robert White who, along with fellow officer Jack Burnett, was first on the scene after the shooting.

Sergeant Burnett had testified just before White took the witness stand that he and his partner had driven to Fourteenth Avenue after hearing on the police radio that Johnson and Thomasson had been shot. He said they slid past the turn because of ice on Herman Street, that they were going "about sixty miles per hour." He said he walked directly to Car 16, found Johnson lying on his back, felt for a pulse, concluded he was dead, picked up the revolver lying at his side, and put it in his coat pocket. Later, he said, he helped load Johnson into an ambulance, handed the revolver to White, and began combing the area for evidence.

White, also a sergeant, testified he walked to Car 45, discovered Thomasson talking on the radio, and attempted to calm the wounded police officer who, while bordering on shock, grabbed his coat and asked him to assist him to his feet. Also, White said he picked up the revolver lying beside Thomasson, helped load the wounded police officer into an ambulance, and handed the revolver to police officer G. L. Lilley. He testified that Burnett and he began combing the area for evidence.

[Note: In March 1988, when Burnett and White were questioned about the night of the shooting, Burnett said he might have opened the revolver used by Johnson to see if it had been fired, that he did not recall for sure. He remembered handing the weapon to White, who immediately handed it to police officer Robert Titsworth, the sergeant in charge of that district. White said the guns were handled by more than one of the investigating police officers, which is unusual in such a case, because they were concerned that bystanders would pick them up.

It is interesting that without further explanation of why he thought it, White said, "There's good possibility that Thomasson arrived there [on Fourteenth Avenue] first, just before Johnson. There's a good possibility Thomasson was shot first. It's a probability it happened like that if he got out of his car shooting."

Among the first group of police officers to arrive on the scene was Titsworth, commanding officer for the slain officers. During the fall of 1987, he admitted he had handled at least one of the Smith and Wesson 38 Specials used by the officers. He said he had searched the area for evidence and had conversed with Mrs. Wayne Thomasson later that night at General Hospital. He did not testify in court, which was peculiar given the number of his peers who did.]

Subsequent testimony revealed that one 30-30 slug was discovered under Johnson, that two 30-30 casings were discovered below the right front floorboard of the Plymouth, that a 22-caliber casing was discovered in the right front floorboard of the Plymouth, that a "stamp machine" that could be used in falsifying money orders was discovered in the trunk of the Plymouth, and that a suitcase with a Student Non-Violent Coordinating Committee decal pasted on its outside and with SNIC reading material inside was discovered in the trunk.

Such discoveries aided the case being presented, because they tied the defendants to three things: the civil rights movement, money orders, and rifles.

[Note: However, the number of 30-30 and 22-caliber casings found on the scene also supports the thought that Thomasson was not shot as many times as the prosecution contended. It is hard to fathom Allen or Canady, who had to have been frantic, taking the time to search for, pick up, and pocket casings before fleeing from the scene.

In March 1987 a copy of the ballistics report sent to the Tennessee Bureau of Investigation was full of interesting information: It said the Glenfield 30-30 held five slugs; two empty casings were found; two slugs were fired by the police department during testing; and one live round was being forwarded to the TBI. It also said the Winchester 22-caliber rifle held seventeen slugs; one empty casing was found; one slug was fired during testing; and thirteen live rounds were being forwarded to the TBI. It did not say Leroy Brown, Jr., had shot the 22-caliber rifle after finding it. That leaves only one bullet from the 22-caliber rifle unaccounted for, provided it was full that night. It said one spent casing from a 38-caliber revolver was being forwarded to the TBI.

Those numbers did not support the theory being advanced by the prosecution team in court, not unless the defendants took the time on a relatively dark avenue to gather empty casings and, during a quick shoot-out, to reload their rifles. The time element did not allow for either of those actions.

Again, the account of the shooting being advanced in 1987 and 1988 by the two surviving defendants in the case was supported better than the one offered by the district attorney in 1968.

When asked to lend expertise to the matter on February 10, 1988, Titsworth agreed to do so. The veteran of almost four decades, who is so respected that he has provided security for eleven U.S. presidential visits, was asked if he thought either Allen or Canady would have been composed enough to pick up empty casings from the 30-30 and 22-caliber rifles before leaving the scene of the shooting incident. "There's no way," he answered. "That's not logical. There's no way they would've known where to look for them, not since they were discharged automatically, and it's doubtful they would've been able to see them if they had known where to look."

Titsworth was reminded that it was the contention of the district attorney, who was acting on the advice of homicide detectives and medical personnel, that Thomasson had been shot a minimum of five times.

"Then what happened to the other empty casings from the 30-30 and the 22?" he asked.]

However, the number of times the police officers shot their revolvers, if any, or how many times they were shot became a secondary matter in court the following day. After substantial debate, in the absence of jurors, from Whitworth Stokes, Hollins, and Shriver, the most interesting, if not the most powerful, evidence of the trial was presented.

FOURTEEN

For Bill Allen it was a dreadful way to start a day. He went into the courtroom fairly certain he would have to face up to a letter he had written more than ten months earlier in Harlem. He knew his defense lawyer, Whitworth Stokes, was going to argue against those words being presented as evidence, but he realized that Judge Leathers probably would rule in favor of the state in the matter.

His fears were well founded.

The first witness District Attorney Shriver called to the stand was John Walker, to whom Allen had sent the letter in which he claimed to have been the only person who used a gun the night of the shooting. Walker had turned over the letter to defense lawyer James Havron, who had been appointed by the court, and Havron had turned it over to the police. Eventually it had landed in the hands of the district attorney, who had promptly leaked its contents to the press.

Allen had to face a signed confession of sorts in court, and it clearly made him appear to be the ruthless one among the defendants.

He had to listen as his fate was all but determined by a broken string of testimony that made him appear guilty of murder. It was testimony welcomed by every defense lawyer in the trial except Stokes, because it clearly shifted the focus of the case from three defendants to one.

Walker, whom Allen considered a faithful friend, said he received the letter and, on the advice of his mother, gave it to Havron. He said he thought it would help Canady and Parker, who about a week prior to its arrival in the mail had surrendered to the Cincinnati police. Then on cross-examination Walker told the jury he and other blacks had been physically and mentally abused by Nashville police officers during the days immediately following the shooting, as well as how Allen and the other defendants were men of enviable character, which led to the state's declaring him a hostile witness.

Shriver waited until the presentation of his case was near completion before focusing on the letter written by Allen. Eugene P. Caruthers, dean of admissions at Tennessee A&I University, confirmed Allen's signature on a 1963 enrollment application form. FBI agents from Washington, specialists in handwriting and fingerprinting, confirmed Allen's signature and thumb print on the letter. So what Allen feared most became a matter of substantial record. The contents of the letter were further highlighted when Tyler McCormick Smith testified that Allen appeared extremely nervous when he and Canady arrived at his house about an hour after the shooting. He said Allen, who had requested to use his telephone, was smoking a lot and kept rubbing the back of his neck.

"That's it for Allen," Shriver said to assistant district attorney John Hollins after the testimony about the letter written in New York. "He's as good as gone."

"True," Hollins answered. "But we've got all manner of problems with Parker and Canady. One of them didn't have a gun. He just drove the car. We haven't proved the other one ever fired a shot."

"But we've got both of them on the scene," Shriver reminded him. "Also, there's the money order angle."

"That's a fact," Hollins replied. "But this is a murder trial, Tom, and we haven't put as much proof up there as we need to."

"Well, if you think that tape was emotional, wait until you hear the doctor and medical examiner. What they're about to say should seal the fate of all of them."

As Shriver and Hollins conversed, Mrs. Wayne Thomasson stood near them and listened. The widow of the slain police officer had heard all of the testimony in the trial, and she was thinking along the same lines as Hollins.

"I don't like our chances with Parker or Canady," Mrs. Thomasson told the startled prosecutors. "It doesn't look like a solid case against them to me."

"Well, Mrs. Thomasson, we'll have one before it's over," Shriver replied.

"I don't know about that," Mrs. Thomasson continued. "Is it

possible to make a deal with Parker in exchange for his testimony against the other two?"

"That's possible," Hollins answered. "It might not be such a bad idea, not with us running the risk of cutting loose Canady. Tom, what do you think?"

"I'm for going after all of them," Shriver declared. "But I'll listen to reason."

"I think we should make a deal with Parker," Mrs. Thomasson said. "It's obvious he didn't shoot Wayne or Pete. I think it's the right thing to do."

By the time Dr. Michael Petrone went to the witness stand, it had become apparent that officers Johnson and Thomasson had died as a result of gunshot wounds administered on January 16, 1968. It also was obvious that most of the slugs had come from a 30-30 rifle. Some evidence had been introduced that strongly suggested a 22-caliber rifle also had been used to wound Thomasson.

But it had not been proved beyond reasonable doubt who actually fired the lethal weapon, or weapons, or that a planned ambush had taken place. That made the forthcoming verdict uncertain and also made it doubtful that the all-white jury would give any of the black defendants the death penalty, as the district attorney had hoped.

The jury had heard a six-year-old boy, Leroy Dunn, Jr., and his father, Leroy Dunn, Sr., testify how the youngster had found the weapons in his front yard. It had heard a battery of firearms experts testify that the slugs and casings found on the death scene matched the rifles found. It had heard law enforcement personnel from Cincinnati and New York, including FBI agents who had been tracking the men, testify about the events surrounding the apprehensions of the defendants, first Parker and Canady four days after the incident, then Allen more than two months later.

But the prosecution was saving two strong witnesses to conclude its case, Davidson County Medical Examiner Petrone and Dr. William C. Alford. Their testimonies were graphic and powerful. The statements made on the witness stand by Petrone were so explicit that one juror, Charles Anderson, became sick and was replaced by alternate W. G. Summers. Since Mrs. Thomasson, the widow of the police officer for whose death the defendants were being tried, was the first witness in the case, by closing with Petrone and Alford the state presentation had begun and closed its case with strong emotional appeals.

Petrone detailed how an autopsy showed large and small wounds caused by bullets, fragments of which were removed from the upper left abdomen and lower left chest, and operational wounds. He said the cause of death was infections in the pancreas, the spleen, and the left kidney, plus an inflammation in the lungs. He noted that Thomasson had sustained a broken hip.

During cross-examination, Eugene Smith, the defense lawyer for Canady, presented an unusual line of questioning. He began by asking Petrone if surgical procedures could have led to the development of the infections that ultimately killed Thomasson. This line of questioning drew numerous objections from the prosecution. Finally, Shriver chose to further question the medical examiner, asking him his expert opinion of the cause of death.

"In my opinion," said Petrone, "Officer Thomasson died as a result of overwhelming toxemia as a result of the pseudomorphic infection, which was caused by gunshot wounds to his abdomen."

Alford was influential, obviously, as he detailed how he had fought seven hours to save Thomasson and how the wounded police officer had been administered fifteen pints of blood during the surgical procedure. He said he had discovered wounds in the left leg, in the left side, in the ribs, with intestines protruding, and in the left forearm. He said a grave situation got better, almost miraculously, and that he thought the patient, who received sixty pints of blood during his two-month stay in the hospital, was on his way to a full recovery. He said he was surprised when Thomasson went into relapse in mid-February, leading to death on March 17.

Shriver had Alford point out various wounds on a diagram. As the doctor marked them, the district attorney counted them, concluding that there were seven bullet holes in Thomasson. After Alford pointed out that a hole of that type could be caused by fragments from a slug or the splintered metal of the police cruiser door, Shriver accepted the thought and settled on six bullet holes.

During cross-examination, Smith got Alford to admit there was no way to tell the difference between entrance wounds and exit wounds caused by bullets. He also got the doctor to admit holes caused by fragments look similar to holes caused by bullets. Such testimony left the number of shots fired at Thomasson unknown or, more importantly in the minds of the defendants, unproved beyond reasonable doubt.

[Note: In retrospect, it probably should have been noted that Thomasson's broken hip could have been caused by a 30-30 slug hitting the bone. That could have caused the fragmented bullet to move in several different directions through his body.

On February 10, 1988, Major Robert Titsworth of the Nashville police department was asked for an expert opinion about what a single slug fired from a 30-30 rifle would do upon impact. "It's hard to say, given the circumstances of this case," he answered, "because

I'm not sure how much resistance the slug got as it passed through the police cruiser door. A slug like that can do numerous things when its path is altered, such as move in several different directions, upward, downward, or sideways, or even change its rotation pattern. It's a powerful weapon, one used for hunting big game, and it can do a lot of damage. For instance, I can remember a case where a man was shot in the waist with a 30-30 slug and was torn to pieces all the way into his chest and both sides because the slug fragmented and sent pieces flying this way and that way through his body." The police officer was reminded that Thomasson sustained a broken hip on impact and was asked what that could have done to alter the direction of the slug. "That could make it do a lot of things, too, because the human bone is a strong piece of creation," he concluded.]

Defense lawyer Robert Lillard, who was representing Parker, thought several ends remained loose. After the state rested its case, he moved for a directed verdict on behalf of his client, pointing out that no proof had been presented that linked him with the firing of a gun. His plea was rejected.

Defense lawyer Smith did likewise on behalf of Canady. He also lost.

Defense lawyer Whitworth Stokes, who was representing Allen, continued to take a subdued posture, making no overtures toward a directed verdict for his client.

Just before expert witnesses Petrone and Alford took the witness stand on behalf of the prosecution, Shriver and Hollins had negotiated with David Vincent and Lillard, who were representing Parker, to secure a plea bargain for him. They wanted Parker to testify against Allen and Canady to solidify their case against the defendants they thought had shot the police officers.

"So what's the deal?" Parker asked Vincent after an adjournment one afternoon.

"You'll get a year on manslaughter," Vincent said to Parker. "But only if you testify against the others."

"And say what?" Parker said.

"That they killed the police officers," Vincent replied. "And that they were laying and waiting for Thomasson after shooting Johnson."

"I want to confer with my father," Parker replied. "Then I'll let you know."

Steve and Correlus Parker discussed the situation, concluding the prosecution was seeking his help in getting an electric chair sen-

tence for Allen and Canady. They were angered, particularly by the
request that he tell the jury that an ambush had been set up.

"I'm not doing it," Steve Parker then told Vincent. "I'm not
lying to save myself and to kill my friends."

"That'll just leave you with a month or so to serve before you're
paroled," Vincent reminded him.

"My son won't be a rat," Correlus Parker replied, ending the
conversation.

So all three defendants returned to court, with Parker still believing the truth would spare them.

[Note: "They didn't make a statement," Chancellor Robert
Brandt said about Parker and Canady. The former assistant district
attorney, who helped put together the case for the prosecution in
1968, was discussing the plea bargain negotiations in March 1988,
more than nineteen years after they occurred. "They rolled, threw
the dice, and lost. They had a false sense of brotherhood about
them."]

If conjecture was apparent after fifty witnesses had testified, it
grew broader when the next person went to the stand and swore to
tell the truth. That was Canady, who was followed by Parker and
Allen as the defense began presenting its case.

All three told interesting stories about what happened the night
of the incident, each mingling truth with fiction.

FIFTEEN

What about the rifles? was the question being discussed outside the courtroom as the murder trial moved toward its conclusion and the defendants readied to testify on their own behalfs. Black observers, who stayed to themselves in the corridor outside the courtroom, and white observers, who were allowed to move about more freely, took contrasting viewpoints. In one corner there was talk about fear of police department brutality; elsewhere there was talk about a cold, calculated ambush.

The answer never came, at least not conclusively, and jurors were left to wonder who put the rifles in the car and who used them to shoot Johnson and Thomasson. Incredibly, neither Allen, Parker, nor Canady chose to offer a reason why shots were fired that night, not even with their lives in the hands of the jury that had heard testimony making all three look guilty of a conspiracy.

Canady went on the witness stand first. He said he was twenty-six years old, from Cincinnati, had graduated from Bowling Green University in Ohio with majors in speech and business, and had been in Nashville two weeks when the shooting took place. He had been in town to work with underprivileged children and to check into the prospects of doing postgraduate work at either Tennessee A&I or Fisk University. He said he resided at 1906 and 1910 Hermosa Street and that he was in the Plymouth because he was catching a ride to his home in Ohio, where he previously had worked as a manager in a large department store.

What about the rifles?

"I had been told they were to be sold."

Obviously, given previous testimony, nobody questioned Canady when he said the Plymouth was parked beside a warehouse on Fourteenth Avenue when the shooting took place. But some people debated the rest of his testimony about the shooting. He said he was seated beside the back right door of the automobile, that Johnson ordered Parker, who was driving, to get out and put his hands against the side of the warehouse, that the police officer ordered everybody to get out and do the same, and that he heard gunfire when he turned at the rear of the automobile and began walking toward the warehouse. He said he dived to the ground between the Plymouth and Car 16, which Johnson had stopped about eight feet behind them, and heard a series of gunfire while on the pavement. He said that when the gunfire subsided, he jumped to his feet, brushed off his pants, looked at Johnson lying dead on the ground, heard sirens, and ran from the scene.

On cross-examination by Robert Lillard, who was representing Parker, Canady again confirmed that the driver had been out of the Plymouth with his hands against the warehouse when the shooting started. Again questioned by assistant district attorney John Hollins, Canady began hinting that Allen was the person closest to the 30-30 rifle used to kill Johnson. He testified that he thought the automobile belonged to Alexander. He confirmed that he had known Parker most of his life, having gone to school with him, that he had known Alexander two years, Allen eighteen months, and Herron one year, and that he had become acquainted with all of them in Cincinnati.

Parker told a similar story about what transpired at the death scene, after testifying that he was twenty-four years old, had attended classes at Central State University in Ohio and Knoxville College in Tennessee, had worked at National Distilleries in Cincinnati, and had flown to Nashville with Alexander five days before the incident.

Parker said he was ordered out of the car by Johnson; had put his hands on top of the Plymouth, as ordered, then against the warehouse, as ordered; he heard Johnson say, "Now all of you boys get out of the car, over against the wall." Then he heard gunfire.

Parker testified he was attempting to drive "to [James Robertson] Parkway" when he noticed "emergency lights flashing." Near the intersection of Herman Street and Fourteenth Avenue he asked, "What are those lights behind me?" Somebody replied, "Police, I think." He said he stopped the automobile at the intersection of Herman Street and Fourteenth Avenue, then at the urging of Johnson turned right and drove to the site of the incident.

What about the rifles?

Parker stated that he had first noticed the 30-30 on Hermosa Street because it was lying across the front floorboard, obstructing his ability to drive. He asked Allen, who was sitting beside the front right door, to "do something with it." He said the rifle was then placed under the front seat. He did not mention the 22-caliber rifle.

The normally articulate Allen was not impressive on the witness stand. He said nothing about what happened on Fourteenth Avenue to incriminate himself, but he was not smooth, often repeating questions before answering. It was an out-of-character performance by an intelligent person.

Allen testified he was twenty-four years old, from Old Hickory, had attended Haynes High School and Tennessee State University, and was the son of W. G. Allen, who worked for DuPont Chemical, and Ellariz King Allen, who worked as a health department nurse. He had lived in Cincinnati, "off and on" for eighteen months, at which time he worked in the research laboratory of a grocery chain, at National Distilleries, and as a youth counselor. He said he had flown to Nashville from Newark, New Jersey, three days before the incident, and that he had lived at 1910 Hermosa Street while attending his senior year of classes, but was hitching a ride to his parents' home when the Plymouth was stopped by Johnson.

Allen said he was wearing a tan suede jacket and Hush Puppy boots when he got out of the automobile on Fourteenth Avenue, as ordered, and ducked behind the front of the Plymouth when he heard gunfire. Then, he said he surveyed the scene quickly and ran along railroad tracks behind the warehouse, going east toward downtown.

When asked about the letter he wrote while in New York claiming to have been the only person who did any shooting, Allen said he chose to write it after his uncle, Lonnie Pinkston, told him by telephone that numerous people "had been beaten in connection."

What about the rifles?

"I was going to give them to my father, W. G. Allen, who collects guns," Allen answered, "or sell one to my uncle, Lonnie Pinkston, who likes to hunt."

With Alexander and Herron still at large, it was impossible for courtroom observers to fully understand what had happened during the shooting. Likewise, it was difficult to figure out what the three defendants did later. Their testimony, which later proved to be laced with fiction, painted interesting pictures for the jurors.

Canady said he ran from the scene and went to a college dormitory to borrow money for a bus ticket out of town. He claimed he ran into Allen at the dormitory, went with him to a house in North Nashville, left him, sold a watch, slept that night in a dormitory lounge, and caught a bus the next morning to Cincinnati. He said he surrendered at the police department in Cincinnati on January 20.

Parker said he ran from the scene and was detained by a night watchman at Carrigan Iron Works, but he continued running after talking to the watchman and heard Alexander's footsteps behind him. He said Alexander and he caught a bus for Cincinnati at 12:50 A.M. and that he surrendered at the police department in Cincinnati on January 20.

Allen testified that he ran from the scene, going up Twelfth Avenue to Jefferson Street, then up Jackson Street to the Fisk University student union building. He said he caught a ride to the Tyler McCormick Smith residence in a red GTO automobile driven by James Hatchett and that he caught a ride to the William Huff residence in a car driven by Herman Harlan. The following morning he telephoned his uncle, Pinkston, and asked him to pick up him and Canady at the Tennessee State gymnasium, and at 11:00 A.M. his mother arrived at the Pinkston residence in Donelson, provided Canady and him a ride to Louisville, and gave Canady and him enough money for bus tickets to New York. Allen testified that Canady got off the bus in Columbus, Ohio, and that he continued on it to New York, where he was arrested in March by FBI agents while in bed.

Other than his failure to disclose that he ran from the scene with a 30-30 rifle in his hand, which he deposited in bushes two blocks away, Allen told the truth about what happened after the shooting.

Parker lied in testimony related to his flight. In fact, Alexander, Herron, and he rode to Cincinnati in an automobile driven by a friend.

Canady also lied on the witness stand. He was with Allen every step of the way.

Whether Canady and Parker frequently lied while making statements to law enforcement personnel in Cincinnati and Nashville after their surrenders is debatable. Nashville police officer Charles Stoner, who testified in court after the defendants, said he interviewed Parker after he surrendered in Cincinnati and that the prisoner told interrogators that "Allen and Canady put the rifles in the car" and that he and Alexander "rode to Cincinnati together."

The testimony by Stoner came just before similar testimony from police officer Robert Russell, the last witness in the trial. It was an anticlimactic close to the testimony. But it set the stage for dramatic debate among jurors, who were charged by Judge Leathers late one afternoon and began deliberations.

SIXTEEN

"**L**ady, if you get in trouble, if somebody is breaking into your house, don't call the police department to come help you, not if you let any of these men go free. They won't be willing to come help you."

Those words spoken by juror W. G. Summers, age forty-five, were aimed toward Mary Hall, age fifty-four, the lone woman juror, after the first three votes among jurors ended in eleven ballots for three guilty verdicts and one ballot for a not guilty verdict.

The coaxing statement from Summers provided the first tense moment among jurors, who had been under sequester for twenty-two days and nights as the trial unfolded. Hall was standing alone, mostly on behalf of Parker, whom she did not want to convict, as she wrote in a diary she kept of the proceedings. In that record she wrote the names of witnesses and their opinions of what had transpired, as well as recaps of what jurors did while under sequester.

Many of the jurors had played poker to pass the hours. All of them, said Hall, had played rook. Summers said he read thirty-year-old magazines because he and the others were not allowed to read newspapers, listen to the radio, or watch television. Marshall Irwin said he and other jurors were taken on brief walks after court was adjourned each day, that is until, as he remembered, they were passed one afternoon by "four or five carloads of coloreds who were going real slow." Hall disputed that claim, discounting it as merely a personal impression on his part.

The position taken by Irwin was not disputable, however, because he, too, fired a convincing verbal shot at Hall after deliberations reached a stalemate. "Ma'am, have you done your Christmas shopping?" he asked. Hall shook her head. "Well, Ma'am, you're

not gonna get to spend Christmas with your family if you don't
come around and agree with us. I'm not budging. I'm prepared to
stay here until after the new year arrives."

Hall was not budging, either, sticking with her opinion that all of
the defendants seemed like nice individuals and that Parker was
merely in the wrong place at the wrong time, with no knowledge of
the money order problem. She was more adamant in her arguments
against the death penalty, which was favored by five jurors.

Had Assistant District Attorney Hollins known what was happening during the jury's deliberations, he would have been more anxious than he was. Perhaps the key prosecution figure in the
courtroom, assuredly the most powerful examiner of witnesses and
the author of a moving closing argument, he was confident that his
case for the state would end in success.

Hollins, age thirty-five, a Vanderbilt University graduate, considered the case against Allen to be a lock. He said the defendant "was
in a box" because of the letter he had written in New York before
his apprehension, "a confession that put the burden of proof on
him."

Hollins had used his examination of Allen on the witness stand to
solidify the case against Parker and Canady, an effort to tie together
the theory the state advanced in the case: "All of the defendants
were involved in the money order deal. All of them were trying to
get out of town to avoid arrest. All of them were going to Cincinnati. They ran through a roadblock formed by police officer Wayne
Thomasson. They were stopped by police officer Pete Johnson.
They did not have intentions of killing the police officers when they
left the apartment that night in the Plymouth, but did so in an
emotional reaction when they were stopped on Fourteenth Avenue
and found themselves with no place to run."

But Hollins knew that getting a conviction of Parker and Canady
might be difficult. As he said, there was "no proof" they handled
guns, "no proof" Parker was in the car when the shoot-out took
place, and "no proof the defendants were laying and waiting to ambush the police officers," as Summers, Irwin, and most of the other
jurors had concluded. The assistant district attorney did think,
however, that a tape recording of Thomasson's asking for assistance
after the shooting was meaningful, "because it made the hair on
your neck stand up. He was like a crying baby."

In summary, Hollins was thinking it would have been difficult for
the jury to convict any of the defendants were it not for the letter
Allen had written, which sealed his fate. That is why relatively early
in the court proceedings District Attorney Thomas Shriver and he

offered Parker the opportunity to plead guilty to involuntary manslaughter and accept a one-year sentence in exchange for his testimony against Allen and Canady.

Hall was thinking like Hollins. From the time juror deliberations
started at about 6:00 P.M. until the twelve of them quit for the night
at about 10:00 P.M., she voted not guilty, but the following morning, she was tricked into changing her vote. At about 11:00 A.M.,
after more than three hours of deliberation, it was announced that
the jury had a verdict.

Hall had compromised with her male peers. She was told the jury
could ask for leniency on behalf of the court for Parker. She was told
a maximum sentence of twenty years was probable and that the men
in favor of the death penalty would reduce their prison sentences for
Allen and Canady to ninety-nine years. It was a tough time for Hall,
who had clearly been the principal target during a summation by
Eugene Smith, the defense lawyer representing Canady. He had remained in eye contact with her during most of his closing argument, which was emotional and lasted almost an hour. She had
remained unshaken until jurors left the courtroom to begin their
deliberations, at which time she secluded herself and sobbed.

Hall was not shaken again until the verdicts were announced and
Judge Leathers polled jurors to confirm them.

Judge Leathers asked jury foreman Lee A. Pendarvis for the verdicts and sentences, one defendant at a time. He announced guilty
of first-degree murder in regard to all three defendants, with
ninety-nine year sentences in regard to all three defendants. But the
jury foreman stunned observers when he requested the judge consider leniency in sentencing Parker.

Somewhat stunned, Judge Leathers contemplated that action for
a moment, stumbled a bit when responding to it, and announced
that state law said it was the responsibility of jurors to set sentences.

Hall was more than a little shaken. She had argued against con-
victing Parker, and she had argued against the death penalty for all
of the defendants. She also had left the jury hung through three
votes, but when Judge Leathers stated that the court could not alter
the sentence, she knew she had been tricked by her fellow jurors,
who had led her to believe otherwise.

Then the judge polled the jurors. All of them confirmed the verdicts and the sentences, with Hall shaking as she reacted affir-
matively. In retrospect, she said, "I said yes, but I didn't want to. I
wanted to say no."

The results from the trial caused a stir inside the courtroom, as
well as outside, with tears and cries of anguish mixing with cheers

and vows of justice. Mrs. Thomasson, widow of the victim in the case, smiled with her eyes laden with tears. A black woman wept openly and fainted.

While reflecting on the case later that day, David Vincent, the lawyer who represented Parker, concluded he should have objected to the verdict on the grounds that the jury had not been properly charged before deliberations began. But he and Robert Lillard, who was also representing Parker, had sat quietly at the defense table as the fate of their client was sealed.

The day after the guilty verdict was announced, Allen, Parker, and Canady were loaded into separate panel trucks and taken to the Davidson County Workhouse—after extended rides around the city.

"Now they're going to kill us," Parker said to himself as he rode alone in the back of one of the trucks for more than an hour. "They didn't get the death penalty, so they'll do it another way."

Those fears were unfounded, but the cells in which the trio were placed made them wonder if they would be better off dead. There was several inches of water on the basement floor where they were kept and roaches were everywhere. Canady grew particularly tense when he was placed in a cell that had an electric lamp dangling near his head.

"Damn, I've got to get out of here," Canady told Allen and Parker, who were in cells within earshot. "I'm going to be electrocuted with this light and this water."

"Be tough, Slim," Allen encouraged him. "It's not forever."

"But be careful," Parker warned.

The convicted murderers were kept there for a couple of days while police officers and guards paraded people to the area so they could have a look.

"There's your bad guys, the cop-killers," an officer said to a man wearing a business suit.

"Then keep the niggers in there where it's nasty," the man answered.

That was not to be. Death row was waiting for three men who had not been sentenced to die.

SEVENTEEN

"**Q**ueen to Bishop Three," Steve Parker said to Bill Allen as he moved a small piece of paper along a larger piece of paper with square blocks drawn on it.

"Darn you, Bitsey," Allen exclaimed.

"What can I say?" Parker responded with a chuckle. "You just can't play the game like me."

They were playing a homemade style of chess in a small cell at the Tennessee State Penitentiary in Nashville. This was almost a year after they had been convicted of first-degree murder in a Davidson County courtroom, but not long after they had been allowed to stray from the individual cells that had been home to them for six months.

Allen, Parker, and Canady had been shipped to death row at the prison after their convictions, although they had not been sentenced to die. The reason, said Tennessee Department of Corrections officials, was they were considered "not in count" while awaiting the results of their appeals.

Also, said Parker, they were erroneously considered threats to peace in the facility.

So they sat in Unit Six, the White Building, and salted away the hours of the first six months with only pants, shirts, shoes, a plastic spoon, and a plastic bowl at their disposals. They were allowed out of their cells only to take showers on Tuesdays and Saturdays—"then just every other Tuesday," reported Parker.

Canady was on the other side of the walk, receiving similar treatment in the cell closest to the electric chair, "Old Sparky," as it is called. His only contact with Allen and Parker came by hollering through the heating and air conditioning ducts.

95

Then, during the spring of 1969 an incredible thing happened. Allen and Parker looked up one morning and saw a new convict joining them. The man placed in a nearby cell was James Earl Ray, who had just pleaded guilty to first-degree murder in the shooting death of the Reverend Martin Luther King in April 1968.

Whether Ray, a staunch segregationist, was placed alongside Allen and Parker to torment them is a matter of speculation. Perhaps he, too, was "not in count." Regardless, it made for an interesting group on death row, especially when none of them was scheduled to die.

Actually, Parker remembered, "We got along just fine. James was OK, sort of comic relief.

"I can remember how he never was able to call me just Parker or Bill, just Allen. It was always Parker/Allen or Allen/Parker. He never got it straight."

But Allen and Parker took notice when the prison warden frequently came to take Ray to his office for private conferences. They smiled when he told them on his return that he was being asked about preparing a book, that he was not being a snitch.

They never discussed the death of King in Memphis.

But they laughed at the guards together, at least at those who tried to add to their misery.

It took a six-day hunger strike in 1969 by everybody on death row, except Ray, to secure a daily newspaper and two sheets of paper and a pencil to use for writing letters.

"Even then," said Parker, "the guards picked on us. Like there was this one dude who whistled all the time, sort of in a sarcastic manner. He'd walk along in front of us handing out paper. Then he'd ask if we wanted pencils. Then he'd break the pencils into pieces and hand us just enough to write with. He was something, man."

Charles Lee Herron and John Alexander were living in Atlanta when they learned that their friends had been convicted of first-degree murder and had been sentenced to ninety-nine years in the state penitentiary.

"I sure as hell can't believe this," Alexander said after he and Herron had stopped at a convenience store on their way home from their construction jobs. The *Jet* magazine they had bought carried the sad news.

"They've got life in prison," Herron said. "Damn. I don't know what all the shooting was about that night, but I know Bitsey was with us."

"He got ninety-nine for hauling ass," Alexander said, shaking his

head. "It looks like staying in Chicago with you was the best decision I've made."

Alexander and Herron had been in Atlanta only a few months
when they heard the news. They would remain together until 1971,
when Alexander, who was using the alias Anthony Williams, received news that there was a lot of construction work available in St.
Louis.

"Be cool and keep an eye out," Herron warned him the day he
left for Missouri. "Remember, we've got friends doing too much
time in Tennessee."

Once Bill Allen, Steve Parker, and Ralph Canady were placed in the
general population at the Tennessee State Penitentiary, they became
model prisoners. No disciplinary reports were filed on the convicts,
which enabled them to mix with fellow prisoners and guards.

In newspapers they read brief articles about their appeals being
turned down by higher courts. They also read troubling articles
that indicated parts of the Nashville community were resisting ac-
cepting the civil rights of blacks.

Music City U.S.A. was growing, yes, in terms of population and
liberalism, but North Nashville and a section of South Nashville—
where most blacks lived—were still embroiled in racial strife. Allen, Parker, and Canady were not shocked to learn that the police
department was still at odds with people living in those neigh-
borhoods. Because they were so close to the situation, they had
trouble understanding that other parts of the nation were experiencing the same difficulties.

In November 1973 another related incident exploded in North
Nashville in the form of a shotgun fired by a police officer. An
article written in *The Tennessean* by reporter Albert Gore, Jr., was
topped by a headline that read, "'Mistake' Cited in Teen's Death."

The story told of how Ronald Joyce, age nineteen, had been shot
by police as he ran from a dice game in an abandoned house to
escape arrest. Police had been told by mistake that a burglary was
taking place; the dispatcher had misunderstood what the caller had
said, so officers thought they were dealing with a major crime when
they arrived. "As they arrived on the scene, the occupants of the
house attempted to flee, and Joyce was shot in the back of the head
when he ignored police warnings to halt."

The death of that black man came nine months after the death of
another black man in South Nashville. Cedric Overton, age twenty-
one, was shot four times and killed by an officer who said he erroneously thought the victim was armed. After it was learned that
another police officer had planted a knife at the scene of the shoot-

ing, several police officers were suspended from the force. A manslaughter trial in that case resulted in the guilty police officer, Jackie Pyle, being convicted of assault and battery and fined ten dollars.

The death of Overton came less than a month after two black teenagers were sentenced to fifteen years in prison for second-degree murder. Preston Leo Britt and Carlos Lindsley crashed a fraternity party on the Tennessee State University campus in 1971, had heated words with Vietnam veteran George Lowe, and shot and killed him.

Those contrasting verdicts and sentences were noted by the Nashville black community, and the death of Joyce by police department gunfire jolted its memory.

On November 27, 1973, members of the Nashville black community announced they would march on the Metropolitan Nashville Safety Building to protest the death of Joyce. "It will be a peaceful memorial march for my brother because an unjust act was committed," said Debra Joyce, a twenty-one-year-old student at Tennessee State.

Meanwhile, Dr. Charles Kimbrough, president of the Nashville NAACP, called for black citizens "to reexamine their shopping habits as a means of protesting racist activities within the Metro Nashville Police Department."

"We believe this incident is a continuation of a chain of judge and jury murders by paranoid police officers," Kimbrough announced.

But there remained questions to be asked on both sides, particularly one: did the police officers tell Joyce to halt before shooting at him?

The police department issued a statement saying the other men in the house that night said they heard such a command. All seven were charged with first-degree burglary before making such statements.

A woman who said she watched the shooting death of Joyce from a couple of doors down Batavia Street was quick to dispute the police department claims. Hester Powell said nobody told the slain black man to halt until after the lethal shots were fired. She said the police officers who arrived on the scene shone a search light on the house, which prompted the young men to run.

Michael Petrone, the medical examiner, refused to release the details of his autopsy report, saying he felt that he worked for the police department and should follow orders given him. "I feel like I am part of the police team," he said, "and if Chief Mott doesn't want certain information released, then I don't think I should release it, either."

The day following the demands from the NAACP, Shriver and

the foreman of the grand jury announced separate investigations into the death of Joyce. Police chief Hugh Mott terminated his investigation and turned over his files to the district attorney. Also, it was reported, the leader of the police department had decided not to suspend any of the four police officers involved.

As this was taking place, approximately one thousand protesters marched on city hall screaming, "No more killing. No more killing."

Racial unrest had hit Nashville with a hard punch again, with mistrust and fear causing a failure of communication between blacks and police officers. While the entire nation was plagued with racial unrest, Nashville was experiencing more than its share.

In September 1974 Shriver presented evidence to the Davidson County grand jury in the case. His indictment charged officer Jimmy McWright with voluntary manslaughter. He managed to present a weak enough case that the grand jury ruled there was insufficient cause to charge McWright with a crime.

All of this came from five to seven years after assistant chief John Sorace appeared at Fisk University in an effort "to improve communication between the police and the community." At that meeting in 1968, Sorace said, "We are building a new police department. The police department is not made up of perfect human beings. We are not always right and we do make mistakes, but we are trying to improve."

EIGHTEEN

Bill Allen, Steve Parker, and Ralph Canady were walking from the baseball field at the Tennessee State Penitentiary in Nashville. The softball game had ended, and they had done their parts to help their team to victory.

Winning behind the wall was important to the three men. They had learned that there is a society unto itself in prison, an existence that must be handled with care, with every conquest important to survival. The point had hit home like a hammer pounding a nail earlier that week when they learned that all appeals of their convictions had been exhausted.

Allen, Parker, and Canady had been incarcerated for more than six years. Almost two of those years had been spent in lockup, which is akin to solitary confinement, or in the death row section of the state prison. Some of the time had been spent at Brushy Mountain State Prison in Petros, about 150 miles east of Nashville.

While at Brushy Mountain, Allen started radio station WBMP, which featured a jazz format, and a newspaper, *The Communicator,* which chronicled prison life and commented on social issues in the free world. Throughout his incarceration he had thought about a vow the trio had made not long after the jury in Davidson County announced that they should be put away for ninety-nine years, or at least until December 1998, as their probation parole date read.

Parker had thought about how the jury wanted to go light on him and how it had requested that the judge consider reducing his sentence, only to discover moments later that state law said it was the responsibility of those determining guilt or innocence to set the penalty for convicted defendants. As the appeal process came and went, he was stunned to learn that law ruled over logic.

100

"At least we're breathing," Parker said as Allen, Canady, and he walked toward the main building at the penitentiary. "I was struggling for air when the jury started giving the verdict. I thought we were going to the electric chair."

"But the jury tried to give you a break, Bitsey," Canady reflected. "They knew you were just caught in the dark that night."

"I know," Parker lamented. "My lawyer screwed up, and my new lawyer said there's no way in hell we'll get out of here."

"I wouldn't be so sure about that," Allen replied. "I've been doing a lot of thinking, especially now that Skin has made his move toward parole."

John Alexander, the "Skin" they were discussing, had been captured near St. Louis in June 1971 after being stopped and arrested by police officers and FBI agents who had received tips about the true identity of a man who went by the name Malike.

"OK, you, the little one, what's your name and why have you been hanging out around this apartment?" an FBI agent demanded of Alexander after three cars had converged on the one in which he was riding.

"I'm Malike," Alexander responded. "It's a name from my native Africa."

"Well, we'll clear that up at headquarters," answered an FBI agent who noticed a pistol in the car.

Once agents knew that the man they had captured was Alexander, the FBI contacted the Nashville police department, which dispatched homicide detective Tom Cathey and another police officer to Bellview, Illinois, to transport him to Tennessee. Once in Nashville, the former fugitive encountered defense lawyer David Vincent.

"What's my best chance?" Alexander asked.

"They're offering a voluntary manslaughter plea," Vincent replied. "That's two-to-ten. I'd take it. Remember, I represented Parker three years ago, and he got ninety-nine years for doing nothing."

Alexander, who was never placed on the FBI Most Wanted list, accepted the advice. He spent about eighteen months at Turney Center in Only, Tennessee—having run into Allen, Parker, and Canady at the Tennessee State Prison just after making his guilty plea. He encountered them as they returned to Nashville after spending time at Brushy Mountain.

Alexander remained extremely quiet during his time at Turney Center. Ultimately, he was sent to a halfway house in Memphis, where he was a cook, then was put on work release in Memphis, during which time he labored at a taco shop.

"Skin got a good break," Canady commented in the exercise yard at the state prison. "But what about Lee [Charles Lee Herron]? He's out there playing basketball and taking it easy."

"I've been thinking about that," Allen replied.

"Lee playing basketball?"

"No, about us having to stay in here at least thirty years, maybe until after the year 2000."

"Well," Canady replied, "it's a fact of life."

"I'm not sure about that," Allen answered. "Remember what we said during the trial, fellas. You know, if we go down together, we're coming out together."

The three convicts had spent much time talking about ways to escape from prison. They had dreamed and laughed, reflected and mourned, and every avenue they considered seemed to run into a dead end. They had even put their hands on free money and had saved enough to keep them afloat if such a successful flight ever happened.

The always optimistic Allen had not given up. Instead, he had developed a friendship with The Man in the bath house in which incoming convicts were washed before they were issued their prison garb. Driven by the thought that Parker, Canady, and he did not deserve to be in prison, he devised a plan of escape. It was his way—the only one available to him—of correcting what he believed was a social wrong.

His plan was for The Man, a prison trusty, to put aside civilian clothes removed from incoming convicts that fit Parker, Canady, and him. Either that, or the trusty could complete the needed wardrobe with clothes issued to convicts who were granted furloughs to attend funerals. Once each of the convicts had a full suit of clothes, they would walk away from the penitentiary wearing the clothes.

"It has been a long time in here for us," Allen told Parker and Canady as they ate lunch in the prison cafeteria. It had been about a week since they had discussed their dismal future while strolling from the baseball field. "Fellas, it's time to leave these clanging doors."

"That means you've talked to The Man?" Canady asked io an excited tone, pushing aside his food tray.

"For real, Blood."

"When?" Parker asked as he pitched aside a plastic fork. "And how can we do it?"

"On Mother's Day, during the picnic on the grounds, at shift change."

"Oh shit!" Parker exclaimed. "That's just three days."

"Right, Bitsey, and The Man makes his drops in our cells on Saturday afternoon. A 42-long shirt, Slim. That's what you ordered and that's what you've got."

When Sunday, May 11, 1974, arrived, Allen was nervous as he walked through an open cell door and surveyed the walk to see if there were convicts or guards moving up and down it. Sweating profusely, he saw nobody, so he hurried back into his cell, pulled a sack from under the mattress on his cot, and opened it. He wondered what his mother had thought when he told her there was no reason for her visit on this special day, that he and his friends had decided to spend it eating with two women friends, neither of whom knew about their plans to escape.

Allen quickly stripped to his underwear, put on civilian clothes, and covered them with his prison garb, a pale blue jumpsuit. He looked at his watch. "Damn," he muttered. "It's almost time." He sat down and acted as if he was writing a letter, smiling when a fellow convict walked past his cell and looked inside. His confounded expression indicated he was wondering why Allen was sweating so much.

"Last call for anybody with a pass to the picnic grounds," called a prison guard in a loud voice from down the prison walk. "The next stroll starts in an hour."

Allen literally jumped from his cot, grabbed a baseball cap and put it on his head, donned a pair of sunglasses, and looked into a mirror. He smiled. "It's the best I can do," he said to himself in a whisper. "I hope the other fellas do just as good."

His fears subsided when he looked out of his cell and saw Parker and Canady strolling down the walk with six other convicts. They kept their heads pointed straight ahead, refusing to glance his way, and Allen wondered whether they were still in the game as he put aside his note pad and walked from the cell.

It was crowded on the picnic grounds, which consisted of forty tables and a lot of real estate covered by grass. The air was warm and pollen filled. At the top of a small hill about thirty yards from where Allen, Parker, and Canady lounged at a cloth-covered concrete table with their two friends, sat portable bathroom facilities that featured two small toilets. Both were situated at the top of a dozen concrete steps, and Allen kept an eye on the bathroom facilities and his watch as he and the others ate a picnic lunch of fried chicken, deviled eggs, and rolls. Not even the swarming flies kept him from concentrating on the plan.

"Well, it's 1:45, almost shift change for the guards and baseball time for us," Allen said. The two women, both twenty-eight and attractive, did not like the sound of that.

"What does that mean, Bill, that it's time for us to leave?" asked one of the women, a Nashville native who had met the three men in 1967. Her disdain for the suggestion was obvious, as was that felt by the other woman, who had also met the trio when the intellectual Allen, a chemistry major, worked the social circuit on campus.

"My God, fellas, we've worked hard on this meal. You don't have to go until after five. Let's sit here a while and catch up on lost time."

"Ah, calm down," Parker responded. "It's just that it'll be easier for you to get out of here before the guards have their shift change."

Ten minutes later, the two women walked away from the picnic table with their food baskets in hand. Allen called to them when they were ten yards away, and they turned to see what he wanted.

"Hey, I almost forgot. I've made you a gift. Can you wait at your car until I get somebody to bring it out to you?" Allen said to one of the women.

"OK, Bill, but just for a while."

"It'll be fifteen minutes, no more."

Prison guards were walking toward the security gate on the picnic grounds when Allen, Parker, and Canady strolled to the bathroom facilities. The guards were preparing to leave after their shift, as their replacements came from the parking lot toward the security gate. The picnic grounds remained crowded, with convicts mingling with visitors, and the sound of laughter made the scene similar to many taking place outside the prison.

"I just saw one guy go into the toilet on the left," Allen said to Parker and Canady as they started climbing the steps to the bathroom facilities. "I'll use the one on the right, then split. You guys go after me, then meet me at the car in the main parking lot."

"If we're not there in twenty minutes, you haul ass, Little Doc," Parker said. "Go without us."

"Don't worry, Bitsey," Allen replied. "I'm gone."

Once inside the bathroom, Allen locked the door, yanked off his prison jumpsuit, and stuck it behind the toilet at the base of the plumbing. He was careful to jam it out of view, then took time to relieve himself, straightened his attire, and exited. He saw Canady standing outside by himself.

"Good afternoon," Canady said with a smile as he moved toward the door Allen had left open.

"I hope so," Allen answered as he walked past Canady, down the steps and into the crowd. He acted every bit the visitor instead of the convict.

Allen mingled with visitors and convicts on the picnic grounds as he made his way toward the security gate. He passed a guard who was going on duty, picked up a Frisbee and tossed it to a child, who ran to retrieve it, then spotted the familiar face of a convict housed on his walk. Turning in a wide circle to avoid encountering him, he kept moving toward the first obstacle he had to clear to reach freedom.

As he reached the security gate, Allen took a deep breath, then continued past a guard, at whom he nodded and waved.

"It's a hot day," commented the guard.

"For sure," Allen replied in a mumble as he moved toward a van used to transport visitors from the main gate to the picnic grounds, then back again. He seated himself in the back of the van and waited quietly. The trusty driving the van did a double take when he saw Allen, as if he recognized him, then sat behind the steering wheel examining him through the rear view mirror.

"It looks like you're it for a while," the trusty said after a wait of five minutes. "I guess I'll take you to the main gate now." He paused, and Allen said nothing. "That's if you're sure you want to go."

"For real," Allen answered as he realized the trusty might be suspicious of him. "That'll be good. Thank you."

As the van carrying Allen to the main gate started rolling, Parker and Canady were strolling across the picnic area, staying a safe distance apart but never out of view of each other. When they got to within twenty yards of the security gate, arriving from opposite directions, Parker stopped and acted as if he was tying a shoelace, allowing Canady to move ten yards ahead of him. They moved past the guard at the security gate without fanfare, somewhat hidden by the large group of visitors who exited the picnic area with them.

"Oh shit!" Canady exclaimed. "My legs feel like rubber."

"For real," Parker replied. "But keep 'em moving, man, all the way to the van and on to the car."

One of the women was seated on the hood of her automobile, a seven-year-old Chevrolet, with her eyes fixed on the main gate when Allen walked past a security guard. The other was leaning on the hood of the automobile, looking the other way.

"Oh, my God, look who's coming toward us," said the woman facing the gate. "It's Bill. And he's out of uniform."

The other woman looked up quickly as Allen raised his arms and pointed his palms toward them, as if to urge them to keep quiet. He quickened his pace.

"OK, ladies. Let's stay calm," Allen said when he got within five yards of the automobile.

"I don't know about this, Bill," said one of the women. "What's the deal? You're not leaving."

"Well, I hope so. Bitsey and Slim, too. That's if you'll give us a lift."

"I don't want any part of this," said the other woman. "It's against the law. It's dangerous."

"For real," Allen replied. "But it's time to go. Just stay cool. Bitsey and Slim will be here in a minute. Let's get in the car and wait for them."

Silence prevailed as Allen and the two women sat in the automobile and waited for Parker and Canady to clear the main gate. It was ended when Allen chuckled and pointed at a group of visitors walking toward the parking lot. "Well, girls, here they come. They've made it."

"What now?" asked one of the women.

"Well," Allen answered with some apprehension, "we were hoping you'd give us a ride to Atlanta."

So that is what they did. It was a quiet ride until the five of them crossed the Georgia state line, sighing with relief. A couple of hours later the escapees checked into the Mark Inn on the edge of the city.

Allen, Parker, and Canady gave the two women enough money for their return trip to Nashville, then enjoyed their first night of freedom in seven years.

"I guess going to see the Braves play baseball tomorrow is out of the question," chuckled Canady in a frivolous moment.

"Yeah, Slim, it really is," said Parker. "But the best squeeze play came today down on the farm in Nashville."

NINETEEN

Bill Allen, Steve Parker, and Ralph Canady concluded that the best way to survive on the run was to appear to be walking. So within days of their arrival in Atlanta, they settled into normal lives, finding an apartment and getting jobs to pay the rent.

They received a break when the Nashville police department and the FBI drew blanks while trying to figure out where the escapees were hiding. The search was concentrated in Ohio, based on the theory that most troubled people think home is the safest place in the world, and in New York, because Allen had gone there just after the shooting.

"Excuse me," Allen said to the young lady waiting for a bus at the corner of Ashby Street in Atlanta.

"Yes?" replied Ann Barnwell, age twenty-two, as she surveyed the handsome young man dressed in a pair of khaki pants and a work shirt who approached her that morning in late May.

"I was wondering if you could tell how to get to Rock Street. I know it's in the area."

Sensing a weak opening line from a man attempting to make a harmless pass at her, Barnwell smiled, pointed up Ashby Street, and answered, "Just keep walking."

"Thank you," Allen replied. "By the way, I'm Robert Williams, a student at Morehouse. I'm on my way to work at Bankhead Industries."

"Good," said Barnwell, who was attired in dress slacks and a silk blouse. "I'm going to work, too."

Barnwell adjusted her glasses nervously, looking up the street as if she was anticipating the arrival of the bus. She attempted to ignore Allen.

107

"So your name must be Susie?"

Barnswell offered no reply.

"Is it?"

"No, it's not," she answered as if she was annoyed with the persistent man. "It's Ann."

Barnwell flinched with the slip of the tongue. Allen chuckled as the bus turned a corner two blocks away.

"Well, Miss Ann, I'd like to telephone you."

"Here comes my bus."

"Can I call you sometime?"

As the bus approached the stop, Barnwell quickly reached into her purse, grabbed a piece of scratch paper and a pen, and wrote her telephone number on it. She handed it to Allen as she boarded the bus.

"Never call late," she warned. "Never after nine."

"Right," Allen replied. "And have a nice day."

The lady with the engaging smile was the daughter of a preacher, Elder O. D. Barnwell, and Clovis Barnwell. Intelligent and astute, she was an active worker for civil rights, and those attributes helped her as she attempted to digest the conversation she had had at the bus stop.

"There's something unusual about that man," she said to herself as the bus rolled along streets. "But there's something about that smile that makes me think he's a good one."

That was the start of a blistering romance that picked up heat two weeks later when Allen telephoned Barnwell and asked her to accompany him to a jazz club. She accepted on the condition the oldest of her three sisters, Mary Barnwell, could accompany them.

The suspicions Ann Barnwell had about Allen, or Robert Williams, as she knew him, grew when he arrived for their date wearing casual slacks and a casual shirt. A gifted seamstress, she had made a stunning dress for the occasion, something like a person would wear to church, but it did not surprise her when her escort was the only man in the jazz club not wearing a sportcoat. She thought his style made up for his lack of proper attire.

"Do you mind if I sit closer to you, Mr. Williams?" she asked as the band took a break and her sister left the table to go to the restroom.

"Not at all, Miss Barnwell," Allen replied, taking her hands in his. "I'd like that."

They conversed with ease and agreed to go out another night.

Allen was sharing an apartment on Ashby Street with Canady and Parker, who were also working and playing a lot of basketball at a municipal park in the Summerhill section of Atlanta. All of them were gifted athletes who had earned acclaim in high school, which made their pickup games enjoyable and feisty. That made Canady and Parker a bit jealous when Allen passed up time on the court to socialize with Ann Barnwell.

While Allen and Barnwell's romance was developing during June and early July 1974, police officers and FBI agents in Nashville were all but beating their heads against a wall.

"You can forget about any of those guys being with Alexander," an FBI agent said during one of several meetings held to coordinate the hunt for the three men. "He's as clean as a whistle, has been since being paroled. He's living in St. Louis with his mother."

"What about the other guy, Charles Lee Herron?" asked another agent.

"Your guess is as good as mine. I think he's in California with friends he met in the Air Force."

"Well, we've got to find a tie that binds."

"Gentlemen, if I might inject something, I'd say we're talking about sports and intelligence," suggested a Nashville homicide detective whose department had been under fire because Herron was still at large after more than six years. "They love to play sports, and they're smart. Guards at the prison say they're great basketball players, almost as good as those in college. The rap sheets say they have a fondness for city life."

At the end of a date one Saturday night in July, Ann Barnwell invited Allen to accompany her to church. He declined, saying he planned to visit a fellow worker across town, provided he could find transportation. She asked if he wanted to use her automobile, an Opel, and he accepted.

After noticing the automobile needed gas, Allen drove it into popular Riley's Shell service station. There were five other cars on the premises, which had attendants rushing about, and he grew impatient while awaiting his turn at one of the pumps. He was startled just after moving to the front of the line.

As he glanced at the short man approaching him to take his order for gas, he did a double take. It was Charles Lee Herron. Herron turned at the front of the Opel and started toward an open window.

"Damn, it can't be," Allen said to himself as he recognized the weekend manager at the service station. "I heard he was in Atlanta, but it's unbelievable."

But it was true. After six years, Allen and Herron were reunited for the first time since the shooting in January 1968. Both were so shocked that neither remembered much about what they said. They also exchanged addresses and telephone numbers, tearing apart a paper towel for washing automobile windows, and vowed to get together.

Another familiar name and face came to light that afternoon in Atlanta. Herron informed Allen that Herbert Munford, a longtime friend from Nashville, was living in the city, but he cautioned his friend to stay away from anybody from his past. He felt the FBI would have such people under surveillance.

But Allen could not avoid the temptation. He contacted Munford, who was working at refurbishing houses and businesses, and learned his friend would be more than happy to help the fugitives get started in that trade.

Had the FBI known such contacts had been made, it would have zeroed in on the fugitives quickly. Instead, it was being fed unreliable tips from a business-minded informant inside the Tennessee State Penitentiary.

"The convict seems to be taking us for a ride," an agent in Memphis said by telephone to a Nashville agent after disclosures from the informant were checked out and proved erroneous.

"So he doesn't know where they are?"

"No way. He's just trying to make money at our expense. I don't think the bastard has a clue."

"But he sounded so sure," the Nashville agent said, "like there was a network set up before the escape."

"I don't think they had much communication inside the prison," the Memphis agent replied. "Hell, they just vanished. Poof! Gone in a flash! I'm not sure their families knew what was going on."

"What about the girls, the ones who visited them that day?"

"Just regular people. Nervous at first. Like rocks now. They haven't helped us, and they won't."

"Well, I doubt they sit tight," the Nashville agent concluded. "The hunted run more than they hide."

"But these guys aren't used to being hunted."

They were learning to play the cat and mouse game, though, which is why a telephone call Parker received one afternoon was alarming.

"Bitsey, it's Lee," Herron told Parker. "I've got a problem."

"What's up?" Parker asked.

"I'm in jail."

"Say what?"

"They stopped me because my car was smoking," Herron replied. "I've got to have bail money."

Herron was referring to an old car he had purchased from a man at Riley's Shell Station. He had spent hours working on it, with an assist from his boss, and had gotten it running. What he had failed to do periodically was check the oil pan for leaks.

"We'll be there in an hour," Parker told Herron. "Just sit tight."

"Who's coming to get me?"

"Bill and me."

"I don't know about that," Herron replied.

"But we'll bring my lady with us. She'll come in and post bond for you."

The lady Parker was referring to was Ann Roberts, whom he was dating. She had fallen in with the group but did not know about the past experiences of the four fugitives. She had construed them only for what they seemed to be at the time, nice individuals who worked hard and laughed a lot during leisure hours.

In Parker she had found the man of her dreams. They were in love.

So Roberts was more than willing to accompany Parker and Allen to a police station in an Atlanta suburb. Without the slightest hint of tension, she went inside the building and posted bond for Herron, who had received a citation and a court date. Meanwhile, the two fugitives sat outside in an automobile, watching several police officers come and go, and did not relax until they saw their two friends walking through the front door.

"I'm sweating like a thief in church," Bill Allen told Parker as the two friends walked toward the automobile with smiles on their faces.

"That's two of us," Parker replied. "But be cool about it, Doc. Remember, the lady doesn't know."

"You got it," Bill Allen agreed. "And it's a good thing. She'd be sweating, too, if she knew how hot this street corner is right now."

TWENTY

Love was in full bloom the second week in September 1974. Bill Allen and Ann Barnwell were becoming inseparable, which was obvious on a Monday night when they sat together on a couch and watched a football game on television. Lying on the floor of the duplex apartment in front of them were Charles Lee Herron and Steve Parker. Ralph Canady was out on the town.

"Fellas, I guess you know that we've got a birthday coming up?" Barnwell said. "So Friday night I'm having a party for Robert at my house. My parents are turning over the place to us. There'll be some ladies there."

Parker pulled himself from the floor and started walking to the kitchen to get a beer. He glanced at Allen as he passed the couch. Herron remained on the floor with his eyes focused on the television screen.

"What do you think, James?" Barnwell said to Herron, who was using the alias James Johnson. "Can you guys come to the party?"

"I don't know, Ann," Herron said. "I might have to work Friday night."

"I told Slim I'd go to a game with him," Parker answered as he returned to the room. "Maybe another time."

Barnwell was disappointed to hear their responses, obviously, and it showed as she looked at Allen in disbelief. "Don't these guys like me?" she asked in a whisper. "What's wrong with them?"

Allen spoke loudly, miffed by the inconsiderate behavior of his friends.

"They'll be at the party," Allen declared as Herron and Parker glanced at each other. "These guys love Robert Williams like you do, baby, and so does Slim."

Allen paused, then continued, "I'll explain what they're thinking tomorrow afternoon."

Herron and Parker looked at Allen in disbelief. They could not fathom why their friend, a fellow fugitive on the FBI Identification Order list, was being so free with information. They glanced at each other when Allen shrugged his shoulders, then turned their attention to the game on television. Later that evening, after Barnwell had gone home, Herron and Parker urged Allen to remain quiet about the past.

But their pleas fell on deaf ears.

"She's a good lady, fellas," Allen declared. "She's active on behalf of the cause. I think she'll understand."

Still, it was a nervous Allen who accompanied a confused Barnwell on a stroll the following afternoon.

"Let's go sit on the bus stop bench," he said as they walked hand-in-hand along a sidewalk. "After all, Sweet Lady, that's where I struck oil."

"I know, Robert. I think about that every day I get on the bus to go to work. It's been four months."

"Well, let's sit and talk a while. I'll explain the reluctance Bitsey and Slim had last night. I think you'll understand once you hear what I've got to say."

Allen and Barnwell seated themselves on the bus stop bench. It was a cloudy day, with rain threatening as afternoon became dusk, and Barnwell noticed some uneasiness on the part of Allen.

"Are you in trouble, Robert?" she asked after a few seconds of silence that seemed much longer to her.

"Sort of," Allen answered, his voice cracking.

"So what is it?"

Allen sat for a moment without replying. Leaning forward, he rested his elbows on his knees, his head in his hands. He shook his head, then reached into his shirt pocket and grabbed a cigarette. He watched a motorist pass on the street, then lit the cigarette.

"Ann, I've got a bit of past that we need to discuss," he began.

"Yeah?"

"For real."

"Well, what's the deal?"

Choosing his words carefully, Allen told her about the January evening in 1968 that had altered his life permanently. He told her about the philosophical base that had served as a catalyst for his fears and his response to the shots that had been fired by officers Johnson and Thomasson. He paused frequently and looked at his love, who nodded and, on many occasions, appeared to be fighting back tears. Finally, the book on his life was complete.

"So that's it, Ann," he concluded. "Except I've got to tell you how much I love you, how I've known since our first night out that you're special, the lady for me."

Barnwell rose to her feet and walked a few yards from the bench. She took off her glasses with her right hand, looked at them with a blank stare, and returned them to her nose. She took them off again as tears streamed down her cheeks, then wiped away the moisture with her left hand.

"Well?" Allen asked when she turned around to face him.

"What do I call you?"

"What do you call me?"

"Yeah."

"Well, Bill when we're in private quarters. Bill Allen. Robert when we're in public."

"OK."

"That's it?" he asked in disbelief.

"Yeah. Except you need to know I love you even more now that you've told me. And the same holds true for Lee, Bitsey, and Slim."

Barnwell paused.

"See, Robert, uh, Bill, I know now how much you love me. I know you're a man, too, because it would've been easy for you to avoid me for the rest of your life. Instead, you came clean."

"I've always been honest, Ann. I'll always be."

"I believe that, Bill. And, like you, I've always felt strongly about human rights, equality for all people. So that'll be our bond."

"Then you're staying with me?"

"Forever, if you'll let me. I'm willing to walk through the muck with you."

"Then we've got a deal, Ann, that'll last a lifetime."

That vow was followed by a more formal one on May 23, 1975, when Elder O. D. Barnwell performed a marriage ceremony for his daughter and Allen, whom he still knew as Robert Williams. The ceremony took place in his house, with Herron, Parker, and Canady present.

It had been one year since Allen and Ann Barnwell had met. Less time would pass before the FBI began zeroing in on four men prominent on its seek-and-apprehend list.

TWENTY-ONE

Al Archer and Frank Pickens, somewhat inexperienced agents with less than one year and four years experience, respectively, were talking away the final hour of the work shift in the FBI office in Atlanta when the special agent in charge, Jim Dunn, entered the room.

"Gentlemen, how's life treating you?" Dunn asked with a smile as Archer and Pickens attempted to look more busy than they were.

"Well, uh, everything is fine, chief," Archer stammered.

"And, Jim, there's something we've been wanting to discuss with you," Pickens said.

"What's that?" Dunn asked.

"There's this police officer in town who's convinced he has seen a most wanted fugitive around here, that Charles Lee Herron who we've hunted for seven years," Pickens answered.

Dunn changed moods in a hurry. He became more serious. "Tell me what you know," he asked.

Pickens told Dunn that the officer had seen a familiar face when he was a student at Morehouse University, where the fugitives had socialized frequently. He said that after almost two years, after he studied some wanted posters, it dawned on him that the person in question might be Herron, also that three of the men he was moving around town with might be Bill Allen, Steve Parker, and Ralph Canady.

"What's the deal with this police officer?" Dunn asked Pickens. "I mean, is he reliable?"

"He's as clean as a whistle, as far as I know," Pickens replied. "He has a good reputation. I don't think he's in error, especially since he was in class with the guy."

"What have you guys got going these days?" Dunn asked.

"It's not too heavy, at least not now," Archer replied.

"Then why don't you wrap it up in the next two or three weeks and check into this case," Dunn suggested. "It's a biggie. We've looked for Herron for more than seven years. Now there are three more of them from that Nashville incident out there with him."

Two weeks later, after learning that Herron had been employed at Riley's Shell Station, Archer and Pickens put on blue jeans and sweat shirts and went to visit the place. Armed with a picture taken of the fugitive in the 1960s, they interrogated several people including the station owner, and found all of them only somewhat cooperative.

"I don't know anything about Charles Lee Herron," answered one of the men Archer and Pickens interviewed during their two days in the area near the service station. "But that man there in the picture, he's a brother known in the streets as Kimathi, or something like that. He has an African name. He used to work here at the station."

"When was the last time you saw him?" Pickens asked.

"Lord, man, it has to have been at least a year, probably more. He split from these parts a long time ago."

Undaunted, Archer and Pickens kept asking questions. Finally, they hit on something: "That man you're asking about paid cash for an old car, a 1965 Barracuda, and fixed it up. Then, lo and behold, he got stopped in it because of smoke. I mean he was as mad as hell about that. He carried on for weeks about how the police took him to jail."

"Sir, would you by any chance know who owned the car before Herron, or this Kimathi?" Archer asked.

"That'd be Soap Man. He's a regular around the station. He'll be back by here."

In time, Archer and Pickens located the original owner of the automobile, who provided them with vehicle identification and tag numbers. For three weeks the agents poured through police department files.

"Frank, old buddy, I'm afraid we're barking up a bare tree," Archer told Pickens as they searched late on a Friday afternoon.

"I know," Pickens replied. "We must have looked at 10,000 of these arrest forms."

"Yep," Archer said, "and there's a pile still—"

Archer was interrupted by a suddenly excited Pickens. "Partner, the man we're looking for is Benny Leroy Smith, who was bonded out of jail and jumped ship. And I don't know if it's good or not, but we've an address for him."

While Archer and Pickens were excited about the information they found, they would have been more subdued if they had known that the men they were seeking were living "normal" lives.

Allen had married Ann Barnwell. Parker was working with Allen at Bankhead Industries. Canady was working at Atlanta Tile and Brick. And Herron was picking up pocket change somewhere other than at Riley's Shell Station and was continuing a long-running romance of his own. Ann Allen (a.k.a. Ann Rene Williams) continued to earn her wages as a seamstress.

In St. Louis, John Alexander was trying to reconstruct his life after a stay in prison. He made no effort to contact the other four men. They made no effort to contact him.

So Archer and Pickens went to the address they found on the police department arrest record for Herron, discovering it was nothing more than the site of Atlanta-Fulton County Stadium. Fall gave way to winter, with FBI and Nashville police still baffled concerning the whereabouts of the four wanted men. Angered veteran officers in Nashville carried pictures of Allen, Parker, Canady, and Herron in their wallets as reminders that they were still free while officers Pete Johnson and Wayne Thomasson were dead.

They would have been surprised had they known how smoothly the fugitives were operating in Atlanta. Parker and Canady were playing the roles of most eligible bachelors, while Herron had settled in with a lady he had met a couple of years earlier. They were living free of crime, which helped them establish a reputable part-time house renovation service.

Few fix-up crews, as they were called at the time, were honest enough to do the work without stealing from homeowners. But the four men being hunted so diligently by the FBI were termed "good boys" by those who hired them. They were considered totally trustworthy.

The house renovation business picked up momentum when Parker saved enough money to buy a 1963 white Chevrolet pickup that came replete with redneck decor, most noticeably an STP sticker on its side. He had seen a "truck for sale" sign at a place on Marietta Street.

"How much for the wheels?" Parker asked the owner.

"Three bills," the owner replied. "It's a steal."

Parker thought so, too. He bought the truck for $300, took it home to show it off to his friends, and smiled when Allen came up with an idea to add money to their kitty.

"I'm good with the hands, as you know," Allen told the other three men. "What you say we put them to work, maybe start a home improvement business?"

They all agreed.

So the four of them became part-time carpenters, with much success, and the extra money came in handy for the men and Ann. They were never hungry, but sometimes they wondered where their next plate of food would come from.

The truck involved Parker and Canady in a bizarre and frightening incident one evening.

"Say, what's happening," Parker asked two ladies he and Canady had been visiting at an Atlanta boutique.

"Not much," one of the women answered.

The other was looking outside at the truck.

"That your truck?" she asked.

"Right on," Parker replied.

"Then you'll move me?"

"What do you mean?" Canady asked.

"I've got a new place. I need to move my furniture. When can you do it?"

"It's your call, baby," Parker replied.

"Then it's tomorrow night."

"That's cool," Canady said. "We'll be here."

Parker and Canady arrived at the boutique with thoughts of work and romance dancing in their heads. They accompanied the women to a nice brick ranch house on a wooded lot and were stunned when one of them said, "This is where I live now. This is where my stuff is."

"Why would anybody want to leave a place like this?" Parker thought to himself as Canady and he loaded the pickup truck with furniture.

They did not notice as they sweated, but the leg of a table had disconnected the wire on the truck that fed electricity to the taillights. Nor did they care when the two ladies slipped into the bench seat between them before they started across town with a loaded rear section.

"You guys will never know how much we appreciate this," one of the women said.

"We'll find out, believe me," Canady laughed.

It was then that Parker noticed rotating emergency flashing lights on a police cruiser behind them, a grim reminder of what had happened in North Nashville more than seven years earlier. He pulled the pickup truck to the side of the road and waited for an Atlanta police officer to walk to the open window on his left.

"How are you doing tonight?"

"OK," Parker answered. "And you?"

"I'm good," said the police officer. "But did you know you're missing taillights?"

"No, sir, I didn't," Parker replied.

"And it's against the law to move after dark."

"I didn't know that," Parker answered.

"Have you got your license?" the officer asked.

Parker reached for his back pocket, knowing that he did not have a license to operate a motor vehicle in Georgia.

"Doggone it," Parker said. "Is it in the box [glove compartment] or in the back?"

On cue, Canady leaped from his seat and ran to the rear of the pickup truck, as Parker searched the glove compartment without success. Canady began digging through the furniture on a spurious license hunt.

"What kind of identification have you got on you?" the officer asked.

"A work badge from Bankhead Industries," Parker replied, while reaching for his identification card.

"OK," said the police officer. "I'm going to give you a ticket, just the same. Just show your license to the folks at headquarters when you pay the fine."

"For sure," Parker replied.

As the officer drove away, Parker and Canady breathed sighs of relief. They continued toward their destination.

After the furniture had been taken inside an apartment building, Parker and Canady walked back toward the pickup truck in the parking lot. Before they could get to it, a giant of a man, at least six feet, six inches and 250 pounds in weight, leaped from an automobile and pointed a single-barrel shotgun at them.

"What the hell is going on?" he swore at Parker.

"What do you mean?

"I mean, damn! You bastards are messing with my furniture and my woman."

"Come again?"

"Don't give me that shit. You've stolen my woman and my furniture. What gives you the right to go into my house and clean it out?"

Parker swallowed hard, then said, while looking down the open barrel of the gun, "Sir, you misunderstand. We just pick up extra cash moving people. That's the deal."

The man, who was so mad he was trembling, turned the gun on Canady. "So what have you got to say for yourself, you son of a bitch? I've got every reason in the world to drop you two thieves right here."

Canady did not pause before responding. Using a French-African accent, which he had learned from friends who worked with him at Atlanta Tile and Brick, he offered a most bizarre explanation.

"Sir, I know not what you are speaking of. You see, I am thousands of miles from home. I know not a single thing you say."

The man was somewhat amused and smiled, then lowered the weapon. Shaking his head, he laughed. "Aw hell, the bitch ain't worth it anyway."

Parker and Canady walked to the pickup truck and rode home counting their blessings.

TWENTY-TWO

Agents Al Archer and Frank Pickens were despondent as they drove away from newly constructed Atlanta-Fulton County Stadium. They had hoped to zero in on Charles Lee Herron that afternoon.

"Well, we're back to square one," Pickens sighed. "We came looking for a house and ended up with a football stadium."

Then they spotted their silver lining in a dark cloud, a United States Postal Service employee who was making his appointed rounds. "Let's ask the mailman a question or two," Archer suggested. "You never know."

Not only did the mailman know the neighborhood, he had a good memory.

"Not only do I remember the man you've got there," he replied as he looked at a Most Wanted poster, "I recall his house and some of the mail he got."

"Such as what?" Pickens asked.

"Well, for starters he got a lot of letters from a woman up in Delaware. I'd bet my life she has been down here to see him a few times."

"What else can you tell us?" Archer asked.

"I can remember seeing a lot of faces around here," he said with a smile. "I'm good at recalling faces and names—and addresses, obviously."

Pickens was quick to produce Identification Order posters on Allen, Parker, and Canady. "Yes sir, I've seen them all from time to time. But, gentlemen, that's been quite a while."

The FBI now had the name of a woman from Delaware, as well as her address.

121

Herron, who was at the top of the FBI Most Wanted List, was living with his lady friend. Parker and Canady were sharing an apartment on Ashby Street. Two of their neighbors, Bill and Ann Allen, were living on Wellington Avenue and considering a move into a larger apartment, since she had just learned that she was pregnant.

These plans did not make the James Leftowich family happy. The man and woman, both in their seventies, had taken to the group who lived in their neighborhood. They liked them so much that they had invited them to have Christmas dinner at their house in 1975. They were crushed when they learned their youthful friends might be moving.

"Who'll keep the house in working order?" James Leftowich asked Allen when the move was first mentioned. "Who'll tidy up the yard? We've gotten to where we count on you folks to help us."

"It's not like we're leaving the country, Mr. Leftowich," Bill Allen answered, while thinking that might not be such a bad idea. "We'll check in with you from time to time."

But there was little time for fun and games. All four men, and Ann Allen, were working fulltime, and the FBI was getting closer to them by the minute.

"Our guys in Delaware have talked to Cynthia Brown," Al Archer told Frank Pickens early one morning in the FBI office in Atlanta. "I got the call last night."

"Is she willing to cooperate?" Pickens asked.

"It looks that way. But you've got to go get her."

"I've got to go to Delaware?"

"That's right," Archer replied. "The lady will talk to us only after we escort her to Atlanta."

In just a few days Pickens was on an airplane headed for Delaware, where he encountered a woman who was not totally convinced she was doing the right thing. However, she was concerned enough by FBI involvement in the case to at least answer a few questions.

"Yes sir, that's correct," Brown said to Archer and Pickens, "they're sort of freaky the way they try to stay in shape. They run. They lift weights. They play basketball, a lot of basketball, all over the city. I've heard them say they have to stay in shape because there's no telling when they'll need the stamina. After what you've told me, I understand that statement much better."

By the time Brown returned to Delaware, Archer and Pickens had the names of others who had gotten to know the fugitives.

"Basketball, man, basketball. That's their game," said a man interviewed by the agents.

"They're into an African fraternity or some group like that," a woman replied. "They've got African names. They socialize with some African nationalists."

"Yes, I'm familiar with them," another man, a mechanic by trade, answered. "I've seen them working in the neighborhood. Good carpenters, those fellas. Sharp and honest. They do good work. And they're marksmen, too. I've heard them practicing their shooting with 45-caliber pistols down by I–20."

"No, I've never heard of them causing any trouble," said one woman. "But I've heard they're good shooters. I think Herron might be the most devoted to the guns. I've heard he even sleeps with his pistol. I haven't heard anything like that about the others."

"They're good guys, real hip," declared another man. "Herron even walks like jive, up on his toes, bobbing and weaving like Ali, the boxer. They're smooth with the ladies. They're smart. They're clean. They're sharp fellas."

"If I were you, I'd check out this African man, Omar Kah, who lives in that neighborhood you're talking about," a woman suggested. "They hang out with him a lot. His wife is an American lady, Theresa Smith, a nurse. You might want to talk to her. She's more than a little cautious. I'm not sure she likes having those mysterious guys coming in and out of her house."

With weary legs and worn shoes, Archer and Pickens returned to the FBI office in Atlanta and began spreading the news.

"It's coming together, little piece by little piece," Pickens declared by telephone to an agent in Memphis. "At least we've got a few things to watch now."

"It sounds to me like you're getting close to Herron for sure. The others must be nearby for the nabbing," the Memphis agent commented.

"Yeah," Pickens replied, "but headquarters has made it clear that we want all four at once, not just one."

"Mmmm, I see. In other words, we're using a big net, even with Herron on the Most Wanted list."

"That's right," Pickens said. "And if we're going to get them that way, it might be at the Kah residence. They're in and out of there, but never as a group. In fact, I'd say they're too smart to go anywhere as four."

Pickens paused for a second, then asked, "By the way, what's the mood in Nashville?"

"There are a lot of mad policemen over there," the Memphis agent answered. "The wounds are deep among them. And, get this, there's talk that some policemen might have had a hand in the prison escape, that they wanted Allen, Parker, and Canady out so they could get them."

"That's unreal," Pickens replied.

"I know, but that's the word. They got out of town too quickly."

"Well, I'm not getting into something as wild as that," Pickens commented. "I've got enough to handle here."

The burden on Pickens and Archer increased on an early spring afternoon in 1976 as they sat in an unmarked automobile down the street from the Omar Kah residence.

"If that's not Allen, I'm not an agent," Archer told Pickens as they observed a man wearing blue jeans and a matching jacket emerge from the house and move toward an automobile parked curbside.

"He's clean looking," Pickens observed, "just like we've heard. He doesn't look like a radical."

"Well, let's get a closer look," Archer replied as he started the automobile and began following the fugitive at a distance of one block. "You wouldn't want to look peculiar if you were in his situation."

"Keep your distance," Pickens warned. "He might be leading us to the other three."

Instead, Allen was going to a liquor store. He parked in a small lot in front of the store, spoke to a woman who was leaving, and went inside.

In a flash, Pickens was out of the automobile and moving toward the front door. "Remember, it's four or none," Archer reminded his partner as he moved toward the first close contact anyone in law enforcement had had with any of the fugitives since the escape from prison.

Pickens was dressed in blue jeans, an old shirt, and sneakers. He looked more like a hard drinker than an FBI agent, by design.

"Hello, my man, what's happening?" Pickens said to Allen as they waited to pay for their purchases.

"It's you," Allen said with a smile, engaging Pickens in hip conversation.

"For real," Pickens answered. "And I'll be better when I get a drink under me."

Allen paid for his bottle and turned to leave. "Go easy on it, my man," he joked. "It's bad for you."

Pickens nodded and watched Allen move toward the door. In the parking lot, Archer sat shaking his head and thinking how good it would be to arrest a highly wanted fugitive.

As hard as Pickens tried to get outside quickly without drawing attention to his undercover operation, Allen was gone in a flash, not back to the Kah residence, but to a destination that remains unknown to the FBI.

"Those guys you're chasing, well, they play a lot of sports," the anonymous male caller said by telephone to FBI agent Pickens, who was seated in his Atlanta office.

"Tell me about it," Pickens answered. "We've heard that. In fact, we've watched basketball games on every damn court in Atlanta during the last two months."

"Well, there's a big game planned on the south side this afternoon, in Lucille Park, and I'm hearing they'll be involved in it."

Pickens thanked the caller, smiled, and told Archer what he had learned. Then he contacted the special agent in charge of his office. The information excited him, especially since Archer and he had been on a wild goose chase of sorts while tracking the fugitives.

"We'd like to go full guns on this one," Pickens said during a hastily called meeting of FBI agents.

"I can appreciate that, Frank," said the special agent in charge. "But it remains a fact that we can't put everybody in the city on this case. We've got other duties to deal with, bank robberies left and right, all kinds of crime."

"We understand that," Archer answered. "And that has been a problem for us. We get close, and then we can't stay with them because everybody has something else to do. I'm not arguing that point, you understand, but I'm with Frank on this one. I'd like to take our best shot."

"OK, we'll give it a good go. But remember it's still four or none. That's orders from above."

"Fine," replied Pickens. "So what's the deal?"

"You and Al get close to those basketball courts," the special agent in charge said. "We'll have help outside the park, under wraps."

Later that day, Archer and Pickens were crouched in thick bushes not more than thirty yards from the basketball courts under surveillance. Outside the park sat fifteen FBI agents in as many unmarked automobiles. In the sky over Atlanta an airplane flew within quick striking distance of the area.

"Damn it's hot," Archer complained to Pickens as they waited and watched with binoculars around their necks and with a walkie-talkie nearby.

"Spring in Georgia is always like this," Pickens reminded him. "You should know by now."

"Well, I hope the sweat is worth it," replied Archer, who, like his partner, was dressed in ragged clothing.

Basketball players came and went as they watched. Soon they saw Canady and Parker walking past an automobile parked in a nearby lot.

"I think this is it," Archer said as he looked through binoculars. "There's two familiar faces. The one with the small beard, the goatee, looks like Herron and walks like that woman said he does."

"If it's not Herron, it's two of the others," Pickens replied. "But not Allen. He's the only one we've seen."

"I know," Archer answered. "And it's hard to tell while working with mug shots that must be ten years old."

The men they were watching were Parker and Canady, who frequently played basketball in the park and obviously knew several of the other men there. They engaged in a few handslaps, waited for a game to end, and took their turns on the court, going one-on-one on the vacated end.

"We think we've got two of the suspects under surveillance on the court," Archer spoke into the walkie-talkie, alerting agents outside the park. "We'll watch a while longer and see if the other two show up."

They waited for perhaps thirty minutes as Parker and Canady played basketball.

"I don't think all of them are going to show up today," Pickens finally said.

"I agree. And while we can't grab those two, we can at least trail them."

"Right," Pickens answered. "But we've got to be sure about their identities."

"Well, that'll take a closer look," Archer commented.

"Right. So I'll take a stroll."

Parker and Canady were sweating profusely on the court as Pickens took the long way around on his stroll from the thick bushes. The concrete was hot. So was the FBI agent as he mingled with bystanders and got closer to the action.

"Agent Pickens is walking near the court," Archer spoke on the walkie-talkie to his fellow agents outside the park. "He's looking for a positive ID. The suspects are still playing their game. Be on alert."

As Pickens strolled past the fugitives, like a man walking for exercise, he attracted keen eyes.

"Be cool, Bitsey," Canady warned Parker as he braced himself on defense.

"What's the deal?" Parker asked as he went into a stall on offense, dribbling the basketball deliberately as if he was attempting to catch his breath.

"I think that man is a cop," Canady replied. "He has the look. He isn't here to play."

"Keep playing," replied Parker, as he made a move toward the basket, forcing Canady to resume the action.

Pickens continued his stroll, eventually working his way back toward Archer. Parker watched him out of a corner of his eye, then alerted Canady after a basket.

"Slim, we've got to get the hell out of here. Give me an easy basket and a handslap. Then it's to the car and out the other gate as quickly as possible."

Parker made a jump shot to end the game, pointed at Canady, and said, "That's two dollars you owe me, Slim."

Canady laughed and answered, "Only if you can catch me, Blood."

"Well, Slim, let's make it look good. They're watching us."

As Canady started running toward the white 1963 Chevrolet truck, acting more like he was capping an afternoon of exercise than attempting a getaway, Archer threw down his binoculars and picked up the walkie-talkie.

"They're on their way out," he warned agents outside the park. "They've been spooked. All cars stand by. They're moving toward the gate. Alert. Suspects are on the move. Do you copy?"

"That's 10–4," an agent answered. "But I don't see them."

"Suspects are moving into traffic, going north," another agent reported. "I can't get to them from here."

"Is the plane overhead?" asked another agent. "Do you copy up there?"

"That's 10–4," radioed the agent in the airplane. "We're looking. Nothing yet."

Archer and Pickens were hurrying toward their unmarked automobile parked inside the park.

"They can't beat this," Archer said. "We've got to catch up with them. They'll go straight to the others."

"Maybe," Pickens replied. "They might be too shrewd to do something like that."

Pickens paused, then said, "But that's our men."

Parker and Canady remained tense as they quickly moved through traffic, weaving their way toward safer ground. "If that wasn't a cop, we're sure as hell taking a lot of chances in this traffic," Parker exclaimed.

"It was, man," Canady said. "No doubt. And if there was one there, I'll bet there were others."

"Well, let's take a long ride in the country," Parker suggested, "then make our way toward home."

The mood was not pleasant at the FBI office in Atlanta that night. Agents fought against the realization that they had muffed a golden opportunity.

"Well, they'll be back. We'll just have to watch a lot of basketball until we see them again," Archer commented, trying to remain positive. "That's the only way we'll figure out where they're hiding."

"That's only if they don't leave town," Pickens answered. "I'll bet the house they're out of here."

Still, the two FBI agents stayed on guard at the park almost daily.

But Parker and Canady knew better than to return to the basketball court in Lucille Park.

TWENTY-THREE

A waitress was removing plates and utensils from the table when a Nashville police officer and an assistant district attorney began discussing a subject important to both of them. They had heard that Steve Parker and Ralph Canady had been spotted by law enforcement authorities in Atlanta. Both were dismayed that they had managed to elude apprehension.

"Let's hope the local newspapers don't hear about it," said the assistant district attorney. "Every time there's the slightest mention of that case, my office gets turned upside down."

"Yes, sir," the officer agreed, "and it's like an earthquake hits our place."

"Well, I guess it's a good thing nobody picked up on the comments your boss made to that reporter from Cincinnati after those guys escaped a couple of years ago."

"What do you mean?"

"I mean our folks up there read them with interest, especially the explanation he made as to why Allen, Parker, and Canady were tried in the death of Thomasson, who died second, instead of Johnson," the officer answered.

"You mean the part where he said Johnson and his wife were estranged, that she didn't want to prosecute the case?"

"That's right. I wouldn't think this is the type of matter you'd want the public to know about the two police officers. Such a statement aroused interest in his character, at least his love life."

"I see. Well . . . so tell me, is there anything new on your end?"

"Well, yeah, there is," the officer answered. "I think the FBI has something more in Atlanta."

"I've heard a little."

"Does the name Herbert Munford mean anything to you?" the officer asked.

"It's vaguely familiar."

"It should be. He's one of them, another troublemaker from North Nashville."

Herbert Munford, a friend the fugitives had visited in Hubbard Hospital on the afternoon before the 1968 shooting, had been spotted in Atlanta. Through keen investigation, the FBI had linked him with Allen, Parker, Canady, and Charles Lee Herron, prompting agents to embark on somewhat heated interrogations.

But Munford, who had set up the fugitives in the house renovation business in Atlanta, refused to cooperate with the agents. He consistently denied knowing of their whereabouts, as did other friends. Although he was under surveillance from time to time, the FBI finally stopped interrogating him, at least for a while, and, like the fugitives, he continued to have a relatively smooth and easy lifestyle.

For sure, with the narrow escape Parker and Canady experienced at the basketball court behind them, and with all the fugitives warned of how dangerous their situation was, the friends managed to remain somewhat calm during the summer of 1976, as the United States moved toward its two-hundredth birthday.

"Hell, we don't have anywhere to turn," Herron said one afternoon as the four fugitives contemplated their futures. "The FBI is all over Omar and our other friends to the point that we can't go around them, and it's just a matter of time until they find out where we live."

"That makes sense," Parker agreed. "Maybe it's time to get out of here, to move out of town."

"I was ready to go after the basketball episode," Canady replied.

"But you don't know for sure that it was the police watching you," Allen objected.

"Right," Canady agreed. "But I'm confident of it."

"Well, I think it's best to stay put," Allen said. "The quieter the better, you know. Besides, my lady is pregnant."

"I'll buy that for a while longer," Herron conceded. "But, Doc, we've got to be ready to move, just in case."

After talking with Omar Kah and Munford, as well as others who had been with the fugitives, agents Al Archer and Frank Pickens were convinced the four men had left Atlanta. Still, they remained alert.

As for the fugitives, they were constantly on guard.

The chase picked up on an August day in 1976. Allen and Herron were on their way to play in a pickup basketball game in Four Square Park. As they moved along an interstate highway near the stadium, where the baseball Braves and football Falcons played their games, they noticed they were being followed.

"He's coming off with us," Allen told Herron when he turned off an exit ramp.

"Maybe it's his exit, too."

"But he has been on our ass for a while now, Lee," Allen answered. "Let's stop by Willie's house and see what happens. Maybe see if the other fellas want to come play some hoops with us."

Both men were profoundly concerned after they stopped to visit friends in a neighborhood just a few blocks away. As they talked to their pals in front of an apartment, they noticed the suspicious automobile drive past them a couple of times. They also noticed the arrival of another automobile, similar in make. They decided it was time to leave.

"Let's make a quick loop at the next street and come back to meet them," Herron suggested to Allen after they noticed both automobiles were tailing them.

"Hang on, Lee. It might get bumpy!" Allen muttered as he glanced into the rearview mirror.

They made their turn quickly, and reached an entrance ramp to the interstate before the men they erroneously thought were FBI agents could recover enough to catch up with them. As Allen and Herron headed toward the duplex apartments on the other side of the city with fear gripping their hearts, they saw the two automobiles zipping through the neighborhood they had exited.

"Let's get Bitsey and Slim and get the hell out of Atlanta," Herron yelled as they drove toward Wellington Avenue. "It's time to go."

"For real," Allen agreed. "And quickly."

They followed through on that plan, as hastily as they formulated it. Within one hour the four fugitives packed their clothes and left Atlanta for Pittsburgh. Parker was in such a hurry after he spotted a police cruiser in the neighborhood that he jumped out of his pickup truck and left it parked in his driveway. In fact, they all left their vehicles parked on Ashby Street and Wellington Avenue because they had persuaded an unsuspecting friend to rent an automobile for them, promising him they would return it to the agency the next day in Washington, D.C.

"Sweet Lady, it's time to go," Allen told Ann Allen as he packed his clothes in preparation for his departure from Atlanta. "I'll call you tonight or tomorrow morning and let you know what's happening."

"When will I see you again?" Ann Allen asked. "And what about our baby?"

"It'll all work out in time," he replied. "For now, check out some telephone booths. Write down the numbers, and we'll talk that way in the future."

Parker was on the telephone saying goodbye to Ann Roberts, his chief romantic interest.

Then they were gone, with the four of them leaving good enough jobs, some happy memories, a super friend in Ann Allen, and more close encounters with law enforcement officers than any of them wanted to know about.

TWENTY-FOUR

Pittsburgh was not to be the fugitives' home in the late summer of 1976. They had sympathetic friends there, to be sure, but the Iron City was in a depressed state and unemployment was running high. The four friends had little chance of finding work.

So they stayed in the city for only six weeks before moving to Baltimore. Even that short time was almost too long for Bill Allen.

The incident happened late one afternoon when he accompanied two friends to a bar in the Wilkinsburg area of Pittsburgh. As they drank beer and talked, the man noticed that they were being watched by a man in a business suit who was standing near the front entrance.

"I'd say you've got a problem," he told Allen. "There's a man watching us like a hawk. I've seen him around. He's either a police detective or an FBI agent."

"You're kidding!" Allen responded. He started to look over his right shoulder, then decided against it. "This can't be. They can't know we're up here."

"It's for real, man. You keep drinking and talking. I'll keep watching."

Several minutes later, after another round of beers had been served, the man near the door left the bar to confer with his partner at an automobile parked nearby.

"Put some money on the table and let's split," Allen's friend said. "He's gone. He went right. We're going left. Let's roll it."

Allen and his two friends hastily left the bar, which drew the attention of people near them. Looking to the right, they saw two law enforcement officers conferring beside a parked automobile. Walking away along the sidewalk, they reached their parked auto-

133

mobile, got into it, and moved toward the congested intersection. As they turned left onto a main thoroughfare, they noticed that the lawmen were hurrying into their automobile to give chase.

The head start—about two blocks—was a blessing for Allen. A few blocks up the main thoroughfare, with the trailing automobile fighting traffic more than a block behind, his friend pulled his automobile into a bus stop at the right curb.

"I'd say this is the end of the line for you," he told Allen, who was squatting on the rear floorboard.

"I agree," Allen said as the woman opened the right front door and pulled the back of her seat forward.

"You better hurry," she warned.

"Right," Allen replied as he rolled out of the automobile. Landing in the gutter beside the sidewalk, he jumped to his feet and walked to the corner of the building in front of him. Once there, he leaned against the wall and watched the automobile following him move through the intersection in pursuit of the automobile he had just left.

"Thank God!" Allen thought to himself as he rubbed his face in disbelief, at first without noticing the pedestrians gawking at him. "We've got to get out of this place."

But where would Allen and his three friends go next? Given the events of the past three months, that was a good question. "Baltimore," he thought as he rode a city bus to tell his fellow fugitives about his close call. "It's not far away. It's nearer Ann in Atlanta, and it's big enough to hide in."

"We've got to go," Allen told his friends as a debate raged behind closed doors in their apartment on Batavia Street. "If that was the FBI, and I'm pretty sure of it, they'll be closing in on us."

"You're not just paranoid?" Canady asked.

"Hell, no," Allen retorted. "That car was hot on my tail when I hit the gutter."

"You think they caught up with your friends Sunshine and Barbara?" Herron asked.

"I don't know," Allen said. "But if they did, which is likely, they're putting all kind of heat on them."

"Then I better get on the phone and see if I can find us a place to stay in Baltimore," Parker replied.

So Baltimore was where they went next, and all four of them began to work at refurbishing houses. Maryland was a good choice, for they quickly developed lifestyles that did not attract further attention from the law.

"You're kidding me," the FBI agent in Memphis replied to a call from Washington.

"You read the greenie [a report from headquarters], didn't you?" asked the Washington agent.

"Yeah, I saw it, and I guess I can believe it was Allen in that bar. But was the other guy Washington?"

"That's unconfirmed. We're still not sure about him. But it's a pretty good bet he's their money bag, the one keeping them alive."

"Are the agents in Pittsburgh still watching his house on Batavia Street?" the Memphis agent asked.

"Yep. They've got his place under what you'd call sporadic surveillance, a look every now and then. And they're asking questions at his bank, too, trying to find out where he gets all his money and what he does with it."

"Don't you think they should pick up the pace?" asked the Memphis agent. "If it was Allen, it's doubtful he and the others will stay in Pittsburgh."

"For sure. But it's impossible to tell where they'll go."

"Well, it won't be Cincinnati. I'm sure they know we're all over their families and friends. And it won't be Atlanta, not after our near-miss there."

"Let's give New York a good look," the Washington agent suggested. "If Allen went there once, it's safe to say there's a connection up there for them."

In Atlanta agents Al Archer and Frank Pickens continued to work on the case. Shortly after the fugitives left the city in a rush, they had gained access to an apartment where they discovered beer cans and a tube of toothpaste, which they took to the fingerprint lab.

"There's no doubt about it now," Archer reported to the Memphis regional FBI office. "We've got prints on both Allen and Herron."

"It's too little too late," admitted the Memphis agent. "They were there, but they're gone. So what are you guys up to now?"

"We're trailing the former Miss Barnwell, the woman who's married to Allen," Archer replied. "And we've got a line on some other women, known companions."

"Will they talk?"

"I don't know. But it won't be long before we find out."

Not a day passed without Allen fretting over his wife in Atlanta, where she was living with her parents. By then she had told her mother and father about how her husband was wanted by the FBI, and she had encountered a sympathetic response.

Although the abrupt departure of Bill and his friends from Atlanta forced her to confide in her parents, it was a good move on her part. She was being trailed by FBI agents, one in particular, who was convinced the Robert Williams who was her husband was an escapee from the Tennessee State Penitentiary.

"Well, my love, you're twenty-four years old, old enough to make decisions for yourself," Elder O. D. Barnwell told his daughter on the night she told him about Bill Allen. "You made an important one when you chose to marry him. It's a lifetime thing, Ann, this marriage, so we'll all have to make the best of it."

"I know, Daddy, and that's what I plan to do."

"Well, Ann, that's good. Your mother and I realize you and Robert, uh, Bill, have a special love for each other. We'll support you. But we're not gonna lie for you. We love you, Ann, but it's your situation to handle."

Dealing with a long-distance marriage was compounded by the birth of a son, Sekou Lumumba Williams, on August 31, 1976, less than one month after the fugitives had hustled out of Atlanta. Ann Allen looked over her shoulder while at the grocery store; she gazed into the front yard before leaving her house; she surveyed the congregation at church from her seat at the organ in the front of the sanctuary. At times she thought people were following her and looking at her as if she was a criminal.

She knew her fears were well founded.

When Sekou Williams was born to Ann Rene Williams, the alias Ann Allen was using, at Southwest Community Hospital in Atlanta, he was given African first and middle names with an American last name. In Nigeria the name Sekou means "Say Who," which was a question worth contemplating when he entered the world.

But the FBI knew the identity of his father, which is why a dozen agents watched the hospital day and night, hoping the fugitive would visit his child. When a proud grandmother, Clovis Barnwell, took her daughter and Sekou Williams home from the hospital, law enforcement personnel simply changed positions.

One night Ann Allen was sure she was being watched as she stood in a telephone booth and talked to Bill Allen. They communicated by his calling certain pay telephones at specified days and times.

"Yeah, baby, I'm fine," she replied. And so is Sekou. He's kicking like crazy. He's like his dad, too wild to tame."

"Good. He'll need some spunk," Allen replied while sitting on the couch in a tiny apartment in Baltimore. Herron was seated in a chair across the room.

"So how's it going for you and the other fellas?"

"Great, Sweet Lady. We've got some work in the inner part of the city that'll keep us in diaper money for a while. It's pretty nice, really. And, baby, it's looking like we'll be together soon."

"That'd be good, Bill, because I'm scared down here alone. I'm being watched a lot."

"Ah, Ann, you're probably a little paranoid."

There was a pause in the conversation as Ann Allen looked over her right shoulder and noticed the familiar face of a man standing beside an automobile parked curbside across the street. Her face mirrored concern, and she quickly turned it away from the man.

"It's him, Bill, the same man I saw in the maternity shop not long ago."

"What man? Where?"

"He's across the street watching me. It's an FBI agent, Bill. I know it is. I'm hanging up and going home. Call me at number five next week."

As Ann Allen hung up the telephone, without a sign of panic, Bill Allen attempted to talk to her on the other end of the line. "Wait, Ann. Ann. Ann. Damn, she has gone," he exclaimed as he slammed down the receiver.

Ann Allen walked the long way home that night, looking around at every turn but seeing nobody suspicious. She entered her house with sweat on her brow and nausea in her stomach. "God, please help me," she prayed as she moved toward her bedroom for needed rest.

Such leisure did not come for Ann Allen. A few weeks later there was a knock at the door of her father's house. She was sitting on the couch, with Sekou Williams lying on a blanket on the floor. Her father answered the summons.

"Reverend Barnwell, we're FBI agents who'd like to talk to your daughter about the whereabouts of William Garrin Allen and his friends."

"Sir, I don't know who you're talking about," Reverend Barnwell replied. "And my daughter is just home from the hospital with a baby son."

"We know, Reverend Barnwell, and that's what we'd like to discuss with her."

Ann Allen looked over the back of the couch toward the agents and yelled to her father, "It's OK, Daddy. I don't have anything to hide."

With the FBI agents seated across the room from her and firing a battery of pointed questions, Ann Allen stood her ground. She said she was familiar with Bill Allen, yes, but that she did not know where Parker, Canady, Herron, and he were living. That was the truth because she refused to let her fugitive husband tell her his whereabouts so she would not have to lie about it.

The questioning continued for several minutes. When the agents became exasperated, they began getting pushy.

"Let's talk about those telephone conversations you've had in pay booths all over the city," one of them said to her.

"That's enough," said Reverend Barnwell, who leaped to his feet and ran to the side of his daughter. "You leave my daughter alone. Don't you ever bother her again."

"Frankly, Reverend, I'm shocked," one of the agents replied. "You'd think a religious man like you would want murderers brought to justice."

"Let me tell you what this religious man thinks right now," shouted Reverend Barnwell, as he started walking toward the front door of his house. "He thinks it's time for you to get your damn asses out of my house."

"You're aware of harboring laws, aren't you?" one of the agents asked, somewhat frazzled.

"Gentlemen, you can put your damn cuffs on me if you like," Reverend Barnwell replied, "but you're gonna have to have an arrest warrant to do it because it's time for your asses to hit the streets."

Reverend Barnwell paused as the agents walked toward the front door. Then, as a parting shot, he said, "And, dammit, you stay away from my Ann."

For several weeks after that visit to the Barnwell residence, Ann was stopped by FBI agents Archer and Pickens and asked about her husband and his companions. At times she became frivolous with them.

"Are they in Florida or still in Pennsylvania?" Pickens asked after she was accosted at the front entrance to a library.

"Have you read *Roots*?" she replied.

"We know they're not in Atlanta," Archer replied, dismissing her question. "So why don't you tell us where they are?"

"It's a beautiful afternoon, huh?" she responded. "It's a nice day to sit under a tree and read."

"You do know where they are, don't you?" Pickens asked.

"No, not really. I told you we decided against me knowing so I wouldn't have to lie to you. I'd say that was a smart decision, wouldn't you?"

By late fall the exchanges between Archer, Pickens, and Ann Allen became almost comical. They would part company with a laugh, as well as a vow to talk again in the near future; then in a few days they would meet again.

"It's incredible how pleasant that woman is with us," Archer told the FBI agent in Memphis. "She's cool under fire, too, except when the subject turns to race relations. She's like all of the others then."

"How's that?" asked the Memphis agent.

"It's the same story over and over," Archer replied. "They all contend the fugitives are political prisoners, victims of the civil rights movement. And they say it's for that reason that they don't trust us."

"How are you handling it?"

"I try to assure them that it's not a conspiracy, that the bureau wouldn't get involved in something like that," Archer replied. "That we're just doing our job, attempting to get some fugitives back to Tennessee. That we'd like to accomplish that as safely as possible. I've even told them that things have calmed down a lot in Nashville since 1968, that maybe people would be more understanding now."

"I bet that went over big," the Memphis agent laughed.

"That line really gets a rise out of Ann Allen," Archer agreed. "The Roberts woman, too. They both say we don't have any idea what happened in Nashville that night."

"Well, I guess it's best that you stay soft with them. They're not wanted, you know. They're sort of like victims of circumstance."

However, the interrogations got tougher for Ann, especially on December 20, 1976, when she gave FBI agents a somewhat detailed account of the recent lives of the four fugtives they were tracking.

During an interview at FBI office in Atlanta, she told agents that she had lived with the four men at 259 Wellington Avenue just after she and Bill Allen were married on May 23, 1975. She said they moved to Elinor Place in June 1976 to make room for the arrival of their first child. She said she had no idea they were wanted by law enforcement personnel.

Ann Allen told them that Parker had taken a wife, the former Ann Roberts, who used an African name Akebu. She said all of the fugitives had used such names: Onaje for Bill Allen, Damel for Parker, Kimathi for Herron, and Amadu for Canady.

She also told the agents that all four men had left in a hurry during the summer of 1976, after Bill Allen and Herron had been spotted by authorities while en route to a basketball game. She said her husband had telephoned her shortly thereafter and told her they were in New Orleans.

Ultimately, FBI agents found it pointless to ask her anything, but they continued watching her daily, often driving past the Barnwell residence.

That is why Ann Allen was so shaken on a Sunday afternoon when she answered a knock at the door and discovered Bill Allen standing on the front porch.

"Hello, Sweet Lady," he said to his wife. "I've come to see my baby boy."

Allen spent several hours at the Barnwell residence that day. Much of it was spent with Ann lecturing him about taking such chances. Then he kissed his son and left in the middle of the night.

Meanwhile, across the city Roberts was wrestling with a situation with which Ann Allen could empathize. The woman who had fallen in love with a fugitive, Parker, was pregnant. She had told the prospective father the news less than two weeks after the fugitives had left Atlanta for Pittsburgh.

"Why didn't you tell me you were wanted by the law?" Roberts asked him as they talked by telephone.

"I didn't want to burden you with it," Parker told her. "It's not your problem."

"It is now," Roberts answered. "You're going to be the father of my child."

"And I'll love him or her forever," replied Parker, who also had an eight-year-old daughter, Stephanie, who was born about seven months after the shooting in North Nashville. She was living with his parents, Sadie and Correlus Parker, in Cincinnati.

"I hope so," Roberts replied.

"You can count on it."

At that moment, with his picture on post office walls throughout the nation, Parker had no idea he would sit in the Tennessee State Penitentiary in 1988 and talk with obvious pride about his daughter, who at the time was an honor student and a member of the Central State University marching band, and his son, Naeem, who was living with his mother in Atlanta.

"I'm living for the day when the truth will set me free," Parker said, "when I can meet them face to face and explain the entire story."

However, the fugitives did not have time for much contemplation. The FBI remained in hot pursuit of four fugitives who were about to split up. Allen and Herron would leave Baltimore, and Parker and Canady were staying put.

TWENTY-FIVE

"It's a big city and it's booming," Bill Allen said as Charles Lee Herron, Ralph Canady, Steve Parker, and he sat in an apartment in Baltimore and discussed their futures. "It's the kind of place I want to be."

"That's fine with me," Herron replied. "If nothing else, it's farther from Nashville than Baltimore."

"So what about it, fellas?" Allen asked as he directed his gaze toward Canady and Parker.

Parker shrugged his shoulders.

"I think I'd rather stay in Baltimore," Canady answered. "I like it here. And, of course, I've got a lady to consider."

"I think I'll stay here, too," Parker decided. "I don't like the idea of moving around too much."

"That's a good point," Canady agreed. "Beside, it's getting obvious they don't know where we are, or else they would've caught us by now."

"Well," Allen said, "I'm going to Texas. I've got some skills. I've got to find an opportunity to use them."

"Then I'm with you, Doc," Herron pledged. "It makes sense to me. And it also makes sense that they'll have a harder time tracking us in pairs than with us all together."

So for the first time since they were reunited in Nashville in March 1968, two months after the shooting, Allen, Canady, and Parker were about to be separated.

It turned out to be a good move because it further confused police and FBI agents who were tracking them. Not only would they go in opposite directions, they reasoned that evening in Baltimore, they would establish themselves in normal jobs or careers. After all, Her-

ron had avoided incarceration for more than eight years, while the
others had survived for almost three years since their bold escape in
Tennessee.

Obviously, the FBI was on edge, a mental hardship agent Joe Bonner discovered when he was handed chief responsibility in the case
after being transferred to Memphis. After having investigated bank
robberies and organized crime for seven years in Youngstown,
Ohio, he was considered seasoned enough to take jurisdiction over
the perplexing case.

"We've got an old dog for you," the special agent in charge of the
Memphis office told Bonner just after he arrived in Tennessee during June 1977.

"Yeah?" Bonner asked. "What's that?"

"Charles Lee Herron and the three parallels."

"Mmmm. I'm familiar. It's an 88."

"Right. A social bomb ready to explode on us. Big in Nashville.
Big all over. At FBI headquarters, too."

Bonner spent the next two weeks reviewing the case, from the
night of the shooting to the near-miss in Pittsburgh, and to the
contrary ways of Ann Allen during interrogation. He smiled when a
fellow agent saw him reading in the file room one afternoon and
said, "Oh, my God, you've been handed that one." He was amazed
by much of what he discovered in the files, which included all correspondence related to the case, plus newspaper clippings from
Nashville, and he was astonished when he learned that he was to file
weekly reports with FBI headquarters in Washington.

"So, Joe, tell me what you think," asked agent Claude Curtis,
who was preparing to retire from the Memphis office after overseeing the case.

"I think I've got a monster on my hands," Bonner replied.
"Except we're chasing four men who are as quiet as mice. They
don't look over their shoulders. They just keep moving along with
new lives."

"That's right," Curtis answered. "And that's what makes it so
hard."

"Who's the brain in the group?"

"I don't know. But I'd say Herron is as cagey as any we've
hunted. He's a mystery man."

"Judging from what I've read, he's the philosophical base that got
the others in trouble in 1968," Bonner commented. "An Air Force
vet who got frustrated trying to advance as a postal clerk. I noticed
somebody quoted him as saying he doesn't care about two mules,
that he wants and deserves more, like equality for blacks."

"That's where it seems to have started," Curtis agreed. "It's a racial thing, at least according to Nashville."

"I know that's what they said," Bonner answered. "But where's the proof of that? It's all too sketchy. I've talked to agents in Nashville who agree."

"Uh huh," Curtis concurred. "But don't forget that it isn't our responsibility to investigate murder cases, only to get the fugitives returned to Tennessee."

"Right."

"And, Joe, I'd appreciate you doing one thing for me," Curtis asked.

"What?"

"It's been a tough one, buddy, and there doesn't seem to be anybody to reach out to. But if you get lucky, give me a call and let me know about it. I've lived with this damn thing too long to forget it."

"You've got it," Bonner conceded. "But only if you'll do me a favor before you get off the case."

"What's that?"

"Tell me where to start looking."

"Anywhere there's a good-looking woman," Curtis laughed.

Future telephone calls placed by Bonner proved that Curtis's advice was accurate. He learned that FBI agents in Atlanta believed that Ann Roberts and Ann Allen knew the whereabouts of the fugitives, even that they thought Roberts had provided the four frightened men with an automobile to use in their flight to Pittsburgh. Two other names were also prominent on their list of people closely related to the manhunt: Herbert Munford and Omar Kah, an African living in Georgia.

Because of the influence of Allen, who had set up a part-time photographic services business in Atlanta, Parker set out to become a photographer. He purchased a good camera and searched Baltimore for subjects. That led him to an interesting rendezvous with a young woman, a meeting almost as accidental as the one he had had in Atlanta with Ann Roberts.

Parker had met Roberts when he spotted her standing beside a stalled red sports car and stopped to lend assistance. They became lovers and, eventually, the parents of a son.

Parker met Joyce Goodman while shooting pictures at a fashion show in spring 1977. "Excuse me," he said to her after he stumbled over her while positioning himself to photograph models on stage.

"Sure," Goodman replied with an exasperated sigh. "But please be more careful."

"I'm sorry," he said again after he stepped on her foot a second time.

She said nothing.

"I don't know why I'm taking pictures of these ladies when a beautiful one like you is right beside me," he said.

She smiled.

"Really, I'd like to shoot one of you."

Goodman was flattered enough to agree to pose for him. The smooth-talking Parker also persuaded the lovely twenty-year-old elementary education student at Coppin State College to give him her address and telephone number so he could send her prints. Soon they were dating, then falling in love, sharing a house, and parenting two children. She knew nothing about his past.

Eventually, Parker decided that photography was not the right profession for him, so he got into the merchandising business on the sidewalks of Baltimore. He became what is commonly known as a street vendor, which was not an uncomplimentary profession in that area, and he made a good living selling air-brushed T-shirts, balloons, and all manner of trinkets. He took advantage of the vast ethnic heritage of the city beside the harbor, working hard on Pratt Street during various festivals to polish his substantial business skills.

Parker was laying the groundwork for two rewarding business ventures that would come later, a landscaping business and a downtown gift shop. Meanwhile, Goodman was working hard to secure a college degree and eventually became a special education teacher.

Parker, who was using the alias John Collins (with an accompanying J. C. moniker), and Canady did not see much of each other after the fugitives went their separate ways. Their athletic prowess mandated that they play basketball and run together, and their common bond as men wanted for a crime dictated that they would visit each other occasionally. But for the most part, they attempted to establish separate lifestyles, a new beginning of sorts.

Canady had already displayed managerial skills while working in a Cincinnati department store the year before the shooting, so it was not surprising that he obtained employment at Katzenstein's Framing, a reputable wholesale clearing house. Once there, he built up so much confidence and trust from the owner that he was the only person the owner trusted with a key to the front door. Later, the proprietor purchased the fugitive he knew as Elmer Marcella Diggs a 1980 Subaru.

Canady, who also used the alias Charles Meadows, became more active than Parker in his pursuit of female companionship. He solicited and obtained the friendship and love of Elaine Kirsey; together, they produced three children, which put a financial strain on their relationship.

Needing more money to support his family, Canady secured a second job at Red Coat Janitorial Services. He worked at Katzenstein's Framing during the day, opening the business every morning, and at the janitorial service during nights, managing three crews.

Incredibly, one of the buildings Canady was in charge of contained the local FBI offices. While Canady knew better than to show his face in that building, he had many telephone conversations with the men who worked there.

Meanwhile, Allen and Herron were attempting to find work in Texas. Using the aliases James Adams and David Denison, respectively, they were trying to make a go of it in the house renovation business. Allen also had established a custom photo processing business in the garage of the house the two fugitives were renting.

The two newcomers to Houston got a break in August 1977, when Allen was hired at Arden's Picture Frames and Gallery.

"I don't know what we have available," said Keith Hoak, the owner of the gallery, when the two men met.

"Well, I've got to find something quickly," said Allen. "I can't wait around long. I've got some other stops to make."

Allen left the gallery that afternoon and walked along a city street toward another interview. As he walked past FBI headquarters, which was three blocks away, he heard an automobile horn blowing. When he turned around, he was stunned to see a woman employee from Arden's Picture Frames and Gallery running toward him.

"We've got a job for you, Mr. Adams," she said. "We didn't want to let a man like you get away."

Allen smiled at the woman and nodded.

"Then I'll take it," he replied, before walking toward an automobile taking him to his place of employment.

In leisure hours, which were plentiful for the two men, Allen and Herron moved about the city seeking various forms of recreation. Herron found favor with Ruby Caldwell, and they started a lengthy relationship. Allen, who was using the alias J. D., accompanied them on many occasions while escorting a woman named Betty Lou, whom Caldwell labeled an extremely religious woman with strong allegiance to her church.

By fall 1978, Allen had established himself as a gifted craftsman. His reputation gave credibility to a suggestion he made to management at Arden's Picture Frames and Gallery.

"You're needing more help, right?"

"We sure do," Hoak replied.

"Then I'd like for you to consider hiring my friend David Denison. He's quite gifted when it comes to this type of work."

"If he's good enough for you," Haok said, "then he's good enough for me."

So Allen and Herron worked together framing pictures in a back room at Arden's Picture Frames and Gallery, even as FBI agents did business with the owners in the showroom.

Life on the run was slowing down some. All four fugitives were gainfully employed, while Ann Allen and Sekou Williams sat nervously in Atlanta and wondered about their futures.

TWENTY-SIX

Bill Allen had left the alias Robert Williams in Atlanta and Baltimore. While working in Houston, he was known as James Adams. Herron used the aliases David Denison, Lawrence Connor Johnson, and James Johnson. They supplemented their incomes at the art gallery by remodeling houses.

Allen also had another alias at his disposal—Arthur Robinson—which he had happened upon by accident. While riding a city bus in Houston, he was surprised when a boarding passenger kicked a tote bag that was sitting beside the aisle two rows in front of him. The impact knocked a wallet to the feet of Allen, who picked it up, looked inside, and found interesting identification forms that included a military card and a driver's license. The real Arthur Robinson was born in Istanbul, Turkey, as the son of an Air Force officer. Allen was fascinated with the disguise such a background would afford him, and he had the forethought to immediately use it to secure a passport.

There was no money in the wallet. But Allen was making more than enough to get by. He was earning a name for himself in art restoration at the gallery and on the side for well-known collectors. He also was coaching the Orioles' little league baseball team. Every time he saw a police officer pick up a son at practice or after a game in South Park, he remembered the night of the shooting. By now it seemed so long ago—it was more than a decade—so he continued to build his future while forgetting the darkest hours in his history. In essence, he had developed a philosophy: live today, find good in the past, and dream about the future.

Allen had already learned it was foolish to take chances while on the run, but a telephone call from his uncle in Nashville, Lonnie Pinkston, prompted him to make a daring move. His father was sick and growing weaker by the moment, and it was time to visit him for the last time.

By then, new conflicts had come and gone at the Nashville police department. The city had been sued more than a few times by blacks who thought their civil rights had been violated, as well as by families whose members had been shot and killed in confrontations with Nashville police officers. Little emphasis was being put on apprehending Allen, Herron, Parker, and Canady.

But there were veterans on the force who thought otherwise, and they carried wanted posters of the men on the FBI Identification Order list, with Herron on the FBI Most Wanted list. They regularly talked about what the fugitives had done to their fellow police officers, and some of them made routine stops at the Allen residence in Old Hickory just to see if their son had arrived there for a visit.

Without reason or logic, a rumor developed among police officers that Herron had been seen in Nashville dressed as a woman. In reality, Tennessee was the last place any of the four fugitives wanted to be.

Still, Allen had to return home. He drove into the city late one night, wearing sunglasses and with a coat collar pulled snug around his neck. Driving to his house, he motored within blocks of the shooting scene in 1968 and within a mile of police department headquarters.

"Hello, Mom," Allen greeted his mother after arriving at his house and hugging her. "How's Dad doing?"

"I'm glad you're here," she said. "He's getting weaker every day."

Allen went to his father.

"Dad, I wish you could see Ann [Allen] and Sekou [Williams]."

"I bet they're something, for sure," his father said in a weak voice. "It isn't like you to pick anybody bad."

Later during the emotional conversation, Allen reminded his father of something he had told him when he was a child.

"Dad, do you remember how you said it's OK for me to stick up for what I believe is right? You know, when things were real bad for blacks all over the nation."

His father nodded.

"Well, Dad, I've done that. I just didn't realize I'd have to pay such a price for it."

His father smiled and answered, "I know, Bill. But sometimes that's what makes it worthwhile."

His father paused, with a tear falling to his cheek, then said, "And that's why I'm so proud of you."

Allen left later that evening, not long before dawn, and drove back to Houston. He contemplated going on to Atlanta to see his wife and son, but he thought better of it.

He had already determined he would not return to Nashville after his father died, knowing that his family would understand why. It was a wise choice because the FBI had agents and informants at the funeral, just in case.

The Sweet Lady in his life was becoming a little impatient, too, somewhat frustrated and a tad devilish. All of those characteristics were displayed one 1979 morning after she looked out the front window of her house in Atlanta and saw an FBI agent sitting in a car.

"Dammit, that's enough," she declared as Sekou Williams, three years old and starting to ask questions about his father, played on the living room floor.

"What's wrong, Mama, what'd I do?" Sekou asked after hearing his normally cool mother's anger.

"It's not you, Ku, it's them," she replied. "And it's nothing a telephone call can't fix."

So she walked to the telephone sitting on a coffee table, grabbed the directory, and sat down on the couch. Turning the pages to the number she wanted, she dialed it quickly.

"Yes, ma'am, is this the Atlanta Police Department?" she asked of the lady who answered. "Well, this is Ann Rene Williams at the O.D. Barnwell residence on Cairo Street, and I've got a suspicious character parked in front of my house in a green Chevrolet. He has been out there several days. I'm afraid he's going to burglarize the house or kidnap my son."

She repeated her description of the man and the car, then paused before thanking the woman. Hanging up the telephone, she turned toward her son and extended her arms to him.

"Now, Ku, let's go out back and play a while. It might be fun."

Soon she saw what she wanted, two Atlanta police officers confronting an annoyed FBI agent who knew what kind of ordeal he was about to experience.

"OK, fellas, I've got my hands on the steering wheel," the agent said. "There's no reason to get anxious. I'm an FBI agent who has had his surveillance screwed up."

"Let's have some identification," one of the officers responded.

"OK, I'm reaching for it now, easy like, with no problems," the agent said as he slowly moved his right hand toward the inside pocket on the left side of his coat. "You guys take it easy, too."

After looking at the identification, one of the officers apologized and asked a question trying to secure more proof. "Sorry, chum, but we had a complaint. So what's agent Flo Davis doing these days?"

"He's tracking that troublesome Top Ten 88, Herron, Allen, Parker, and Canady," answered the agent, who followed with a statement that further proved his identify. "And I guess that sweet blond is still working the front desk over at your precinct."

"OK, buddy, I guess we screwed up this one," one of the officers acknowledged.

"Yep," the agent replied. "And I'd appreciate it if we could bypass a report on it."

"For sure."

"And if you don't mind, spread the word that we're watching the Barnwell residence. We don't need another screw-up if we get some action going down around here."

As the FBI agent and the police officers smiled, Ann Allen chuckled loudly.

"What's so funny, Mama?" Sekou asked as he dropped a play truck to the ground and ran toward her.

"A lot, Ku," Ann Allen replied. "See, honey, the fish just wrapped the hook around a stump. That has the fisherman a little upset."

Ann Allen got her satisfaction in difficult ways while she lived in Atlanta. She reaped a lot that day while playing cat-and-mouse with the FBI, because that was the last time they bothered her. She and her son left the country not long afterward.

"Hello," Steve Parker said to the man who was calling about a newspaper advertisement he and Ralph Canady had placed. "Yes, that's correct. It's home repair work. And I'm sure you've read all of the requirements. I mean, you're bondable and all that, aren't you? It doesn't matter if you don't have a driver's license, just that you're bondable. It's what I call good business."

There was a brief pause.

"Fine," Parker said. "Now if you don't mind, I'd like to ask you some personal questions. You know, just to be on the safe side. I've got your name, Rick Walker. Now, Rick, what's your date and place of birth?

"And your address and telephone number?

"OK. Yeah. Well, that's fine.

"What are your parents' names?

"Do you have a social security number?"

On and on the questions went until Parker had enough information to use in getting other identification. He was, in essence, about to become the second Rick Walker in Baltimore, now all he needed to do was to go to the courthouse and apply for a replacement birth certificate. From there, it was clear sailing. In Parker's mind he was merely being resourceful—surviving—not being deceitful at the expense of an innocent victim.

In this way Parker and Canady were looking toward their futures after having to glance over their shoulders every day since their escapes from the Tennessee State Penitentiary in May 1974. Their new identities, they reasoned, along with their pleasing personalities and keen abilities to articulate, would allow them to settle into the mainstream of life more comfortably.

It worked well for Parker, whom many Baltimore citizens knew as Rick Walker, a constantly smiling street vendor who was becoming a serious businessman. Others felt the same way about Canady, who used the aliases Elmer Marcella Diggs and Charles Meadows while working at a wholesale warehouse during the day and a janitorial service at night.

In late 1977, after Bill Allen and Charles Lee Herron had left Baltimore for Houston, Parker rented an old apartment for $185 per month. He helped his landlord, an elderly man named Larry, with repairs to pick up extra cash. When a financial crisis arrived, he merely tinkered a bit with the plumbing. After doing that one day, he discovered that he was not quite as shrewd as he thought.

"Didn't you tell me you wanted to get in one of those old places downtown?" the landlord asked him.

"Right, Larry, because I'm thinking about opening a store down there. It'd be great to get my own shop, a place where I can become more established. But they're sort of expensive."

"Well, Rick, I'll be honest with you," the landlord said. "The guy who owns those buildings, as well as the apartment you're in now, lives in California. I haven't seen him for several years. That's why I've been able to rent this place to you so cheap."

"I see."

"So I'll make a deal with you. If you'll quit breaking all my pipes and stuff like that, I'll see if I can get you in one of those places on North Liberty at a decent price. Like, well, what about $300 per month?"

Parker smiled at the elderly man, who returned the gesture, and he immediately resumed his dream of having his own business. He knew the dwelling in question. It consisted of two floors on a street front in a depressed downtown area and could rent for three times that much. The news that he might be able to have it for three hundred per month did wonders for his wallet and his patience.

So it was an encouraged Parker who kept on working as a street vendor while Joyce Goodman, the love in his life, continued her studies toward a degree in elementary education at Coppin State College. She was living at home with her parents, and she was pregnant, which caused her to call a meeting with Parker.

"Rick, I've got something to tell you," she told him after they exchanged jokes and laughs while seating themselves on a Baltimore park bench.

"What's that, baby?"

"I'm pregnant with your child."

"Oh, I see," he said as he took a hard gulp. "How far along are you?"

"Quite a few months. And I'm wondering what you think about that."

"I'm happy about it," he replied. "I love you, baby, and it'll be exciting having a child with you."

"Good," Goodman answered.

"But I've got to be honest with you," he said, interrupting her chain of thought. "Joyce, you see my lifestyle. You know I'm sort of happy-go-lucky. I'm always looking for the best deal for me. It's written in stone."

"I know," she agreed. "That's why I wanted to talk to you now about this."

"Well, don't worry. I mean, I'm here for you now, and I'll take care of the baby every day while you get serious about your work at college."

There was a pause as she waited to hear the rest. "But it won't be easy," Parker said. "You know, I might be here one day and gone the next."

As Goodman nodded, Parker thought to himself that it might be time to tell her about his troubled past. He decided against it, however, because he concluded it was not her burden to bear. The child was enough for now, and they left the park that afternoon tied to each other only by love, the baby in her womb, and a vague commitment.

Fortunately, sales on downtown sidewalks were excellent. Parker was able to sell earrings, T-shirts, trinkets, or, as became the case almost by accident, designer jeans at a discount price.

"What's up, Rick?" the long-haired young man who drove an old automobile asked him one afternoon.

"I don't know, man, unless it's you," Parker answered. He had seen him frequently in the area.

"I'll see you soon," the young man said. "Hang out for a few minutes. I've got a deal for you."

When he returned, he took Parker to his automobile, announced that he was a regional distributor for a jeans company, opened the trunk, and presented the street vendor with several odd lot pairs.

"See what you can do with these," he suggested with a wink. "Let's see some salesmanship."

"I'll move them in a hurry," Parker replied. "It's easy cash."

That it was. He was selling a popular brand of jeans that normally sold for more than twenty dollars a pair for half that much. Soon Parker and his supplier expanded their lucrative business to other parts of the city.

"Damn you!" the department store manager swore as he ran toward Parker and his vending cart on a city sidewalk.

"What's wrong, sir?" Parker asked.

"I'm selling those damn jeans inside for twenty dollars, and you're out here selling them for ten dollars. I thought you were only selling trinkets and T-shirts. I can't make a dime with you doing this. You've got five minutes to get your ass out of this neighborhood before I call the police."

Parker was gone in less time than that.

But he was not discouraged. He kept selling from a cart on city streets and was close to achieving the financial stability he needed to move into his own store.

His good fortune received another boost on April 18, 1978, when Goodman presented him with a daughter, Tierra Nicole Walker.

The mother and child settled in her parents' house, while Parker continued to live in his apartment at Chelsea Terrace while working to establish his business at 226 North Liberty Street.

"Rick, I've got a place for you downtown," the elderly landlord told him.

"Great, Larry. When can I move into it?"

"It's your call."

"Then I'll start getting it ready."

Parker did that, first soaping the front display window to let pedestrians know that after a long lapse the depressed neighborhood was about to have a new shop. Then he cleaned up the downstairs area, where he would conduct business, and made the upstairs area suitable for living quarters. When police officers and nearby citizens stopped by for a look, he told them he was moving his vending trade indoors. He had no reason to think he would be selling anything other than what he had previously been selling from his cart.

"So this is what you're selling in here," a man named Earl said as Parker straightened merchandise in the shop while his daughter gurgled on a countertop.

"That's it. It's a little of this and a little of that for now."

"Have you thought about flowers?" the man asked.

"No, not really."

"Well, Rick, why don't you come outside and take a look at what I've got in my truck."

With Tierra Walker in his arms, Parker walked outside, taking the first steps on a prosperous journey.

"Everybody loves flowers and plants," the man said as he pointed toward a wide variety in his truck.

Parker agreed.

"Then let's take these inside at no charge and see how it goes. I'm back and forth from Florida a lot. I've got enough to keep you stocked."

So the child, who was only a few months old, watched the men empty the truck, taking the flowers inside and transforming what had been little more than a trinket shop into an appealing business.

Parker had received the break he needed.

TWENTY-SEVEN

Anyone interested in the four fugitives' lives in 1978, ten years after the shooting in North Nashville, could have found ample evidence at the post office. From coast to coast, their pictures appeared on fliers under the words "Wanted by FBI." In retrospect, it is hard to comprehend how nobody had recognized them.

Charles Lee Herron was on the FBI Most Wanted list, a society of ten picked by agents because of the seriousness of their crimes and the severity of the threat they posed to the well-being of society. Since Tennessee authorities had concluded that he had not fired a gun during the shooting, his inclusion on the list presumably had more to do with the bureau's not having been able to find him than with anything else.

Bill Allen, Steve Parker, and Ralph Canady were on the FBI Identification Order list, which means that they were wanted badly enough for wanted posters to have been distributed. By now they had been free on escape from the Tennessee State Penitentiary for four years.

One flier noted that the four had "resided and worked together doing home repairs, roofing, carpentry, yard work and other odd jobs." Then, in a surprising statement, it declared: "These fugitives may still be closely associated with one another and engaged in selling marijuana."

The fugitives were doing nothing of the sort, although they were together in pairs, Allen and Herron in Houston and Parker and Canady in Baltimore.

Parker and Canady were running a lot, and not just from law enforcement personnel; they were in training for a marathon. Can-

155

ady, a track star during his high school years, continued to train for the 26.2-mile race. Parker was shocked on the day of the race when he spotted Canady struggling about two miles short of the finish line at Memorial Stadium in Baltimore.

"Damn," Parker said to himself as he watched Canady running, "the Candy Man looks like he's 150 years old. I've got to boost him."

So Parker dashed to the side of his struggling friend, clapped his hands, and hollered, "Come on, Slim, you can make it." He ran alongside Canady the rest of the marathon, encouraging the fellow fugitive until he reached the finish line.

Meanwhile, John Alexander, who had served his time in prison and had been set free in late 1974, was having a rough go of it while trying to reconstruct his life in Cincinnati. In February 1975, two months after he found employment as a construction worker, a cast iron pipe weighing fifteen hundred pounds fell on his left leg. Repairing the damage took massive reconstructive surgery—with rib bones placed in the limb—and he was deemed unfit to work.

The man whose flight had precipitated the shooting and who had separated himself from the others involved, was handicapped for life.

Joe Bonner, the FBI agent in Memphis who had been given jurisdiction in the case in 1978, endured many sleepless nights over the next two years. A tireless worker who had many other responsibilities, he had become frustrated while wrestling with government bureaucracy, a stumbling block that proved most worrisome just after he inherited the case.

"Damn, they're the best I've ever seen," Bonner said to himself after getting out of bed at 2:00 A.M. and moving to a reclining chair in his den. "They've never looked back. They've moved forward without trouble. They've completely restructured their lives.

"And, dammit, their families and friends are as mentally tough as they are. We knock, but they won't crack. We harass the hell out of them, then hear them laugh at us. Hell, maybe the families don't know where they are."

Bonner paused to take a sip of the milk beside him on a table. Leaning back, he closed his eyes, then opened them in a flash.

"But I bet they've got friends who know where they are. That's it. Herbert Munford. He was with them in Atlanta, but he's moved to Silver Springs [Maryland]. He's the tie that binds them."

The next morning Bonner rose early and hurried to the office, where he began the paperwork for a petition for help. Later that morning he called FBI headquarters in Washington.

"There's a Herbert Munford who got those guys started in business in Atlanta," Bonner told the agent in Washington. "He's working for a bottling company in Silver Springs. What do you think about turning up the heat on him? Concentrate in the Washington-Baltimore area, just to see if maybe they're staying in contact."

"We'll get back to you," the agent answered. "Maybe it's logical."

Bonner became disgusted when he read the airtel sent several days later. He learned that there would be no concentrated surveillance of Munford. Not enough agents were available, and the bureau could not determine which office should be in charge of such a long-term investigation in the Silver Springs area.

"Well, that makes the job tougher," Bonner muttered as he pounded his desk. "Can you believe this? I'm sitting in Memphis because the bureau won't let me leave my territory, not even for a trip to Nashville, and I can't get a commitment from Baltimore or Washington."

The decision not to focus on Baltimore obviously was a mistake, because Allen, Parker, Canady, and Herron were living there when Bonner had his brainstorm. But they were not staying in contact with Munford. They knew it was just a matter of time until somebody figured out that he was the person they had visited in a Nashville hospital on the afternoon before the shooting.

Ann Allen and her son, Sekou Williams, had found refuge in Africa. In fact, Williams spent a year and a half living with godparents in Gambia, beginning in the fall of 1979. Ann had sent him there so he would not have to deal with the strain of FBI agents constantly harassing him and his mother in Atlanta. When the child returned, he was speaking three languages, none of which was English, except for yes and no. His experience made his mother and father confident that if they were to find freedom in Nigeria, he would not suffer cultural shock.

Having spent four months in Gambia herself, Ann Allen knew she would favor the move. While there she had played the part of an honored goddess during a ceremonial dance, an experience that made her speak in tongues, as she had on numerous occasions in church with her father in the pulpit.

Until the winter of 1980, when Parker and Canady visited their friends in Houston, the fugitives had been fending for themselves and had only talked by telephone on occasion since splitting up three years earlier. They had a happy reunion, replete with long jogs together in the morning and tennis and basketball in the afternoon. It was then that they seriously began formulating a plan that they hoped would bring them true freedom living in Africa.

"I don't know if it's like books say it is," Herron said during a discussion about the matter.

"That's true," Canady answered. "But if it is, well, it's definitely what we're looking for."

"I agree," Allen replied. "Judging from what Ann said, it's a heavenly place. We'd settle in nicely. We've already got the African names."

"So let's do it," Canady suggested. "After all, we only need financial funding and smart thinking."

"Then let's make a pact," Parker said. "Whenever one of us makes it big—strikes it rich—then we'll pool the money and make the move."

At that time, it appeared that Parker had the best chance for financial success. His shop on North Liberty Street in Baltimore had been incorporated and named This Rare Earth, with Goodman listed as president on papers issued in January 1980.

Business was beginning to boom. Not only was Parker selling flowers, brass items, and trinkets, he was also supplying several corporations with plants for their lobbies. In addition, he decorated display windows for various shops and took care of individuals' lawns.

The man known to patrons as Rick Walker became such a respected businessman that several entrepreneurs stopped by his place to see how he had turned a once desolate area into a busy shopping domain. Visitors discovered that he was running an interracial enterprise; a cheerful older white lady served as his chief clerk. His young daughter, Tierra Walker, was becoming the darling of the neighborhood.

Incredibly, his success came following a near financial disaster. One evening he was attempting to balance the books of his financially struggling business in his apartment above his shop.

"Damn, I've overloaded myself," he swore to himself. "I'm in need of money, and there isn't any around. I'm going to lose it all."

Then came a welcomed memory.

"I've forgotten my money in the mayonnaise jar!"

The cash he remembered, about eight hundred dollars that he had saved during his time as a street vendor, was buried in the unfinished basement of the apartment he had rented before moving downtown.

"I can't just go over there and tell them I forgot about it," Parker thought as he contemplated how he could retrieve his money. "They'll wonder where it came from. It'll cause too much suspicion."

Then he remembered that he still had a key to the place.

It was just after dark when Parker arrived at his former residence. He had been told it was to be refurbished, but after parking his automobile two blocks away and walking to his old apartment, he saw that the work had not been completed. When he opened the back door and went inside, he stumbled over boards and smelled fresh paint.

Then he walked downstairs to the basement, turned on a lamp, and began digging. What Parker did not know was that a neighbor from across the street had noticed the light and had telephoned the police department.

As he emerged from the apartment with a smile on his face and his money in hand, he saw three police cruisers moving along Forest Park Avenue. He turned and ran. With the mayonnaise jar stuffed into a coat pocket, he hurried inside a candy store he had frequented many times.

"Hi, Rick," said the clerk. "I thought you had moved downtown."

"I have, gal, but I'm back for a visit."

"Well, it's good to see you," she answered. "Would you like a Coke or something?"

"Hey, that'd be good."

So he seated himself in the rear of the candy store, sipped on his soft drink, and talked to an old friend for more than an hour. Then, with his nerves tingling, he said goodbye, walked to his automobile, and returned downtown, eight hundred dollars richer for the experience.

In Houston, Allen and Herron were living like regular citizens. Staying cool, they learned to survive as normal people in the crowd.

That was difficult to do, however. Both men were working in houses in all sections of the city, including one dwelling that belonged to a Houston police officer. While they worked on the roof, four officers were playing poker inside. As they got into their van to leave at the end of one day's work, they were stopped by the officer who owned the house.

"Hey!" he shouted from the front porch. "How about playing a few hands?"

"That's a kind offer," Allen replied, "but we're really too pooped tonight."

"You two guys are OK," the officer laughed. "You're good men. Just let me know anytime you want to play."

Inside the van, Herron sat holding his breath in disbelief. "Poker with those guys?" he asked in amazement when his friend seated himself behind the steering wheel. "Get real, man. Damn, Doc, I could have four aces in a game like that and still feel like the pot was going to somebody else!"

Allen laughed and extended a hand to Herron for a soulful slap. Looking at the sun setting in the west, he adjusted the volume on the radio and drove away.

TWENTY-EIGHT

Bill Allen was sitting on the front steps of the house he rented on Southcrest Street in Houston. The Nigerian friend had brought him good news on the warm fall afternoon in 1981.

"So that's the way it looks to me," Dr. Frank Uwa said. A Nigerian businessman, he had brought welcome news to his friend. "It won't be long until you'll be on your way to freedom, you, your wife, and your son."

"That's great, Frank," Allen replied. "It's our big chance. I won't let you down. I'll work day and night to get the job done right."

"I'm glad you're pleased, Bill. It's my pleasure to assist a good man who needs a break."

No sooner had Uwa closed the deal with Allen to ensure that a one-way trip to Africa was forthcoming, than Charles Lee Herron appeared on the bicycle he was riding. The frantic cyclist, who was late for the meeting, turned a corner and pedaled toward the driveway at breakneck speed, barely avoiding an approaching motorist.

"Like I said, I'm indebted," Allen continued after he spotted Herron pedaling toward them. "But, Frank, I was wondering about my friend there on the bicycle. I invited him to join us today. I'd like to include him."

"David Dennison?" Uwa asked with mild surprise as he rubbed his stubbled beard.

"Well, yes," Allen answered. "He's David Denison to you. To me, he's Lee, Charles Lee Herron, one of the men I told you were with me that night."

"Oh, I see. Well, perhaps I need to go back to the drawing board and make it a trip for four. But, understand, that's after we complete our work over there."

161

"That's cool," Allen replied. "But the number might grow to seven or eight, maybe more. You see, I'm obligated to make a couple more calls about this. The other fellas might want to join us over there."

Allen had his life more under control than at any time since he had walked away from the Tennessee State Penitentiary seven and a half years earlier. It was just a matter of time, he reasoned almost daily, until he and his family—his wife, Ann Allen, and their, son Sekou Williams—would see their plan become a reality. Since 1976, they had imagined being reunited in Nigeria, where they would blend into the society like three small trees in a large forest, forever private. When Ann Allen and Sekou Williams enjoyed their time in Gambia, it solidified their desire to seek refuge on the distant continent.

Uwa was the friend that could make that dream happen. A successful businessman in Houston, he had contracted to furnish the inside of a theater being built in Nigeria. He in turn had contracted with Bill Allen to do much of the work, such as installing seats, and had done so with the understanding that his assistant would remain in Africa for the remainder of his life.

.The proposed change of residence became possible because Bill Allen had refused to become complacent in Houston. Although he was considered a pillar in his neighborhood, a personable young man who seemingly had arrived out of nowhere armed with a pleasing smile, quick wit, and warm disposition, he had other concerns on his mind. Instead of putting down roots, he had made contact with Uwa, whom he hoped would pave the way for him to move overseas with his family and friends.

The work Allen and Herron were doing at Arden's Picture Frames and Gallery was going well. They were so talented that they received contracts from local museums and reputable collectors to do art restoration work for them. In addition, their house renovation business was going so well that they were able to put money in the bank, a luxury not possible during their early years on the run.

"Perhaps it'd be better to stay here," Herron responded when Allen told him about the opportunity to move to Nigeria. "After all, life isn't half bad for us now."

"But we won't have to look over our shoulders in Africa," Bill Allen replied. "That won't change as long as we're in this country. Remember what we decided last year."

"That's a point, Doc," Herron agreed. "And I'm sure the FBI won't come after us over there. But I'm comfortable with things the way they are."

"Would you rather I check into it?" Bill Allen suggested. "I mean, I can go over there for a while and see if it's really what we want. Then you and the other fellas can decide."

"I'd like that."

Parker and Canady were still living in Baltimore. Both had established normal lifestyles there, but they already had decided to go to Africa, regardless of whether or not Allen or Herron, who had been on the FBI Most Wanted list longer than anyone, decided to stay put.

Parker was doing well. His downtown gift shop and landscaping business were booming, and Goodman, his live-in lover and the mother of one of his children, had established a good reputation in the Baltimore school system.

Canady was doing well at two jobs, the wholesale clearing house and the janitorial service. He, too, had children and a live-in lover.

But as comfortable as they were, they realized Nigeria would be a safer place for them than Maryland.

So Bill Allen's plan to work in Nigeria as a scout brought their interest close to a reality. With Nigeria clearly in his sight, Allen shipped almost all his possessions, which included more than twenty thousand dollars in art equipment and construction tools, to Africa for use as he established himself there. He then flew to Port Harcourt to claim his possessions, with no intention of returning to the United States. He planned instead to get settled as he and Uwa completed their work, then to telephone his wife to inform her that the time had come for her and their son to join him.

"We're on the verge of being free for good," he told his wife before departing.

"That's the news I've wanted to hear. It's getting more lonely by the day in Atlanta."

But his joy soon turned to despair on a warm day in Port Harcourt.

TWENTY-NINE

An excited Bill Allen went to claim his belongings in Port Harcourt. Instead, he came upon a confused shipment clerk who had dreadful news. The art equipment and construction tools had been stolen on the high seas.

"I'm sorry, sir, but all of the crates are empty," the shipment clerk apologized. "It's something that happens from time to time. I'm sure you had them insured."

"But how could this happen?" Allen asked while rubbing the back of his neck.

"I'd assume they opened the crates in the Gulf of Guinea," the shipment clerk replied. "It has happened before."

Allen kicked the crates in anger. He had only insured the shipment for $10,000. Throwing up his arms in anger, he went to complain to the shipment supervisor, but his complaints accomplished nothing, and he was just out of luck.

While Allen was working for Dr. Uwa, he noticed opportunities for a thinking businessman. He saw that people in the area had to send film to the United Kingdom to have it developed, and he noticed many wrecked automobiles along the side of highways that needed to be salvaged. He also observed lumber mills throwing away sawdust that could be recycled.

Allen told Uwa what he saw and how he thought he could turn such opportunities into profitable ventures. The successful businessman was impressed enough with his ambition that he began to teach him the basics of import-export trade.

He did not tell Ann about his shipping loss until he called her upon arrival in New York City. He was not prepared for her reaction.

164

"Well, don't be apologizing to me again, Bill," she chastised. "I'm tired of hearing that all the time."

"I'm sorry, but there wasn't anything I could do."

They had a rare strained conversation. Finally, Ann delivered an ultimatum.

"Bill, I'm tired of hearing about us doing this and us doing that in the future. I'd say you better get your act together now. Your son is getting older. Why, he'll be going to school before long. He's either going to do that in Houston, with us living as a family, or he's going to stay in Atlanta with me. You've got to get us settled."

Bill swallowed her words with difficulty, fretting over them as he recalled his walk along the docks in Port Harcourt. As he thought, he remembered seeing businessmen in Nigeria who were busy with imports and exports. Even as he chatted with a customs official in New York City, who presented him with a $9,450 insurance check to cover a $23,000 loss, he thought about becoming a middle man in the commodities market.

"Why not?" he asked himself. "It doesn't cost much to arrange business deals between people who have money."

So he began studying the commodities market in earnest as he continued his work in art restoration, remodeling houses, and photographic services. At the Houston Public Library, he read books on the subject. What he could not find there, he ordered.

Allen also traveled to New York to study the import-export market. He spent two months in Baltimore doing the same, mixing his haphazard educational process with working with Steve Parker at the landscaping firm. On rare occasions he traveled to Atlanta where he visited Ann Allen and Sekou Williams, checking into airport motels and spending a lot of time flying kites with the youngster.

Meanwhile, FBI agent Joe Bonner, the man on the hot seat, had run into a dead end in Memphis. His frustration had been aggravated by a telephone call from the FBI section chief, in charge of nationwide fugitive cases.

"Joe, I'm calling to relay a message from my boss [Nick O'Hara]," the caller reported. "He's pretty upset about the lack of progress in the Herron, Allen, Parker, and Canady cases."

"That's two of us."

"Well, he has instructed me to call you and tell you your efforts on the case aren't satisfactory. He said he wants you to know this has become a national embarrassment for the FBI."

"How in hell does he think I feel?" Bonner retorted. "It's not like I'm sitting on my thumbs. Hell, all I can do is develop leads and keep pushing. Don't you think I'd give an eye and a tooth to catch those guys?"

"Yes, but he's—."

"He's worried about his own butt," Bonner interrupted. "Well, I'm not concerned about mine. I'm doing the best I can with this nightmare, given the restrictions of having to sit in Memphis and write report after report when there's nothing to report."

Bonner paused to regain his composure, then said, "Remember, pal, I was the guy who wanted to put on some heat in Baltimore, and I'm convinced to this day that they were there at that time. Where they're at now, well, that's anybody's guess."

"I'm just relaying the message, Joe," the agent declared. "We're as frustrated as you on this one. That's why the section chief wants you to do some thinking, to come up with an innovative way of catching these people."

He paused, then continued, "And he won't take no for an answer. He wants it resolved."

"That's bullshit," Bonner shouted. "But you can tell the section chief that Joe Bonner is doing the best he can and will continue to do so. It's not like everybody in America is anxious to give us a lead on this thing. Hell, their family members are getting downright surly. I'm hearing Mrs. Canady is thinking about filing a harassment suit against the bureau."

The FBI did get a tip not long after that, albeit an erroneous one, but it prompted a definitely innovative approach to seek-and-apprehend procedures.

"Joe, I'm telling you there's a chance one of them, Allen, is in Gambia," agent Flo Davis told Bonner from his office in Atlanta. "The girl, Cynthia Ann Brown, has gone all over Atlanta bragging about having been with her man."

"You're kidding!" Bonner retorted. "How in hell would he get a passport?"

"I don't know," Davis answered. "And we don't know what name he's using or where the passport originated. But street talk has it she's his girl and she's pregnant."

"I thought that girl messed with Herron," Bonner told Davis. "You're sure it's Allen?"

"He's in Gambia, Joe," Davis assured. "Trust me on this one. He has been spotted over there."

"We don't have an extradition treaty with Gambia," Bonner reminded Davis.

"Right."

"Then we'll have to do something tricky. And I'm the guy who'll have to figure out a way to get the son of a bitch out of Gambia and back to the United States."

A fugitive wanted badly by the FBI, Allen was fast becoming a serious businessman. He got to know traders in the Houston area, and on a cold day in 1982 an incident happened that almost led to the end of his freedom.

Two of his friends—Nigerian business partners—were at odds over the excessive use of a credit card. They argued and fought, until Bill Allen took it upon himself to bring peace between them. He thought he had made progress with them when one of the men asked Bill to drive him to the home of the other man.

When they arrived at the house, they parked curbside and walked toward the front door. When they saw the other man walking toward them with a grin on his face, they smiled. Suddenly, the man they were visiting pulled a pistol from one of the pockets and aimed it at his business partner. Bill Allen was standing between the barrel of the gun and the target.

Bill Allen dived to the ground as a shot was fired. The first bullet hit the man accompanying him in the side. He heard another shot and saw the victim fall to the ground after being hit in the back by a second bullet. As the man with the gun began to run away, Allen started to do the same thing, then stopped after a few steps and returned to his friend's side. Loading him into his Monte Carlo, Bill transported him to a hospital emergency room.

An hour later, he was sitting in a Houston Police Department cruiser being questioned about his involvement in the shooting.

"Why would you shoot that man?" an officer asked. "What's your motive?"

"I didn't shoot him, sir. I was trying to make peace between the two of them, him and the other guy."

"Then who's the other guy?"

"I don't know his name."

"Let's get this man to headquarters," an officer said. "He sounds guilty to me."

So Allen was transported to the city jail, where he was interrogated for two more hours.

"So you want us to believe this other guy, a phantom subject, shot your friend?" a homicide detective asked.

"That's right. That's exactly how it came down."

"Where's the gun?"

"I guess he took it with him."

"Or you dumped it."

"Sir, I'm telling you I don't own a gun."

Finally, Allen was taken to a booking room, where a formal charge of attempted murder was to be lodged against him. This meant he would be fingerprinted.

Just before he was charged, however, an officer came into the room and told the interrogating officers that the victim, who was in the hospital emergency room, was telling the same story about what happened.

Allen accepted the officers' profound apologies, then hurried from the building, free and unfingerprinted.

THIRTY

It had been a long day for Joe Bonner. He had worked almost a dozen hours, spending time on bank robberies for the most part, and the hot sun pouring down on Memphis made the heat on the summer afternoon almost unbearable as he turned his automobile toward home.

"Well, I've got some horses to check and some reading to do," he said to himself as he drove into his driveway. "If it's innovation headquarters wants, innovation they'll get!"

As Bonner watched horses run in the pasture behind his house, he thought about the fugitives who had made his life so challenging and, at times, so miserable for more than four years. "They're more free than those horses," he said to himself as he watched them gallop. "They're not fenced. They've got an entire nation at their disposal. And, dammit, one of them might have an entire continent."

After dinner, Bonner sat in his recliner and read about life in Africa. He focused on Gambia and thought about ways to infiltrate the society there.

"Honey, you oughta get some sleep," Merry Bonner told her weary husband. "I can tell something has you stressed to the limit."

"It's that 88," Bonner answered. "And I'll be a son of a bitch if I know what to do about it."

He paused as his wife, who was not accustomed to his discussing business, waited for more information.

"It's amazing. Every police department in the nation has information about them. Fingerprints and pictures. I've even thought they were all dead, but the reports on all unidentified male blacks who have died don't indicate that. And I've checked on aliases from California to New York, thinking they're using names found in newspaper obits. But that's not bearing fruit."

Bonner paused, then said, "Now we have word that one of them is in Gambia."

"So that's why you're reading all of that stuff."

"Uh huh. And I might have come up with something, provided headquarters will go for it."

The following morning, a weary Joe Bonner contacted FBI headquarters in Washington to present an unusual proposition.

"Why not?" a somewhat angry Joe Bonner asked when his plan was rejected later that day.

"Because we can't get the State Department or CIA involved in this. That's just too much to ask."

"I'm telling you, my research indicates this Kah man, Omar Kah, knows about these people," Bonner insisted. "Perhaps he has a weakness we can use. Maybe money. We need to locate him, verify the information we've got in hand, and find a pressure point."

"What's his tie to Allen?"

"I'm not sure," Bonner replied. "But we've heard they've had contact, that they might be doing business."

"What kind?"

"Hell if I know. But Omar Kah is the minister of trade in Gambia, or some such muckity-muck, and I'm telling you he might be open to an approach. You know, the bureau has already offered a reward in this case, so maybe for the right amount of money he'll deliver Allen to us, get him back in the United States. Then all we've got to do is arrest the son of a gun. Regardless, we need to probe Kah. We need to make him roll over for us. Besides, we need contacts over there."

"It's a no go," the agent reminded Bonner. "It's too risky, and it's too expensive. This thing has been testy enough without the CIA getting involved. The FBI can't get rapped for meddling in Gambia. It'd be an incident."

"That's final?"

"That's it. You've got to find another way to close the book."

"Fine," Bonner replied. "But let me ask you a few questions."

"Go."

"How many agents do we have in the streets, those actually doing leg work?"

"Maybe twenty-five hundred."

"OK. And how many people do we have in this country?"

"You know the answer."

"OK," Bonner said. "So you'll agree it's not easy tracking four of them, especially when they're living free of crime?"

"Right. But you've got to find the key to the door."

Not long afterward, Bonner arrived at work one morning and discovered a new man in the office.

"Who's that guy?" Bonner asked Bill Beavers, the special agent in charge of the Memphis office.

"He's a retired agent that headquarters wants on the Old Dog 88s," Beavers replied. "He's supposed to be a wizard when it comes to fugitive cases, and he's been hired under contract."

"Well, shit. Damn, Bill. It's not like I'm a slouch. What does this do to my integrity? I mean, hell, it's embarrassing. The bureau has never done anything like this before."

"I understand, Joe. But it's something headquarters wants. It's getting testy in Washington, and the pressure is getting unbearable up there because the people in Nashville are very impatient."

"So what do I do, sit and watch some over-the-hill, Hawaiian-shirted Rent-a-Cop fail miserably?"

"No," Beavers replied. "Keep working on it. And help the guy when he asks for it. Remember, he was hand-picked by the bureau."

For two weeks Bonner watched the agent prowl around the office and mull through his files without saying anything to him. He was startled when the man approached his desk, introduced himself, and asked for a brief meeting.

"Have a seat," Bonner told him "Let's talk about the case."

"I've got one question off the bat."

"What's that?"

"Where do you think those guys are?"

"I'll tell you this much," Bonner replied. He smiled with the satisfaction of knowing the retired agent had come to him with the ultimate question.

"What?"

"You couldn't find them if they were stuck up your ass!"

Eventually, the agent returned to Chicago. He had produced no viable leads in Tennessee, and Joe Bonner regained control of the case.

"You know," Bonner told a fellow agent, "no matter how softly or loudly you march, or how long and hard you work, it's difficult as hell to catch four quiet mice in a forest."

THIRTY-ONE

It was a birthday present Ann Allen had wanted since 1976, when her husband had hastily left Atlanta. Now it was June 24, 1983, her thirty-first birthday, and she and her son were at their new home in Houston. She felt that she was part of a real family again. No longer would her son have to answer questions about where his father was. Just before he started elementary school in Atlanta, Ann Allen had told Sekou that his father was being hunted by law enforcement officers. As she explained, she had traced much of the civil rights movement for him, recalling the work of the Reverend Martin Luther King, Jr., and had made sure that Sekou Williams understood that his father was a brave man. As a precaution she had taught him how to use aliases, and he had adapted wonderfully well.

During the summer of 1983 there was no need for such careful plotting. One month before his family arrived, Bill Allen had rented a house on the south side of Houston with an option to buy. He was doing fine at Arden's Picture Frames and Gallery, and Charles Lee Herron and he still were picking up extra money remodeling houses. He also was doing photographic services work out of the garage of his house, and he was learning the ins and outs of the import-export business, with hopes of starting a lucrative trade company in the near future.

The Allen family was becoming just another of many in Texas, except that they continued to use aliases. Bill Allen was James Adams at work and Robert Charles Thomas otherwise; Ann Allen was Virginia Kelley Thomas; and Sekou Williams was Sekou Thomas. Bill was known as Coach Adams by the little league baseball team.

Ann Allen found a church for her family and became the organist

172

for services. They developed many friendships at church, as they did in their neighborhood.

During the fall of 1983, Ann Allen was moved to help a two-year-old girl, Shana Wilkerson, in her quest for enough money to have liver transplant surgery. She helped organize a talent show held in a Houston city park, replete with gospel music, magicians, and mimes, and the effort raised three thousand dollars. When the $200,000 needed for the surgery was in hand, Shana Wilkerson Day was held in Houston, with Ann Allen receiving a proclamation from city hall. Her picture was taken alongside the ailing child.

Meanwhile, Bill Allen narrowly averted a trip to city hall for less enviable reason.

"Oh, my God, what's this?" he asked as he looked into the rear-view mirror of his automobile and saw the flashing lights of a police cruiser. He pulled to the side of the street, got out of his automobile, and waited for the officer to approach him.

"Hello, officer," he said. "What's the problem?"

"Could I see your driver's license?"

"Sure," he answered. "What'd I do?"

"It's just a routine check," the police officer said as he gazed at the driver's license. His eyes widened a bit before he fixed his stare on Allen.

"Mr. Adams, your driver's license is a couple of weeks past due."

"What? I didn't know. I'm sorry about that."

When the officer looked into the back seat of the automobile, he noticed carpentry tools lying on the floorboard.

"What's that about?"

"The tools?"

"Yes, the tools."

"I'm a part-time carpenter," Allen explained. "I work at Arden's Picture Frames and Gallery full-time and renovate houses part-time.

"I see," the officer replied. "It's just that a lot of tools have been stolen in this area in recent months."

"I've got receipts for all of these. I'm just trying to make an honest living, sir, that's all."

The officer smiled. "Aren't we all, Mr. Adams? But not all of us have an expired driver's license."

"I know," Allen chuckled. "And like I said, I'm sorry about that. I'll be more than happy to pay the fine. After all, it's obvious I'm guilty."

The officer smiled. "That won't be necessary, Mr. Adams. You've been honest with me. You seem like an OK guy, which definitely isn't the case with everybody I stop. I'm going to give you a break. Just get the driver's license renewed quickly, like tomorrow."

"Thank you, officer," Allen replied. "I'm appreciative. You've saved me some money I need."

After they bade each other polite farewells, Allen got into his automobile, placed his hands on the steering wheel, and breathed a sigh of relief as he prepared to leave what had been a precarious situation.

On the east coast, where Parker and Canady were living, a similar moment took place during the summer of 1983. It was as if the long arm of the law was reaching toward the fugitives.

"Oh no," Parker said to himself as he noticed the emergency flashing light of the cruiser. "You stupid idiot," he said as he glanced at the speedometer and noticed he was going seventy miles per hour in a fifty-five miles per hour zone.

"You're in a bit of a hurry, huh?" the officer asked.

"Yes, sir. I'm trying to get home before dark."

"Where's home?"

"I'm from Georgia originally," Parker replied. "That's where I'm going now. But I work at This Rare Earth on North Liberty Street in Baltimore."

"Why is this a Georgia driver's license?" the officer asked. "Haven't you made the move to Maryland?"

"That's what I'm doing now," Parker replied. "I'm attempting to finalize things in Georgia, then get back up here for good."

"Just sit tight," the police officer advised before he returned to the cruiser.

Parker watched the officer as he talked on the radio. He thought about making a run for it but decided that staying cool had worked well in the past.

"OK, Mr. Walker, you do work at This Rare Earth," the officer said upon his return to the automobile. "But there's this matter of you going too fast to deal with."

"I know, sir," Parker agreed. "And I'm sorry about that. I was in too much of a hurry, for sure."

The police officer looked at his watch. It was 2:50 P.M. He looked at Parker, then said, "It's your lucky day, Mr. Walker, because it's almost time for me to get off work. I'm ready to get home, too. I don't want to deal with this right now. I'm going to let this slide."

"Great," Parker said. "You've saved me a lot of time and money."

"That's true, pal, but I'd advise you to get your Maryland driver's license and then slow this damn thing down."

Parker left the scene with a nervous stomach and drove home ever so slowly. There he found three people waiting for him. Sundiata Ayenda Walker, his son, had been born on January 7, 1983, at Provident Hospital.

That evening, as Parker rested in his bed, he dreamed of moving to Africa, which he and Goodman had discussed before naming their son. The notion gave him added motivation as a businessman. After all, it would cost a lot of money to move a family of four overseas, especially when another family of three, the Allens, and Herron and Canady were anxious to make the move with them.

A move to Africa was not in the mind of the FBI, to say the least. Agents were more perplexed than ever. They had no idea that Allen and Herron were in Houston, and only token evidence that any of the fugitives were in Baltimore. The case had prompted so much frustration that the chief responsibility for the manhunt was moved from Memphis to Nashville in 1983, with agents Rai Patton and Dan Hodges replacing Bonner as its chief tacticians.

This action came after the FBI had toyed with and abandoned an unusual course of action in 1982.

"Joe, I've received a strange telephone call from headquarters in Washington," special agent Bill Beavers told Joe Bonner. "They're thinking about dropping Herron from the Top Ten list."

"Say what?" Bonner asked.

"It's true. And I think we both agree it's a little unusual that he's on there in the first place. Hell, all we've got on the guy in the fourteen years since the shooting is a smoking tailpipe in Atlanta."

"Yes sir," Bonner said. "And in all the correspondence out of Nashville I never have figured out what's fact and what's fiction about the shooting that night."

"Fine," Beavers said. "So headquarters wants you to get off a teletype to them, a request to drop Herron from the list, something they can use to initiate the action."

Bonner took great pains in writing the requested teletype. He rehashed the case, including FBI activity during his five years as agent in charge, and concluded that it would be in the best interest of all concerned to remove Herron from the Most Wanted list.

FBI agents in Washington found no resistance to Bonner's proposal. The Nashville office agreed, as did the U.S. attorney in Nashville. Then came a scathing teletype from Washington.

"Joe, I want you to read this," Beavers told Bonner when he received the teletype.

"Son of a bitch," Bonner swore after reading the uncomplimentary message. "What do they mean who in the hell wrote that stupid teletype? I did it at their request. What do they mean when they say we're gonna intensify the manhunt? That's not what they said originally. And they're saying I'm out of line because I suggested such a thing. Damn, Bill, it was their idea!"

"That's correct, Joe," Beavers replied. "But it seems there was some strong resistance at the upper level in Washington, as well as in Nashville. The county DA, Tom Shriver, and some people in the police department didn't think much of the proposal. They immediately started jumping up and down when they heard about it."

"So it's politics?"

"I'd say it's more of a case of pressure. This entire ordeal is a hot topic in Nashville. At any rate, headquarters has changed its mind. We're going after them with more of a vengeance. As the folks in Washington said, we've got to live up to the demands of the public."

"Fine," Bonner replied. "But did they offer any advice on how to do that?"

"No. At least nothing conclusive. However, they did say they were thinking about making Nashville our base of operation."

"That's just super," Bonner snorted. "I live with this damn thing day and night for what seems like a lifetime, even get close a few times, and they're about to pull the rug out from under me."

The rug was yanked by FBI headquarters. The new man on the spot was Rai Patton. He had requested the assignment upon his arrival in Tennessee after he had heard that province over the case would be moved to Nashville.

"I'm somewhat familiar with the case," Patton said. He had spent several years on assignment in San Juan. "It's not like we haven't kept up with it."

"Fine," said the senior resident in charge of the Nashville office. "But you've got a lot of homework ahead of you. We've got fifty-one volumes on Charles Lee Herron alone."

"Then let me get out of here and get started."

Patton began his sizable task in January 1968, thinking his study of the shooting would allow him to learn a lot about the personalities involved. An agent with training and expertise in the psychology of criminal behavior, he was as surprised as Bonner had been when exploring the basic facts.

"What's the deal with these guys?" he asked Bonner by telephone one afternoon.

"What do you mean?"

"I'm surprised by the personalities involved, Generally, it's a violent criminal with a long history of bad behavior that shows up in a case like this. We've got four who don't fit the mold."

"I agree."

"We're talking well-thought-of guys. And the hell of it is they haven't done anything since then. Violent criminals don't turn their lives around like that, at least not while on the run."

"Yep."

"So what have we got, one of those freakish things where all sorts of unusual elements prompt a shooting?"

"A lot doesn't fit," Bonner answered. "But that doesn't change things. They've been convicted. Three of them escaped from prison. It's ours to settle."

"They're close, Joe, tightly woven," Patton declared.

"Uh huh. Quiet, too."

"Then if we get one, we'll get another one. They're not running as individuals."

Interstate flight after a prison escape is a federal offense that brings the FBI in on a case. Patton was convinced the former convicts received inside help when fleeing in 1974, and so he attempted to develop informants inside the Tennessee State Penitentiary. "What I've got are a bunch of guards and convicts who claim to know more than they do," the agent said to himself one evening. "Either that or I've got some smart cookies on my hands who won't talk."

What Patton had, more than anything, was a fugitive case that had become an embarrassment to the FBI. For all practical purposes, the FBI had drawn nothing other than a series of blanks since Allen, Herron, Parker, and Canady had left Atlanta eight years earlier.

THIRTY-TWO

On her thirty-second birthday, Ann Allen presented her husband with their second son. It was now June 24, 1984.

It was an eventful year indeed for the fugitive on the FBI Identification Order list and his family. With a move to Africa squarely in their sights, they continued to live as ordinary people.

In January Ann had announced to Bill that she was pregnant. She did so with much trepidation, since finances were a constant headache, and she was delighted to see her husband's happiness. Sekou Williams was also pleased to learn he would soon have a baby brother or sister, especially after he was told that he was to become one of the first group of siblings in Texas to take part in the childbirth procedure.

"Do you mean I'll be in there with you when it happens?" he asked his parents.

"Exactly," Bill Allen replied to his son.

"I couldn't begin to do it without my little man Sekou there holding my hand," Ann told him.

The educational experience Ann and Bill Allen had planned for the benefit of their son created more than a few anxious moments for the prospective mother and father. Administrators at Jefferson Davis Hospital in Houston were so excited about the plan, they wanted to film the historic occasion.

"It could get testy," Bill told Ann as she drew near to the due date. "I mean, the last thing we need is for television stations to be flashing our faces all over Houston and the rest of the state."

"I've thought about that," she replied, "and there's no need for you to worry. We'll show up at the last minute, just in the nick of time."

She was correct about that.

"On Ann's birthday, the family rushed to the hospital. She was already in labor, and shortly thereafter Sulaiman Onaje Thomas was born, with his brother holding one of Ann's hands during the delivery and his proud father holding the other. Meanwhile, hospital workers were unable to film the process because the quick pace of her labor did not allow them enough time to set up.

The Allen family had avoided the unwelcomed exposure. The same was true when the four of them left the hospital.

As Ann was being rolled to the front door by a nurse, with Sulaiman wrapped in a blanket in her lap and Bill and Sekou walking alongside, they saw four Houston police officers standing beside the entrance. They kept walking, until a voice stopped them in their tracks.

"Hold on a second," an officer spoke. "Let me see who you've got under that blanket."

The nurse stopped the wheelchair, and two of the officers walked toward it. Ann pulled back the wraps and said, "It's a darling son."

"Well, isn't he a dandy!" exclaimed the officer whose words had halted their exit.

"He's that, for sure," said the officer who joined him for a look. "He'll be a linebacker, a terror in the NFL, hopefully with the Houston Oilers."

"Let's hope so," Bill replied as the officers laughed and stepped back.

"Well, for now, I'd just like to get him home," Ann replied, prompting the nurse to continue rolling her toward the front door.

They got into their car and left as a family. Ann and Bill were convinced the incident was just further evidence that they were on a roll toward good fortune.

Two months earlier, Bill Allen had registered the A. Robinson Export Trading Company at the Harris County Courthouse in Houston. The company's papers in his hands were visible proof that his months of research into the business were providing dividends. When his second son was born, he was already executing small contracts with the Laminah Trading Company, which was operated by Alhaji Laminah Thompson in Lagos, Nigeria, and members of the Rubber Trade Association in New York. So Bill Allen was a mobile businessman the remainder of the year, making several trips across the nation in search of lucrative deals.

During the Democratic National Convention in 1984, Ann Allen was moved by a stirring speech made by the Reverend Jesse Jackson. Without telling anybody about her plans, she designed a doll in honor of the civil rights activist turned politician. She wrote a letter to him requesting permission to market it and received a positive reply from his wife, Jacqueline Jackson. In January 1985 a copyright was issued.

Bill did the silkscreen work from the pattern Ann created, Ann did the sewing, and neighbors assisted them stuffing the Country Preacher Dolls. About two hundred dolls were produced, of which sixty sold at thirty dollars each, and the family received national acclaim. Newspapers in Houston and Portland published stories about Ann Allen, with her using the alias Love Robinson, wife of Arthur Robinson. One story included a picture of Ann, the doll, and her two sons. Bill smiled on the publicity, even commending Ann for a job well done, but he worried that the exposure would prompt suspicion. His fears were unfounded, however, and he continued to move about the nation in search of a business deal that would give him and his family financial freedom, enough money to make the move to the faraway continent.

The breakthrough came just before Christmas 1985, when he secured exclusive rights to the importation of grain, natural rubber, and a grade of corn from Nigeria. This was cause for celebration, as well as cause for alarm on Christmas Day.

As was his habit, Allen went out early on Christmas Day to visit friends, offering holiday greetings from him and his family. Ann Allen stayed at home with the children and when she looked out a window at the front of their house and saw three police cruisers parked across the street, she almost panicked.

"My God, it can't happen today!" she prayed as she turned to watch her sons playing.

"Thank God," she thought to herself as the police officers moved toward a house across the street to arrest a neighbor. She took a deep breath when Bill pulled to the front of their house, home at last and safe.

Suddenly, the holiday season was again ebullient, with merry carols coming from the stereo and laughing children playing on the floor.

As if the gods of good fortune were smiling on them, only another day or two passed before everyone in the family had more for which to be thankful.

"I've negotiated quite a deal," Bill told his family as they spent a quiet New Year's Eve at home.

"So tell me about it," Ann said.

"I've secured the exclusive rights to import grain, rubber, and corn from Nigeria. It has a chance to become a gold mine."

"What are we talking about?" she asked.

"I'd say \$85,000 in July, with more to come, definitely enough for us to think seriously about making our move to Nigeria. Sweet Lady, I'd say we're close to being free at last."

Rai Patton pushed aside a stack of documents and reached for the telephone speaker in front of him.

"Hello," Patton said in an annoyed tone, as if he expected the interruption would take him away from his pursuit of highly publicized fugitives.

"Rai, we've got some interesting data from the National Crime Info Center," said the caller, who was at FBI headquarters in Washington.

"I hope it's something on Charles Lee Herron and the others."

"You've got it," the caller said. "And it makes you look smart as hell."

"How so?"

"We've got a NCIC teletype on an inquiry made about William Garrin Allen II."

"Where'd it originate?" Patton asked.

"Houston. The same place you suggested all of them might be. He's either out there or he knows somebody who is."

Patton was excited, but his enthusiasm was tempered by bewilderment when he learned that the inquiry had been made by somebody with access to the National Crime Information Center. For the most part, the center provides law enforcement agencies with updates on fugitives, such as aliases they are using and vehicles they are driving, and with data related to goods that have been stolen.

Patton immediately solicited the help of FBI agents in Houston as he went about the task of pinpointing the person who made the NCIC inquiry. He discovered the curious person gained access to the computer by using a general sign-on, which means he or she could have been one of several hundred with such admission capabilities.

"So we've got somebody out here who has a strong interest in Allen," a Houston agent told Patton by telephone.

"We're talking about a law enforcement rep," Patton suggested, sounding dismayed.

"That's what it looks like. And we don't know who."

"That's incredible!" Patton exploded. "We're trying to catch the son of a bitch, and it's looking like he has gotten close to somebody on our side who's helping him. I mean, he's in tight enough with this mystery computer operator that he gave him or her his real name."

"That's how it looks."

"Well, dammit, at least we've got a city to check out."

Although agents in Houston became involved with the case, they did not show the kind of enthusiasm Patton wanted. He continued to have other agents interrogate family members and friends of the four fugitives.

"Young lady, we think you're lying to us," an agent said to such a subject near the conclusion of a short interview. "And we know for a fact it'd be best if you or your mother told us where Bill is."

"Let me ask you something," she answered.

"OK."

"If your brother was out there being hunted by the FBI, would you tell anybody where he is?"

"So you know?" the agent asked.

"I didn't say that. I just asked if you'd snitch on your brother."

"I would if his life was at stake."

"What does that mean?" she asked.

"It's like we've told all of you. As far as the FBI is concerned, they're safe from bodily harm. We'll always do all we can to avoid a situation where somebody gets shot."

"Good," she replied.

"But we can't take responsibility for what other people might or might not do. So if your brother or any of the others gets in a tense situation where people have guns and are quick to use them, we can't guarantee their safety."

"I told you I don't know anything," she insisted.

"Then let's all hope you don't have to look back on this conversation with regrets."

After that encounter, the FBI concluded it was pointless to engage family members in interrogations. Patton, however, thought it was important to make a final pitch to Herbert Munford, a friend who had been suspected of remaining close to fugitives.

Munford had been arrested in Atlanta on a drug-related charge during 1984, and he was scheduled to appear before a grand jury to answer felony charges. This gave the FBI the leverage it needed to propose a deal to him, a lesser sentence or an outright pardon in exchange for information about the whereabouts of the fugitives.

Upon arriving in Georgia, where he was to interview Munford with Atlanta-based agent Flo Davis, Patton discovered there was not enough evidence to indict the man on a felony charge. Local authorities were only able to make a misdemeanor case against him. However, Patton was undaunted and continued with his interrogation.

"I told you I don't know where Doc, Slim, Lee, and Bitsey are," Munford answered.

"But you know them too well," Patton suggested.

"I *did* know them," Munford said. "I won't deny that. We went to school together and lived together in Nashville."

"What about in Atlanta?"

Munford shook his head and looked at his lawyer, who was seated beside him.

"Listen, Herbert," Patton said. "We're talking about fugitives on our Most Wanted list."

"Wait a minute," the lawyer interrupted. "I didn't know that. I thought we were talking about a drug misdemeanor."

"It doesn't matter," Munford said. "I don't know anything about them."

"Well, you might remember better if you're hauled in there in front of the grand jury to answer a felony charge, which won't happen if you cooperate with us," Patton claimed.

"That's it," the lawyer spoke. "It's a misdemeanor and nothing else. No more questions. No more answers."

THIRTY-THREE

Steve Parker and Ralph Canady had been amused upon hearing that Ann Allen had designed the Country Preacher Doll in honor of the Reverend Jesse Jackson and had enjoyed success in marketing it.

But the fugitives living in Baltimore shared the concern Charles Lee Herron expressed when the business venture captured national publicity. The group, which had grown to ten, was getting too near their departure to Africa for something as seemingly harmless as newspaper articles to draw the attention of FBI agents across the country.

Bill Allen had returned from Nigeria and had persuaded the others that a move there would be a good thing. And—almost suddenly—it appeared there would be plenty of money to finance the journey. He was about to make it in the commodities market.

Herron had managed to save some money from his job at Arden's Picture Frames and Gallery, as well as from his house renovation endeavors.

Canady was supporting several children and a live-in lover with his checks from Katzenstein's Framing and from Red Coat Janitorial Services in Baltimore, but he was saving some cash to help finance the trip.

Parker was outdoing all of the others as a businessman in Baltimore, where he had become an example of success through labor and intelligence. He already had done well enough to place his daughter, Tierra Walker, in a private school.

The telephone lines between Baltimore and Houston were filled with encouraging news as the fugitives, who had not been together since Allen stopped off for a visit in Baltimore in 1982, discussed leaving the country.

"There's plenty of work in Nigeria for anybody who thinks," Allen told Parker during one conversation. "There are really a lot of opportunities in photographic services. Anybody who's good with his hands can make it."

"What's the latest on the movie deal?" Parker asked. "They haven't started importing them, have they?"

"It's wide open, man," Allen replied. "If we could start theaters over there, I'm telling you they'd flock to them. It's a good opportunity."

"I hope so," Parker answered, "because, frankly, it's tempting to stay here. I never dreamed I'd be able to do so good with the shop. And Joyce [Goodman], bless her heart, is doing great teaching school."

"You haven't told her anything yet, have you?" Allen asked.

"No way, Doc. Like I've always thought, it's just not her burden."

"That's cool," Allen agreed. "You know, man, it's amazing. I don't guess a dozen people know."

"Yeah," Parker agreed, "and the news would shock a bunch of folks, like at work, man. They'd never understand how we've all made it like this."

Parker was developing a reputation as a business whiz. This Rare Earth had become the most profitable distributor of Dassau Brass in Baltimore. Management at the home office were so pleased that they routinely shipped him various items without his ordering them.

Parker also had been attending Little Brothers Mechandising Shows in New York for several years. As he saw items he wished to market in his shop, he expanded his inventory.

To assist his cash flow, he would purchase two thousand dollars worth of rolled gold from Credit Realty Company, then bond it on the stock market. From the ground up the man on the FBI Identification Order list had learned how to use money to make money.

He was always looking for new ways to make money, such as the mass production of what appeared to be hand-crafted earrings. He initiated that venture with other merchants in the neighborhood and students from the University of Maryland Art School. The students designed the jewelry, and Parker made it in the rear of his shop.

In essence, Parker had a loving family, happy employees at This Rare Earth, and such an engaging personality that police officers would join him on their coffee breaks.

"I'm telling you, Rick, you've got to quit parking overtime on the street," an officer said for what seemed like the hundredth time as they sipped coffee in a neighborhood cafe.

"I've got to park somewhere," Parker replied. "There's nowhere else in this area, and I can't leave the shop every hour to put another quarter in the meter."

"Well, you argue a good case, but if you weren't such a good guy, I'd run you in."

"That's cool," Parker answered. "But remember, it's not like I'm a crook trying to take advantage of anybody. In fact, I think it's my time to buy the coffee."

On other occasions Parker found favor with police officers on horseback. When they came by his shop daily, he was quick to grab a plant or two and rush to the street, where he would feed their horses what they had come to consider part of their steady diets.

As life was going so nicely for the fugitives, FBI agents were wondering if perhaps they were out of the country. It was a perplexing case, if not a laughable one.

Allen had traveled abroad.

Herron had worked within three blocks of the FBI office in Houston.

Canady had managed crews that cleaned up the FBI office in Baltimore.

Parker had spent breaks from work drinking coffee with police officers.

It had been almost twelve years since Allen, Parker, and Canady had escaped from the Tennessee State Penitentiary.

Meanwhile, the FBI was putting a new agent in charge of the case, John Canale of the Memphis office. Telephoned in Greenville, Mississippi, he was asked if he wanted a change in office and informed that he could make the move to Tennessee if he was willing to take responsibility for a special fugitive case.

"Which one?"

"Charles Lee Herron and friends."

"Fine," Canale answered. "I'm familiar with it. I've even chased down a few look-alike leads down this way."

Arriving in Memphis, Canale read through sixty-eight volumes of material during his first two weeks on the job, then shook his head in dismay. He also developed a close working relationship with Joe Bonner, who had been in charge of the case from 1977 through 1982.

"Welcome to the real world," Bonner told Canale when they first met. "How'd you like to get your feet wet in a hurry? Maybe wade through some shit along the way?"

"There seems to be a lot of it out there," Canale chuckled.

"Well, you're the twenty-third agent to take a shot at it," Bonner replied. "What do you think?"

"I think I'd like to solve it," Canale replied. "But if something doesn't develop that I'm not expecting, well, it's gonna be a bitch to deal with. After eighteen years of looking, we sure as hell haven't got much to go on."

"Well, I'm in your corner, partner, because those damn guys have made me old before my time," Bonner retorted. "I've never seen so many roadblocks on one case."

With that said, Canale and Bonner began reconstructing some of the fruitless leads covered by the FBI during the most recent three years.

There had been a report that all of the fugitives were in Africa.

"They're not overseas," Bonner told Canale. "Allen was at one time, but he's back."

"But we don't have a clue what state he's in, right?"

"That's right. We found a department store receipt signed by a William Allen in Baltimore, but we didn't get anywhere with it."

"Hell, he's too smart for that," Canale commented. "If they're gonna sign something, they'll use their aliases."

There had been a report that some of the fugitives had returned to Tennessee.

"Nashville didn't do any good with that tip," Bonner said. "Hell, we heard that Herron was walking the streets dressed like a woman. Can you believe that?"

"I don't know about Tennessee," Canale said. "But I'd bet they'll stay in a southern state. They've got accents. They're partial to this kind of food."

"That's a good point," Bonner agreed. "But remember, John, three of them are from Cincinnati. That's where their families are."

"That was my next question. What about their families? I'm big on working families and friends in cases like this. I'd like to push that."

"Good luck," Bonner replied. "I've thought all along that Allen's sister and mother know where he is. But they're not telling if they do."

"And Canady's mother hasn't been cooperative," Canale noted. "She's holding out all the way around."

"It's the same across the board," Bonner commented. "And it doesn't help that Ann Allen, the wife, has long since been gone from Atlanta."

"Well, what about friends?" Canale asked. "Like what's up with that guy in Baltimore . . . uh . . . that Herbert Munford, the guy we shook down so hard in Atlanta?"

"I tried to push it," Bonner answered. "But there's nothing there to work with. He looks as clean as snow."

"So do the damn fugitives."

There had been a report that the four fugitives were involved in a drug network between Colombia, Detroit, Chicago, and Atlanta.

"They might be smoking some dope, but I'm a son of a bitch if they're selling that Colombian Gold," Bonner told Canale.

"Hell, there've been a bunch of interviews about that in Detroit alone," Canale noted. "And not one person we talked to was familiar with any of them."

"That's right. And the same thing in Chicago and Atlanta. California, too, when we got word they were dealing drugs out there."

"So what have we got?" Canale asked.

"A ghost hunt," Bonner replied. "And agents across the nation who are sick of us asking for help."

"At least we've got our man in Baltimore," Canale sighed.

"You're right about that," Bonner agreed. "If there's an agent's agent out there, it's Joe O'Hara."

THIRTY-FOUR

During the early spring of 1986 the FBI remained at a loss in its efforts to track down Bill Allen, Charles Lee Herron, and Steve Parker. So was the Nashville police department.

As for Ralph Canady, the heat was on. He had gotten mixed up with the wrong crowd in Baltimore. On February 21, as he left work at Red Coat Janitorial Services, some of the workers from the crew he managed asked him to give them a lift into the city. He obliged.

When the automobile stopped at a traffic light, one of his riders saw a familiar face standing on a street corner. "Stop," he asked Canady. "I see a friend."

The "friend" sold him a five-dollar bag of marijuana, and he rolled a joint and began smoking it in a flash. Unfortunately, Barbara Chandler, a Baltimore police officer, witnessed the purchase from less than a block away and arrested everybody in the automobile. Canady, who was using the aliases Charles Meadows and Elmer Marcella Diggs, was taken to police department headquarters, where he was booked, fingerprinted, and told when to appear in court.

With much trepidation, Canady stood before a judge who sentenced him to six months probation. He never completed the term.

On April Fool's Day 1986, FBI agents received a telephone call from Joseph Gregory, a fingerprint expert in the Maryland State Police Identification Division. Gregory had finally run a fingerprint check on the men who had been arrested six weeks earlier for possession of marijuana. "We have an Elmer Marcello Diggs, who was arrested for possession on February 21, matched to Ralph Canady, an Identification Order fugitive," Gregory told agent Joe O'Hara.

189

Since O'Hara had worked with the Memphis office in the man-hunt, the name Ralph Canady rang a bell in his head. He thanked Gregory, then began cross-checking files to make sure the fugitive was the one the FBI wanted so badly.

O'Hara wasted little time before moving into action. He and an-other agent visited Red Coat Janitorial Services that afternoon; they showed a woman supervisor a picture of the fugitive.

"Ma'am, does this man, Elmer Marcello Diggs, work here?" O'Hara asked.

"No sir, not Elmer Marcello Diggs," she answered. "But that man looks like Charles Meadows."

"Is he in the building?"

"No sir. But he'll be here later. He works the evening shift."

"Let's keep this quiet," O'Hara told her. "It's a serious matter. We don't want any talk about it until we're sure."

Being sure meant a positive identification, which O'Hara secured a few hours later when he questioned Don Shaffer, a foreman in charge of the crew that cleaned the FBI office in Baltimore.

"That's definitely Charles Meadows," Shaffer answered when O'Hara showed him a picture of Canady.

"There's no doubt?"

"No sir, none at all."

O'Hara then told fellow agent Roger Schweickert, "Roger, let's get some backups arranged and get ready to make a big hit at Red Coat Janitorial Services."

"That's really our man?"

"Yep."

"Then let's get on with it."

"We're on hold," O'Hara replied. "He doesn't get to work until about 3:00 P.M. Let's show some patience."

"Is he hooked up with the others?"

"I don't know," O'Hara replied.

"Well, maybe we should follow him around a while," Schweick-ert said. "He might lead us to the others."

"I'll debate it with you, if you want," O'Hara answered, "but I think it's wise to take the bird in hand. Remember what happened in Atlanta a decade ago when they had two of them and got a little greedy."

Accompanied by two other FBI agents, and with back-ups sta-tioned outside, O'Hara and Schweickert entered the Red Coat Jan-itorial Services building at 9:00 P.M. They went into a large office, showed a woman supervisor a picture of Canady, told her he was a wanted fugitive, and asked her if he was in the building.

"Yes sir," she answered.

"Could you call him down here?"

She summoned Canady with a beeper, saying she needed to ask him about something. It was only a few minutes until Canady entered the office, looked at the agents, took a deep breath, smiled, and said, "I'm not sure she's the one who wants to see me."

"Hello, I'm Joe O'Hara of the FBI," O'Hara said as Schweickert and two other agents prepared themselves for a possible getaway attempt.

"And I'm Ralph Canady," Canady answered with a smile.

"Then you're under arrest."

"Yes sir," Canady replied. "And I'm sort of relieved by it. I knew it couldn't go on forever. It's like you're out there every day wondering if it'll be the day. It's like you're not sure of anything you do."

"I understand."

"So this is the day for me," Canady murmured as he and four agents began walking from the office.

As soon as Canady arrived at the Baltimore FBI office for a lengthy interview with O'Hara, which resembled a pleasant, at times philosophical, conversation as much as anything else, a teletype was sent to FBI headquarters in Washington. In turn, agents John Canale and Joe Bonner in Memphis were informed of the arrest by telephone.

"Now it's rolling," Canale said with a smile. "Now we might get some information to work with."

"It'll flush the others," Bonner replied.

"Yep, I think you're right," Canale replied. "And if we're fortunate, Canady will tell us some things."

But it was not a talkative Canady whom O'Hara visited with until after midnight. To the contrary, he talked rather matter-of-factly. A soft-spoken, yet upbeat, man, he impressed O'Hara with his intelligence and politeness.

"Do you want to discuss what happened in Nashville that night in 1968?" O'Hara asked.

"There's not that much to say," Canady replied. "Some shooting broke out. Four of us ran."

"I've heard you didn't shoot anybody."

"All I know is Parker and I didn't do anything wrong. There were some bad checks cashed before it happened, but we didn't shoot anybody."

"I've heard Allen did the shooting."

"If that's what you heard," Canady answered. His mannerisms indicated he did not want to discuss the matter much more. "I think Bill wrote a letter that said that. They read it at the trial."

O'Hara nodded and smiled. He noticed that Canady was also composed, as well as personable.

"It's a little late," O'Hara said. "I'd guess you're hungry."

"A little bit."

"Well, we've got some sandwiches, crackers, and candy in our vending machines," O'Hara explained. "How about something to eat and a soft drink before we continue? I'm buying."

"No, thank you," Canady said with a smile. "I don't eat much junk food. I'm a runner, a marathoner, who likes to stay in shape."

"Well that's all we've got to offer."

"I guess some crackers won't hurt," Canady replied. "But I'll take them with water. Those sodas are bad for you."

O'Hara purchased Canady crackers and provided him with a glass of water. Then they continued the interrogation.

"OK, Ralph," O'Hara said. "Let's talk about your situation. You've got ninety-nine years ahead of you. Maybe something can be worked out to help you if you're willing to help us locate Allen, Parker, and Herron."

"What do you want to know?" Canady asked reluctantly.

"Let's start in Atlanta."

At about 1:00 A.M., after Canady had taken O'Hara on a truth and fiction voyage, the FBI agent was informed that the Baltimore police at the nearby Woodlawn detention center wanted to take custody of the prisoner they were to keep overnight.

"OK, Ralph, we'll wrap it up tomorrow," O'Hara said.

"What's left?"

"Well, we've got to fingerprint and photograph you," O'Hara explained. "Then you'll appear in front of a magistrate to answer formal charges. And that'll start your extradition procedure."

"Fine," Canady answered. "So what time do you think you'll be coming to get me?"

"Between 8:00 and 8:30."

"I'll be waiting."

Canady was found hanging in a small jail cell just after eight the next morning. There was barely enough room for his lanky body to hang from the ceiling. As attempts were made to save his life, O'Hara was notified by telephone.

"Joe, there's no reason to be in a hurry to talk to Canady," said the officer who telephoned the FBI office with the news.

"Why?" O'Hara asked.

"Because they've just cut him down. It's a suicide."

"He's dead?"

"He's close," the officer answered.

"Then I'm on my way." O'Hara grabbed his coat and rushed from the office.

When he arrived at Woodlawn Detention Center, paramedics were attempting to revive Canady. His pulse was weak, almost non-existent, as he lay sprawled on the floor.

"My God, can't somebody do something," O'Hara asked in a whisper, when all along he knew it was pointless to try. "It's such a damn waste. He was so intelligent. So engaging. He had so much promise."

Then O'Hara thought to himself, "Suicide? He was a health nut. Mere hours ago the man wouldn't even drink a soft drink because he said it was bad for him. Now this? Now he has killed himself? It just doesn't make any sense."

O'Hara was both despondent and baffled when he returned to his office.

Word spread quickly about Canady's arrest and suicide. In Nashville, some police personnel rejoiced when hearing about the first event and had a ho-hum attitude when hearing about the second. In Cincinnati, his relatives cried and lamented because they had been unable to see him for such a long time. In Baltimore, Parker read about the tragedy in an afternoon newspaper and grieved over the death of a friend. It was April 3, 1986.

Then Parker called Allen in Houston. "Bill," he began. "I've got terrible news."

"What's up, Bitsey?"

"Ralph's dead."

"What!" Allen exclaimed.

"It's true, Bill. They found him hanging in a jail cell. They're saying he committed suicide."

Tears came to Allen's eyes as he asked Parker for details.

"Dammit, it's just not true," Allen insisted. "Slim wouldn't commit suicide. That's just not him. You know that, Bitsey. Hey, man, he had a lady and four kids to live for."

"For real," Parker agreed. "That's what I've been thinking about all day. There's talk in the streets that they killed him, hosed him, and then made it look like he took his own life."

Parker and Allen wondered what Canady had told the FBI agents who interrogated him. They wondered if it was time for the three of them to move. Parker decided it would be best for him to stay put.

Allen conferred with Ann Allen and Charles Lee Herron and decided it was time to move to Jacksonville, Florida. The fugitive in him knew it was time to change scenery, and the businessman in him knew that moving to a port on the Atlantic Ocean would enable him to cut his costs while importing grain, natural rubber, and corn from Nigeria. This would increase his profits on his forthcoming deal.

In reality, none of the fugitives needed to flee, at least not because of what Canady had told O'Hara. In what might have been his final conversation, since there is no record that he telephoned anybody after being arrested, the man they knew as Slim and Candy Man had presented a mixture of fact and fiction, leaving the FBI with no leads to track the others.

Parker, Herron, and Allen were deeply upset by their friend's death. They were tormented by talk that Canady had been physically abused in Baltimore, as well as a report that his casket was not opened during his funeral in Cincinnati. With that on his mind, as well as his uncertainty about what Canady had told interrogating FBI agents, Allen moved to Florida. With Herron, Allen and his family arrived in Jacksonville on April 15.

"That's OK, Joe, because there's not a damn thing you could've done to prevent it," agent Canale told O'Hara after the death of Canady was announced.

"I guess not, John," O'Hara replied. "But it seems so senseless, even though I'm sure he wasn't looking forward to going back to Tennessee."

"I guess that's it," Canale said. "But it's done now. We've got to find the others without his help."

"That's for sure. So what do you need?"

"Anything you can do, my friend," Canale replied. "But let's start by seeing if the others are in the Baltimore area."

"We're checking Canady's residence thoroughly," O'Hara answered. "From there, we'll try to find mutual friends."

"Sounds good."

"And you can be sure I won't sit on it. Now that we've got a break on this case, it's time to pick up the pace. If we're gonna get anything else, chances are good it'll happen in the next few days."

THIRTY-FIVE

Steve Parker was passing through the living room of his house in Baltimore when he glanced toward the television set and saw what seemed like a cruel April Fool's Day joke. The newscaster was completing a report about a fugitive who had been captured, Ralph Canady. On the screen was a picture of the man FBI agent Joe O'Hara and others had apprehended without incident at Red Coat Janitorial Services.

"What's this?" Parker asked himself as the picture faded from view and the newscaster moved to another subject. "This can't be."

But Parker was too street smart to ignore the obvious. "If they have Ralph," he reasoned, "they might have my address." So he slipped out of his house, walked city streets, and waited for the *Baltimore Sun* to arrive in newspaper racks. The news he saw in print was unsettling because it came replete with pictures of Bill Allen, Charles Lee Herron, Canady, and himself.

Needing a friend, Parker found a good one, a woman named Joan Kelly. He went to her townhouse on Freedomway West in Baltimore, where he telephoned Allen and Herron with the news.

Several hours later, Parker learned that Canady had been found dead. He panicked. He attempted to leave Maryland for safer ground, but every erratic turn he made brought worse news.

First, he went to his house and packed his clothes. As he pulled clothes from a closet and a chest of drawers, he gazed from time to time at the foot locker in the bedroom, secured by chains and a large lock. Inside it were various false identifications Canady and he had collected for such an emergency.

Parker knew that Joyce Goodman would return later that afternoon from the elementary school where she taught and would be concerned if she discovered that the mysterious foot locker was gone. "It has been like an anchor," he said to himself. "It's the one thing that has helped her believe I've put down roots. She'll miss it and think I've run out on her."

Then he sat for a few minutes and cried. He had lost a good friend and now he was about to give up a family. However, he could not forget that he was responsible to them, and so he took some stashed money out of the trunk, counted out enough for his family to survive on for several months, and put the rest of it, about two thousand dollars, in his wallet

In his mind he thought time was more precious than it really was, so he packed his belongings into his automobile, walked back inside for a final look around his apartment, got into his automobile, and began driving. He circled his apartment a few times, then moved across town in search of a motel where he could stay that night. "I told Joyce I could be here today and gone tomorrow," he told himself as he drove aimlessly in the Baltimore area. "But I never dreamed it'd happen like this."

Daylight had turned to darkness by the time Parker stopped curbside in downtown Washington, D.C. Getting out of his automobile, he walked into a telephone booth on Georgia Avenue and placed a call to his younger brother, Daryl Parker, who was working at Thistle Downs racetrack in Cleveland. He would have preferred to have missed the conversation.

"Hello," Steve said.

"Ohhh . . ." Daryl Parker realized who was on the other end of the line.

"I've got bad news," Steve began as he started to tell his brother about Canady.

"Yeah," Daryl agreed. "But we all have to go through it at some point."

Steve Parker obviously was confused, so he asked his brother what he was talking about.

"Then you don't know?"

"What? Don't know what?"

"That Daddy died," Daryl answered.

"What? No!"

"It's true, Steve," his brother answered. "We buried him ten days ago."

Parker was even more shaken when he returned to his automobile and drove through downtown Washington, D.C., crying. The only comfort he felt came from the memory of how he and his father always left funerals before they got under way because neither of them liked them. He knew his father, whom he had last spoken to six months earlier, would have understood why his older son was not there when they buried him.

"Maybe I should call Mom," he said to himself as he pulled into a motel parking lot. "No, that'll just make things worse. Sadie will worry even more about me."

So Parker checked into a room and went to bed. He was restless, wondering if there would be a knock at the door at any second, and he contemplated when he should telephone Goodman with the news. He decided to do that the following afternoon when she got home from work.

When Goodman picked up the receiver, Steve greeted her. "Joyce, it's Rick."

"Where are you?" she asked. "I've been worried sick all day."

"I'm near Dickey Hill High School. I want you to meet at the field."

"When?"

"Now. And I want you to come alone. We don't need Tierra and Sundiata around. I've got some important things to discuss with you."

When Goodman arrived at the field, a playground of sorts not far from their apartment, Parker took her hand and began leading her on a stroll.

"What's happening here?" she asked. "I mean, you're so nervous."

They stopped and sat on the ground.

"I'm crushed," Steve Parker began.

"About what?"

"Joyce, Daddy is gone. He's dead."

"What? When? How? Oh, my God."

"And Ralph is gone, too."

"What?"

"And I'm scared, baby, real scared."

"Slow down, Rick," Goodman said. "You're going too fast for me."

"Ralph is dead, baby. They found him hanging in a jail cell."

"Well, Rick, you were a good friend to him," Goodman said as she took a troubled Steve Parker in her arms. "You've always been there for him. Ralph knows that. You know that. I know that."

"But Dad is dead, too, Joyce, and I've got to leave town."

"Why, Rick?" Goodman asked. "What is it you're not telling me?"

Parker took a deep breath as Goodman looked into his eyes, then he turned away for a second, glancing at the ground below them. Looking into her eyes, he began to talk.

"Joyce, my real name is Steve Parker," he began. "Back in the 1960s, I was in Nashville, Tennessee, with some other guys when two police officers were killed. It wasn't our fault, and I was just on the scene when it happened, but they convicted three of us for murder. In 1974, back in Nashville, we all escaped from the prison there. We've been on the run since then."

"So here today and gone tomorrow?"

"That's it."

"And the other guys," Goodman said. "That must be Ralph, Bill, and Lee."

"You've got it," Parker replied. "And not once since then have any of us had any trouble with the police."

"And now you're going to leave."

"I've got to, baby, and I'm not going to tell you where I'm headed. I don't want you to know."

"OK," Goodman agreed. "Do what you have to do. It won't be that bad."

"I'll see you again," he promised, "because I love you and the kids too much not to."

"Then I'll be waiting," she replied. "And so will our precious children."

In Cincinnati, John Alexander read in a newspaper about the apprehension and death of a friend in Baltimore. "I haven't been around Ralph Canady at all since 1974," he said to a girlfriend. "But one thing I know is he didn't kill himself. He wasn't that kind of guy."

Parker arrived in Philadelphia on April 6, 1986, three days after he learned about the death of Ralph Canady. As he was settling into a downtown hotel, Bill and Ann Allen and their children and Charles Lee Herron were preparing for their move to Florida nine days later.

Across the nation, FBI agents were attempting to put together a puzzle while using flawed pieces provided by Canady in an interview the night before his death. They thought they were on to something, when in reality they were as stumped as he had tried to leave them. The fugitives and their families would have relished this knowledge had they realized there was no need to become so active.

"We've found a few people who've seen Parker in the presence of Canady in Baltimore," agent Joe O'Hara told agent John Canale in Memphis. "We don't have firm identification on him, but I'm fairly sure he has been in the area."

"What did you turn up in Canady's house?"

"Not much," O'Hara admitted. "He was as shrewd as the others.

He was careful with his telephone calls, too, because his toll records don't indicate much."

"Have we got any reason to think Allen and Herron are up that way?"

"Negative. In fact, it's my guess Parker has hauled ass, too. Maybe to New York."

"Stay with it," Canale suggested. "And let's remember how unpredictable these guys are. As a football coach might say, expect the unexpected."

"That's a good thought," O'Hara said. "The death of a loved one can make a person do strange things. I imagine Canady's dying has all of them in an emotional state."

Parker was in worse shape than the others. He had lost his father, his friend, and, in a manner of speaking, his family in the scope of two weeks. On his first night in Philadelphia, he drove to a park, got out of his automobile, and began crying.

After sobbing for a long time, he tried to get control of himself. *You've got to get it together,* he thought. *You've got to start over, just like before. You've got to keep living while hoping and praying for the best.*

The next morning, Parker began doing that. He checked the newspaper for rental property advertisements, then drove around the city. Soon he decided that the best place to settle was in the Pemrose Park section near the airport, a recently developed neighborhood with apartments for people new to the area. He had about two thousand dollars in his pocket, and he liked the signs that said "First three months free."

To enhance his finances, Parker negotiated a long-distance deal in which he sold his shop, This Rare Earth, to a friend who worked at a Baltimore beauty shop. He requested that no questions be asked, and she honored his wishes. Also, Goodman and he decided to take their daughter, Tierra Walker, out of the private school she had been attending, a move designed to give them more money with which to survive.

Parker considered contacting Bill Allen and Herron in Houston, just to put together a game plan with them. However, he concluded that one man could hide better than three, especially when a wife and two children would be the constant companions of the other two.

Suddenly thrust into a precarious situation because of her love for a fugitive, two of whose children she had borne, Goodman wondered if and when the FBI would be coming to see her.

O'Hara was tracking leads that informed him that Canady and Parker had been close companions in Baltimore, playing tennis together and attending occasional parties. Agents Canale and Bonner, who knew more about the fugitives than anyone else, were in touch with O'Hara on a daily basis.

"I don't know if Parker will return to Baltimore, but I'm hopeful," Canale told Bonner as they ended another day at the Memphis FBI office. "It's a key for us."

"He might," Bonner replied. "Let's keep Baltimore high on our priority list."

"Well, Joe O'Hara does seem to have some of his friends talking," Canale commented.

"And he'll get to the bottom of it," Bonner replied. "He's a king when it comes to dealing with people."

"But we don't have a damn thing on Allen and Herron," Canale reminded him. "For all we know, they could be long gone."

"Let's be patient," Bonner replied. "Everybody's had a gut-wrenching two weeks, all because Canady screwed up. If he was dumb enough to smoke a little dope, I've got a feeling it's just a matter of time until all of the others do something stupid, too."

THIRTY-SIX

Ann Heath, a thirty-nine-year-old clerk in the Florida Highway Patrol testing center on Norwood Avenue in North Jacksonville, smiled when she asked Bill Allen for his Texas license to operate a motor vehicle. She looked hard at the picture on it after comparing it with a Florida identification photograph he had secured earlier in the day.

"This man is a fraud of some type," Heath muttered under her breath, never looking at Allen who was standing just in front of her. "One of these men looks more Spanish than American. Something is wrong here."

Allen noticed she was slow to react to the pictures. He was anxious to begin his driving test.

"Is there a problem, Ma'am?" he asked.

"Oh no, Mr. Spencer," Heath said. "Just have a seat and wait for a tester to take you for a ride."

Allen smiled and moved toward a bench. Heath took care of another customer and wondered what was wrong with the identification she had examined.

The signature William Spencer, Jr., looked strikingly different on the two forms Allen had prepared. The picture of Arthur Robinson did not match the face she had looked at across the counter.

Allen, dressed in blue jeans, a knit shirt, and sneakers, did not realize her suspicion. He was on the brink of what seemed like a fortune: $85,000 for one deal as a middle man in the commodities market. So he was too preoccupied with more important thoughts to watch her facial expression. He had been in more precarious situations, so he was more concerned about the long wait he had to endure before getting his license.

201

This afternoon, June 18, 1986, had been long, sunny, and humid. He had made several telephone calls for his blossoming import-export business, and there was a lot to do to get his house organized.

Still, Heath had questions that required answers. So after Allen had gone to take his driving test, she asked her supervisor to confirm what she had noticed about the pictures.

"You're jumping to conclusions," the supervisor answered. "It's nothing to get upset about."

But Heath was persistent. "I don't know what this is all about," she said, "but that man isn't William Spencer. For all we know, William Spencer has been harmed and this man has his identification."

The supervisor picked up a telephone and contacted the Florida Highway Patrol office in a nearby section of the shopping mall. The clock on the wall said it was 4:37 P.M., with the Florida sun sinking in the sky.

"I don't know what it is exactly," the supervisor said. "It's just that Ann Heath says there's something that doesn't match. He's a polite man, but the signatures and the pictures look different. Maybe somebody should come over and check him out."

At about closing time, with Heath prepared to leave for the day, Officer Charles Hall entered the testing center as casually as a man strolling through a park. He walked through a rear door, looked at Allen, then at the supervisor, who nodded to let him know that was the man about whom she was uncertain. The highway patrolman approached Allen and began questioning him. After encountering many people who had become agitated during such inquiries, Hall was surprised to find this man cordial and cooperative. Nevertheless, he told Allen they needed to go into an office for a conversation. The officer, who was assisted in the inquiry by Dona McArthur of the testing center, was startled when he requested a military identification card and a Texas driver's license and discovered pictures very different from the one on the Florida identification card lying beside them.

"The pictures and the signatures are definitely different," said McArthur to Hall. "I seriously doubt this man, Mr. Spencer, could ever grow a beard as thick as the man on this photo."

"Who are you?" Hall asked Allen.

"I'm William Spencer, like the form reads."

"Well, the picture looks fishy. I'd like for you to sign your name a few times for us."

Allen realized he had problems. He had signed the name William Spencer only a few times, once while purchasing his house, once while closing a deal on his van, and twice at the counter for the clerk, and he was awkward doing it.

"That's not good," Hall said upon looking at the signatures. "We're going to take you to headquarters for an ID check."

Hall suggested to Allen that they go to the Duvall County Sheriff's Department to verify his identity as William Spencer, Jr. Allen did not object. Hall also asked deputy sheriff C. D. Johnson to transport Allen downtown in a police cruiser equipped with a caged rear seat because he did not want to handcuff the suspect for fear of a false-arrest lawsuit. Allen appeared mildly reluctant when they attempted to place him in the car.

"I'm not ready to go," he objected.

"What's the problem?"

"I left my car keys inside. I need to go back in there and get them."

"I think they're in your pants pocket, Mr. Spencer," Hall answered. "Now get in and let's go."

Hall watched Johnson give Allen a slight push toward the back seat, then got into his highway patrol car and followed the police cruiser.

Allen panicked just outside the Sheriff's Department building. When the two officers started leading him toward the front entrance, Johnson remembered that he had forgotten to turn off the headlights. As he turned toward the cruiser, Allen broke away and began running. With Hall in pursuit on foot, Allen ran into a parked automobile two blocks away, met heavy traffic, and was caught two blocks later. They wrestled until Allen realized it was pointless to scuffle.

"Now, Mr. Spencer, what's this all about?" Hall asked as he and Johnson put handcuffs on Allen.

"I just don't like jails, that's all."

"Well, sir, I'd say we've got to find out who you really are."

"OK, but I'm not gonna let you fingerprint me."

Just before 6:00 P.M., with handcuffs in place, Allen was taken to an identification room. After contending all along that he was William Spencer and sensing what was about to happen, he yanked his arms over his head. "You're not gonna do that because it's not necessary," he objected when the officers attempted to fingerprint him.

"See, I told you we've got somebody who doesn't want us to know who he is," Hall told Johnson as they put the handcuffs back on Allen and led him toward the county jail, where he was charged with resisting arrest and searched. In a shirt pocket was a marijuana cigarette, which led the officers to add possession of an illegal drug to the charges.

Hall summoned a supervisor, Highway Patrol sergeant Tony

Napoli, who arrived just after four officers had forced Allen to be fingerprinted.

Then began an interrogation of the man they wanted to identify. Allen changed his story, telling his name was James Adams, which was the alias he had used a lot in Houston, and that he lied because his driver's license had been suspended.

Allen was placed in a jail cell to await the results of the fingerprint tests. As the hours passed, he began to have hope. If the results were not available soon, he reasoned, the law would allow him to post bond, thus giving him, his family, and Charles Lee Herron time to flee.

Allen telephoned his wife where they were living on Miss Muffet Lane and suggested she, Herron, and his two sons, Sekou Williams and Sulaiman Thomas, leave town quickly. They told him they would wait and help him through the situation and that Herron would attempt to contact a bondsman.

Hall and Napoli did not sit idle. They went to Miss Muffet Lane, arriving at 8:26 P.M., where they discovered Ann Allen and Herron standing in the dark on a screened porch. After two requests, the highway patrolmen were allowed to enter the porch.

"Are you related to William Spencer?" Napoli asked.

"Yes," Ann Allen answered. "I'm Mary Spencer, the former Mary Johnson, and this is my brother, James Johnson. I'm married to William Spencer, but I haven't known him very long. My brother is here trying to help us get settled."

"Well, could you give us a little more information about the man, this Mr. Spencer.?"

"I'd rather talk to him first."

"Yeah," Herron replied. "We need to talk to him or a lawyer before talking any more with you."

"Well, we didn't come here to cause any trouble for you," Napoli replied. "We're just here to get enough information to close the case."

"I'm feeling a little sick," Ann Allen said as she began to tremble, as if she was about to faint.

"Would you like for us to get you medical assistance?"

"We need to find out what's happening here," Herron replied. "And we need to telephone our parents."

Hall and Napoli thanked Ann Allen and Herron for their assistance and left the premises. Then they went to the shopping center parking lot and ran a check on the 1976 GMC van with Texas license plate 351-OHA on it. That did not elicit a cause for alarm, only a report that it was registered in Harris County to William Spencer. They returned to the Duvall County Jail, and Hall went inside to file a report on the case. He also contacted E. C. Crews of the Sheriff's Department identification department and requested the results of the fingerprint tests. Napoli returned to highway patrol headquarters to contact authorities in Houston.

The highway patrol officers were somewhat anxious.

So was Bill Allen as he sat in his cell and kept looking at his watch. When she got the van from the mall, Ann Allen and Herron waited with the unsuspecting children at the house on Miss Muffet Lane.

Hands of clocks moved slowly for all of them: the officers waiting for the identity of the man they had in custody, Bill Allen waiting for word that he could post bond, Ann Allen and Herron waiting for a reason to act. At about midnight Ann Allen went to bed, and Herron paced back and forth across the floor of the living room.

An impatient Hall telephoned a busy Crews and told him how important it was to run the fingerprint test quickly. He was told the results would be forthcoming.

Hall leaped toward the telephone when it rang a few minutes later. "You've got one wanted by the FBI for escape, serving a ninety-nine-year sentence for killing two police officers in Tennessee."

"You're kidding me," Hall exclaimed in surprise. "He's that big? Well, son of a bitch!"

Hall telephoned Napoli with the news, then hurried to the county jail, requested the FBI file on Bill Allen, and set up an interview with the former fugitive.

At first, Bill Allen stuck with his original story, that he was James Adams. Then when Napoli showed him an FBI Identification Order flier, he nodded his head and conceded that he was a wanted man.

Napoli then used the situation to teach Hall some good police work. He handed the highway patrol officer the file.

"Take a look at this."

"Yeah, it's Allen, for sure," Hall replied. "But it's not the James Johnson dude at the house."

"Keep looking."

Hall turned to the next page of the file, saw a picture of Herron, and said, "That's him, sergeant. That's the man at the house. That's Charles Lee Herron, a man who's on the FBI Most Wanted list. He's at the top of the list."

Napoli smiled at Hall.

"Then let's get started on a plan to nab him," Napoli told the excited highway patrol officer.

THIRTY-SEVEN

FBI agents were excited when the Florida Highway patrol announced that Bill Allen was in custody and Charles Lee Herron had been spotted.

Agents were only cautiously optimistic because they had been chasing Herron for more than eighteen years. "There's only a fifty percent chance that he's still at the house," an agent told highway patrol sergeant Tony Napoli. However, Napoli and his fellow officer Charles Hall were more optimistic.

"I'm sure he's still there," Hall said as they returned to Miss Muffet Lane. "He has to be. This is too big to get away from us."

The FBI hoped so, too. Agents Marlen Vogt, Arthur Small III, and Thomas Sobolewski were stationed outside Allen's home on Miss Muffet Lane. They were accompanied on surveillance, which began at about 2:00 A.M., by two highway patrol officers. From their vantage points in the front and the rear of the house, they could see an unidentifiable person moving about inside. It was Herron, who was too tense to sleep.

Hall and two other highway patrol officers were stationed in police cruisers at three intersections in the neighborhood, just in case an escape effort was made. They all waited for additional FBI agents and highway patrol officers to arrive, as well as for a SWAT team.

Meanwhile, Bill Allen sat in his jail cell and listened to talk around him. "Well, we've got a big fish in our midst," an officer had said just after he was identified. "And I understand there's another one waiting to be nabbed."

Then Bill Allen was fetched from the jail cell and taken to an interview room, where he was questioned for an hour by FBI agent

206

Jon Bell. The pieces of a massive puzzle began falling into place at that time.

In Baltimore, Joe O'Hara received a telephone call at home. The caller, another FBI agent, was in Jacksonville.

"Joe, we've got William Allen in custody and have a house under surveillance," the agent in Jacksonville told the stunned and sleepy O'Hara.

"Is Steve Parker with him?" O'Hara asked as he focused on the fugitive he was tracking so diligently.

"That's what we're wondering. There's somebody at that house, a male and a female, and we think the male is Charles Lee Herron. We've surrounded the place but are wondering if you think Parker could be down here, too."

"There's a chance," O'Hara replied. "They're all tight, and they've been in contact. But I'm not sure where Parker is. Hell, I'd have him in custody if I did."

While Bill Allen was being questioned by Bell, with the focus on the whereabouts of Parker, the only one of the five fugitives still at large, law enforcement personnel were quietly assembling outside the house on Miss Muffet Lane. It was quiet in the neighborhood, and Charles Lee Herron was seated on the couch in the living room. He was fighting fatigue, and he kept thinking that he heard movement outside, but wrote it off as his imagination.

Ann Allen shivered in her bed and opened her eyes. Turning on the light on the table beside her, she saw that the clock said it was 4:50 A.M. Her feet were cold, and she wrapped her arms around her body in an effort to get warm. But she was experiencing a chill such as she had never known, one that refused to leave.

"Ann, it's over," said the clear voice in her head, words she attributed to God. She opened her eyes wider, then heard footsteps outside. "Go look outside," the voice commanded.

Ann Allen got out of her bed and walked toward the living room. Glancing at Herron, who was groggy from tension and lack of sleep, she walked to the picture window. Pulling back the curtain a few inches and looking outside, she saw what appeared to be a battlefield, what she surmised to be more than fifty armed law enforcement officers.

"Who's out there?" she asked in a loud voice. Nobody answered.

"It's over, Lee," Ann Allen told Herron, who had leaped from the couch and was walking toward the window. "There are policemen everywhere. They've got the house surrounded."

"So what should we do?" Herron asked.

Ann Allen and Herron sat and talked for about an hour. They

talked about the hanging death of Ralph Canady less than three months earlier in Baltimore. Convinced that Canady had been killed by police officers, they feared Bill Allen was also being mistreated in downtown Jacksonville.

The law enforcement personnel outside waited patiently.

"Lee, I'm going to read from the Bible," Ann Allen told Herron. "I'm going to read you the Twenty-seventh Psalm."

And she did, starting, "The Lord is my light and my salvation. Whom shall I fear? When evil men come to destroy me, they will stumble and fall. Yes, though a mighty army marches against me, my heart shall know no fear. I am confident God will save me."

The army was poised and waiting outside her house, so Ann Allen telephoned her mother in Atlanta to tell her of the situation. She asked her mother to pray for her.

"I'm going to talk to them," Ann Allen told Herron just before 6:00 A.M. "I'm frightened for us and for Sekou and Sulaiman. I've got to find out what those people are thinking. I don't want them to kill us."

So Ann Allen walked toward the door. Reaching for the knob, she twisted it and cracked open the door about a foot and called to the officers. "What's going on? Don't kill us. We want to come out."

Weapons were aimed at the door as she spoke. Seeing them heightened her fear.

"Who's in the house with you?" Vogt asked in a loud voice from his position behind a tree about fifty feet from the front door. He could see Herron standing behind her.

"Only my brother and my children."

"Fine," Vogt spoke as loudly as before. "Nobody's gonna hurt you if you do what you're told. We want you and that man to come out of the house with your hands held high over your heads, with palms pointed toward the sky. We want you to come first, then him fifteen seconds behind you."

Herron was standing behind Ann Allen when she opened the door wider. In a shaky voice she answered, "OK, here we come, both of us."

Ann Allen walked from the house as instructed and was approached quickly by FBI agent Small, who without interrupting his quick pace took her by the arm and moved her several yards to the left. She flinched as he grabbed her, thinking he was being forceful, when in reality he was attempting to get her out of the line of fire if Herron did not follow orders.

Herron exited the house as instructed and was approached quickly by FBI agent Sobolewski.

"You're Charles Lee Herron?" Sobolewski asked.

"Yes," Herron answered in a subdued voice.

Herron was handcuffed and searched immediately, then hustled to an FBI automobile and taken to headquarters for a lengthy interview. During the trip, he said it was knowing his picture was on every post office wall in the country that bothered him and that his strangest feeling came when he was on a city bus in Baltimore and saw his picture in a newspaper being read by a woman seated in front of him.

FBI agent Bell, who had arrived at the house as Herron was being handcuffed, approached Ann Allen, who was standing with Small in the front yard.

"Who's in the house?" he said.

"Just my two sons," she answered just before Bell ordered the house to be searched.

"Ma'am, I'd like for you to go FBI headquarters for an interview," Bell told her.

"Fine," she agreed. "But can I take my sons with me?"

Sekou Williams and Sulaiman Thomas were awakened by their mother. Bell watched as she prepared apple juice, packed diapers, and gathered toys for them to play with on the interview room floor during a four-hour question-and-answer session that shed enormous light on the events of the past twelve years.

The ringing of the telephone beside his bed in Memphis did not sound comforting to FBI agent John Canale. Having had little rest since he had taken province over the case, he reached for the speaker and offered a drowsy hello.

"Is this FBI agent John Canale?" asked the man on the other end of the telephone.

"It is."

"John, this is an FBI agent in Jacksonville. We've got some good news for you."

"What's that?"

"Charles Lee Herron and Bill Allen are in the custody of our office here. They were arrested mere hours ago. Positive IDs are in hand."

"Son of a bitch! How did it happen?"

"You'll have a teletype waiting for you at your office."

Canale did not return to sleep. He quickly shaved, showered, dressed, and drove to his office.

In Philadelphia, Steve Parker tossed and turned as he attempted to rest for what he figured would be another hectic day. He was lonely.

He was scared. And he was concerned about a financial situation that was growing worse by the day.

His fear was heightened that afternoon when he stopped to purchase a soft drink at a convenience store. As he walked toward the entrance, he glanced toward a newspaper rack and saw a headline describing the capture of Allen and Herron in Jacksonville. Forgetting about his thirst, he put a quarter in the machine, hurried to his automobile, and read about the events of the previous day.

"Son of a bitch," Parker swore. His life had been turned upside down by three apprehensions in less than three months. "I'm the only one left out here."

That afternoon, citizens across the nation read and heard a bizarre story about the ending of life on the run for Allen and Herron. Many were surprised at how long Bill Allen and Charles Lee Herron had remained free, and many were shocked to learn that the fugitives had developed enviable lifestyles while being tracked in at least five states.

In Atlanta, Pittsburgh, Baltimore, Houston, and Jacksonville, people who had been closely associated with Bill Allen and Charles Lee Herron expressed astonishment upon learning the men they had considered good guys were being called hardened criminals.

As for Ann Heath, the highway patrol clerk whose alert questions had led to the captures, she was moving toward heroine status.

As she answered the telephone beside her bed the morning of Herron's arrest, her supervisor told her she had done well. "Your attention to your work has led to the apprehension of two fugitives from the FBI's Most Wanted list. I thought you might want to know."

Heath was tired, and it was her day off. So she hung up the telephone and returned to sleep, only to hear it ring again.

"Ann," said her supervisor. "The FBI wants to talk to you at their headquarters."

She dressed hurriedly, so fast that she put on makeup en route to FBI headquarters. Upon her arrival, she wanted to hide.

"Oh Lord," Heath muttered under her breath upon seeing television and newspaper reporters. "Those guys really must have been bad."

In subsequent days Heath received letters from many people, including William Webster, the director of the FBI, who praised her for identifying the fugitive. Two days later, Nashville police chief Joe Casey commended her for finding men wanted in "the ambush slaying" of two police officers. Florida Governor Bob Graham presented her a certificate of merit.

But more than anything else, work took on an increased tension. The nervousness was reflected by a humorous event one afternoon after most people thought the excitement had subsided. When a balloon popped in the testing center on Norwood Avenue, clerks and supervisors leaped from their seats and onto the floor.

THIRTY-EIGHT

Ann Allen smiled as she thought of what her neighbor had said in June 1986 to her. "We all know you and Bill well enough to go to bat for you," she had told her less than a week after the arrests. "He isn't the type of person who should be in prison. Why don't you get enough names on a petition to get him out?"

Ann Allen thought about those words, then decided to do something about the situation when she learned one of the few statutory grounds for executive clemency in Tennessee is exemplary behavior while on escape. Certainly, she reasoned, her husband qualified for such consideration.

So Ann Allen, thirty-four years old that week and the mother of two children, got busy as Bill Allen and Charles Lee Herron sat in a detention center in Nashville awaiting what promised to be lengthy legal proceedings. Before she was finished, she had more than three thousand signatures from people in Atlanta, Baltimore, Houston, Jacksonville, and Nashville on a petition that claimed that her husband had proved himself productive enough on escape to be set free for life. She was given an impressive video presentation in which many people in Houston said they would be responsible for the convicted murderer the remainder of his life if the Tennessee Department of Corrections released him from prison. She solicited and received signatures from guards and officials at Brushy Mountain State Penitentiary, where her husband was incarcerated from the fall of 1986 through much of January 1987, when he was transferred to the Tennessee State Penitentiary in Nashville.

On December 9, she appeared before the four-member clemency board working under the direction of Lamar Alexander, then in his final month as governor of Tennessee.

A smartly attired but nervous Ann Allen sat in front of the board, which consisted of two men and two women, as she presented her evidence. She experienced what she took to be a sympathetic audience during the fifteen-minute hearing and was hopeful of a positive result until Ed Hoover of Chattanooga, a clemency board veteran, got into a heated debate with another member. The board finally concluded that the debt to society had not been paid.

Although she was disappointed when she left the room, Ann's determination was not dampened. She kept working on behalf of Herron and her husband as an unusual chain of legal maneuvers unfolded.

First, Davidson County district attorney Thomas Shriver moved to have Bill Allen arraigned on a first-degree murder charge stemming from the death of police officer Pete Johnson. He filed the charges after it appeared the convicted murderer had a chance for executive clemency.

The appointment of Sumter Camp as defense counsel was a blessing for Bill Allen. The thirty-three-year-old lawyer believed strongly in civil rights and was a bright courtroom tactician respected by his peers and Davidson County judges. A man with unbridled enthusiasm, Camp studied the circumstances surrounding the case, noticed a lot of presumed facts that did not add up, and launched a strong effort on behalf of Allen.

Camp immediately challenged the indictment of Bill Allen on grounds of double jeopardy and of the amount of time that had elapsed. His efforts were unfruitful, and in October 1987, Allen and Camp considered dropping the appeal process. The convicted murderer was anxious to return to court to tell his side of the story, but he finally decided to keep appealing in an effort to buy valuable time to prepare a more solid defense.

Allen also kept hoping that financial help would materialize. Not only were his wife and family living on the barest of means, he didn't have enough money to pay transportation for the character witnesses who wanted to travel from Maryland, Texas, and Florida to testify for him on his behalf at the trial.

Legal maneuvering became more complicated during summer 1987 when Herron was allowed to make an interesting plea and the final fugitive on escape, Steve Parker, was apprehended.

Herron pled guilty to two counts of voluntary manslaughter, as John Alexander had done in 1971, and was given a two-year sentence. Because most of that time had already been served since his apprehension in Jacksonville, Herron was also charged with interstate flight, the first such case of its kind heard in the Nashville district of federal court. His first trial ended with a hung jury, with

214 ──────────────────────────────── On the Run

only one juror holding out in his favor, so he decided against a retrial. Herron pled guilty to interstate flight from Texas to Florida, received a two-year sentence, and was paroled from a federal facility in Terre Haute, Indiana, in January 1988.

The Herron trial for interstate flight shed interesting light on the entire case. The most revealing matter came when U.S. Attorney Joe Brown admitted during his closing argument that Nashville police had been guilty of undue force while dealing with blacks during the 1960s, particularly on the morning after the shooting on Fourteenth Avenue. He pointed out that such physical behavior by law enforcement personnel had been documented on the witness stand, where William Bostic testified that an ignited cigarette lighter had been placed under his testicles. The revelation of excessive force on the part of the police department provided Allen and Camp with a line of defense for the forthcoming murder trial, especially since Allen was prepared to admit that he fired lethal shots from a 30-30 rifle, but only with provocation based on a fear for his life.

As the Herron trial for interstate flight neared its end, the name of Steve Parker began to circulate in legal circles. Outside the courtroom it was stated that the fugitive, whose whereabouts was unknown by most individuals, was ready to return to Nashville to face prison escape charges. Almost two decades of discussion about the case had shown that his involvement in the shooting was too slight to merit the ninety-nine-year sentence that had been handed out in 1968. Two weeks after the Herron trial ended, District Attorney Shriver was asked for an interview in conjunction with this book.

"I'll talk to you in detail after the William Allen case is resolved," Shriver answered. "Who knows, maybe we'll have the other guy [Parker] to prosecute, too."

THIRTY-NINE

In Memphis, agent John Canale, who had enjoyed good fortune during the six months he had been in charge of the case, was putting together a plan to apprehend Steve Parker. He was in almost daily contact with Joe O'Hara in Baltimore.

"I've got a feeling Parker will return to Baltimore," O'Hara told Canale by telephone. "He has too many contacts in this area not to be thinking about it."

"Maybe so," Canale answered. "Hang in there. He ditched his car when he left, but he could come back."

"I'm gonna stick with it," O'Hara agreed. "I've got a hunch, if nothing else."

"Do you know about Herbert Munford?" Canale asked. "I still think he knows something. He was mighty close to them in Atlanta."

"He's clean," O'Hara answered. "So what else have we got? Like, has anything turned up in Houston?"

"Nothing. Except more of the same, information that Allen and Herron were good guys who kept their noses clean."

"Sort of like Canady."

"I guess," Canale replied. "You can bet your ass they're not like most of the fugitives we chase."

Meanwhile, Steve Parker was becoming more despondent. His normally clear mind was crowded with thoughts that came quickly and without order, but one thought kept repeating itself: "Turn yourself in and hope the truth will save you."

"That's what I'll do," Parker told himself as he showered.

"No, I can't," Parker thought as he dressed following the shower.

215

"They won't believe me, not in Nashville. Besides, I've been out here for more than twelve years without getting caught."

"Maybe I better give it up," he then told himself as he crawled into bed that night. "There's no telling what they've learned from Doc and Lee. After what happened to Slim, there's no way to know what they might do to make them spill their guts."

"Hell, Rick, get smart," Parker said to himself as he tossed and turned in bed, using the alias he had come to like. "Doc and Lee won't bail out on you."

Parker was correct, for neither Allen nor Herron was willing to tell FBI interrogators anything they thought would help them find the remaining fugitive. On the other hand, they both underestimated the investigative skills of the agents who had been assigned to the case.

"Joe, I think we've got a break," Canale told O'Hara by telephone. "There's a link between Parker and a female companion."

"Great! Have you got a name?"

"Yeah. And what's even better, it looks like she's in your city. Long-distance telephone records indicate some contact."

"Let's have it," O'Hara exclaimed while reaching for his pen. "It looks like we're finally getting a fair chance to do some real police work on this case."

"Uh huh," Canale agreed. "And it looks as if Joe O'Hara gets to have most of the fun."

Actually, O'Hara and other FBI agents in Baltimore developed headaches and holes in the soles of their shoes during the next month. They tirelessly combed the streets trying to find Joan Kelly. Finally, on a tip from a neighbor, they zeroed in on her apartment.

After observing the apartment for several weeks, they saw a man who at a distance resembled Parker. O'Hara and three other agents approached the front entrance on a July evening, stopping just short of an open door and glancing at one another before stepping inside.

"Don't anybody move," O'Hara told the two couples standing inside the apartment. "Let's stay calm."

"What's this about?" one of the men asked.

"I'm Joe O'Hara of the FBI," O'Hara said as he pulled identification from his coat pocket. "We're looking for Steve Parker."

"Who's that?"

"Who are you?" O'Hara asked as he pointed at the man who had first spoken. He resembled Parker, down to a closely trimmed beard.

"I'm not him. I'm afraid you've made a big mistake."

"OK," O'Hara admitted. "But I don't guess any of you would mind answering a few questions."

Parker was not in the apartment that night. However, in questioning the men and women who were there, O'Hara learned some valuable information, especially about a Toyota Parker had been driving in Baltimore.

"I'm not sure what the relationship is just yet, but Joan Kelly and Steve Parker are pals," O'Hara told Canale. "There's more to it than the simple fact he drove her Toyota from Baltimore to Philadelphia in early April."

"It certainly looks that way," Canale agreed. "One of the aliases listed on his Identification Order form is Damon. She has a son by that name."

"Yep," O'Hara said. "We might have muffed the raid on her house. But in time we'll find there's a connection."

As summer turned to fall in 1986, Parker remained in Philadelphia, almost daily studying his dwindling bank account. He agonized over being away from Goodman and his children, who remained in Baltimore, and he was frustrated because although he wanted to work, he was afraid he would be identified if he attempted to find employment. So after living as a fugitive free of crime, he began selling marijuana on a small scale and, to a much larger extent, various forms of drug paraphernalia.

"You seem to have the contacts to get me some good deals," the owner of a head shop said, as he presented a deal to Parker. "Why don't you make some money while saving me some?"

"I don't know about that," Parker answered. "It isn't my kind of environment."

"Get real, Rick," the owner laughed. "You've got connections. After all, you've moved a few nickel bags of grass, right?"

"Yeah, but only when I've been in a financial squeeze. I'm not proud of it."

"OK. So what? I'm offering you a chance to make good cash."

Parker took him up on the offer, stashed away as much money as he could save, and again started thinking about moving to Nigeria. To help along that goal, he decided to begin a mail order business similar to the brass trade he had developed so successfully in Baltimore.

It was a cold winter, to say the least, both for Parker and for the agents chasing him. As for Allen and Herron, they were locked up in Nashville wondering what was going on with their friend and his family.

"Word circulating in Nashville says Parker is thinking about turning himself in," Canale told O'Hara by phone during April 1987.

"Where's it coming from?" O'Hara asked.

"I understand his family contacted a lawyer [Richard Dinkens] to check out a few things [about the social climate in Nashville]," Canale answered. "I've heard he's about ready to give it up, to take his chances in Tennessee."

"Is the Cincinnati office doing any good with his mother? Or his brother in Cleveland?"

"Nope. They're as quiet as everybody seems to be in Baltimore."

"Mmmmm," O'Hara replied.

"So how are you doing with the mystery car caper?" Canale asked.

"That's the main reason I called," O'Hara answered. "I've got a name and an address on the guy who's driving it. I'm going to see him this afternoon."

"Then what?"

"I'm hoping I'll eventually find out that Parker registered the darn thing and obtained a license to drive it. It's obvious the Rick Walker name he's using is just a street alias. He has to be using another name to get whatever documents he needs. He can't survive as a phantom man every place he goes."

O'Hara began making progress when he visited the man driving the automobile.

"All I did was answer a classified ad," he explained. "A lady named Joan Kelly sold it to me."

"I see," O'Hara said. "Can I see the receipt?"

The receipt was signed by Joan Kelly, or so it appeared, but her address was listed as just off Windsor Mill Road on the west side of Baltimore. O'Hara knew the house he had raided about a year earlier was on the east side of the city.

"Are you willing to take me to where you bought the car?" he said.

"Sure."

Their trip added to O'Hara's confusion. The parking lot in which the purchase was made was in front of an apartment complex so large that the owner of the car could not identify the unit in which the woman lived.

O'Hara realized he would have to pursue a different path in his search.

Armed with the date of purchase, he went to the newspaper and requested records of classified ads run near that time. After searching for a day, he discovered the information he was seeking.

The woman who had purchased the classified ad was Joyce Goodman, not Kelly. She had listed her place of residence as the large apartment complex he had just visited. Suddenly, there were two mysterious women linked to the fugitive O'Hara was chasing.

Most of the people O'Hara questioned said they had never heard of Goodman. Others admitted that they had heard of her, but didn't know where she lived.

Finally he struck pay dirt.

"Yeah, man, I know her," said a man who lived in the neighborhood. "She's the school teacher."

"He bought it at a used lot just up the road," the man called Fats told Agent O'Hara.

For the next several days, O'Hara methodically pored through records at the used car dealership. Just before he was about to quit one afternoon, he found a document indicating a man named Ronald Coleman Walker had purchased a 1978 Cadillac.

O'Hara immediately fed the serial number of the car into an FBI computer. Again, he saw the name Ronald Coleman Walker. He fed Walker's name into the computer and learned that Ronald Coleman Walker had a Maryland driver's license, complete with a place of residence, and had been stopped for speeding on Interstate 95 in Delaware.

"My gosh," O'Hara said to himself. "We've either been looking on the wrong side of town or the son of a gun has two places of residence."

O'Hara fed the name Ronald Coleman Walker into law enforcement computers in all fifty states and went home that night weary but anxious to get surveillance under way at another location the next day.

Ultimately, O'Hara and another agent met Goodman face-to-face. She already had heard that a lot of questions were being asked about her relationship with Parker when he encountered her at her home.

"Miss Goodman," O'Hara began, "I assume you know that Rick [Parker] is wanted by the FBI for escape from prison."

"No," Goodman answered. "That can't be."

"Ah, come on, lady," said the other agent. "You're not coming clean with us."

"Frankly, I'm shocked," Goodman replied. "I'm a little shaken by this."

"Yes, ma'am," O'Hara agreed. "We'll give you some time to regain your composure."

It was not long before O'Hara and another agent returned to visit

Goodman. By then, they were more sure of her relationship to Parker. Still, she told them nothing of consequence, knowing all the while that the time the father of her children would remain free was becoming shorter by the moment.

"Miss Goodman, can I take a look at the contents of that envelope?" O'Hara asked after noticing an envelope with "Rick" written on it sitting on a table.

"Yes."

Inside the envelope was a note that said, in essence, "I miss not seeing you for such a long time. Get in touch." It was signed by a person named Fats. Under the signature was a telephone number.

O'Hara was quick to call the number, and equally fast in getting together with the man named Fats. He told them Parker had once dated his deceased sister in New York and at one time had driven an older model Cadillac.

FORTY

Steve Parker was feeling chipper on the morning of June 21, 1987. He was en route from Philadelphia to Baltimore, even though he had heard that the FBI was asking a lot of questions about him in his neighborhood. The urge to see Joyce Goodman and his son and daughter was too strong for him to worry about how dangerous it was to be going home.

He planned to stop off in Maryland for a couple of days along the way to Virginia, where he planned to open a post office box in the name of Rick Walker and to check out the possibility of beginning a mail order business.

"If they catch me, so what?" Parker told himself as he drove along the interstate. "I'm tired. And innocent, too. So maybe it won't be that bad to go back to Tennessee and take my chances."

Parker was taking a chance, for sure, in returning to Baltimore. Under the direction of FBI agent Joe O'Hara, the house Goodman and her children were living in was under periodic drive-past surveillance.

"I'm telling you, John, if this isn't it, it might not happen for us," O'Hara told John Canale by telephone on June 24.

"So he's back in town?"

"That's what his neighbors are saying," O'Hara answered. "It came out of the blue. Boom. A telephone call: 'Mr. O'Hara, I just saw Rick Walker drive past my house in a big Oldsmobile.'"

"I'll be damned," Canale laughed. "He's not nearly as smart as I thought he was."

The next afternoon, Parker drove back into Baltimore, arriving at

221

about 4:00 P.M., about the time O'Hara and several other FBI agents took shooting practice at the local range. "Keep driving until after 5:00 P.M. before going to the apartment," he told himself. "Even FBI agents stop working at that time of day."

But Parker was wrong. He also miscalculated the special sense an FBI agent develops through experience.

At 4:40 P.M. he stopped at a fast-food restaurant and purchased a fish sandwich and a soft drink.

At 4:45 P.M. FBI agent Tom Moore, who had been driving past Goodman's residence off and on during the day, decided to take one more look before heading to his office.

At 4:50 P.M. Parker stopped at an intersection not far from his house, waited for traffic to clear, and turned toward a nearby park where he planned to eat. What he did not realize was that Moore was in an unmarked automobile opposite him near the intersection.

"Well, I'll be damned," Moore said as he drove past the Oldsmobile and began looking for a place to turn around. "That looks like our man."

As Moore turned around his automobile, with Parker still in sight, he reached for the radio in the glove compartment. "I've got a look-alike on Steve Parker, IO fugitive," he announced before stating his location and requesting backups.

After Parker drove down a side street and stopped at the edge of the park, Moore took another look at him and concluded he was indeed the wanted fugitive. He anxiously awaited the arrival of other agents.

The wait was short. Moore was joined on the scene by FBI agents Mike Garrett, Jerry Dougher, Greg Tessier, Sam Wichner, and Roger Kuhleman.

Parker was jittery when he got out of his automobile and stood beside it eating the fish sandwich and drinking the soft drink. His nervousness grew when he glanced over his shoulder and saw six automobiles converging on him. He took a gulp and began walking in the direction of the park. His second glance at the agents, who by now were out of their automobiles and only a few yards from him, told him the high-powered rifles in their hands were proof he had nowhere left to run and hide.

"Hold it, pal," Moore called as Parker walked away from them ever so slowly. "Don't panic. Don't get yourself killed."

Parker stopped in his tracks.

"If you've got a gun on you, Steve, let us have it."

Parker was confused by the name they had used. He had used his alias so long he thought of himself as Rick Walker, not Steve Parker.

But he understood the command and answered, "I've never carried a gun."

"Are you Steve Parker?"

Parker stood silently. Again, the name did not connect.

"What?" he asked, confused. "I'm Rick. Now tell me which one of you is Joe O'Hara?"

Another agent produced a wanted poster with Parker's picture on it as the other agents stood with their rifles trained on the wanted man.

"Let me see that," Parker asked.

He took a look at the wanted poster, and it all came back to him with a jolt. "Oh, my goodness. Yes. I am Steve Parker."

Parker was read his rights, then he was placed in an automobile and transported to FBI headquarters, where he was questioned by various agents as they awaited the arrival of O'Hara. In talking with several agents, he learned that the surveillance on his house had been going to last for only five more days. The atmosphere was so warm he drew a chuckle from the men who had arrested him when he attempted to telephone his brother, Daryl Parker, to tell him he was in custody.

"Hello," said an agent monitoring the call. "Who is this?"

Steve Parker smiled and said, "I'm Steve. I'm under arrest. Now, who in the hell is this?"

"This is FBI headquarters, buddy."

"I know. I'm in the building with you."

Steve Parker answered the telephone when it rang a few minutes later.

"Hello, this is O'Hara. Who is this?"

"Joe, it's Steve Parker, the guy you've been chasing."

O'Hara laughed, playing along with what he perceived to be a joke.

"I'm not kidding," Parker answered. "They've got me. So, Joe, when are you coming down?"

"I'm on my way."

O'Hara's interview with Parker was not as lengthy or as formal as the one he had staged a little more than fourteen months earlier with Ralph Canady. The case was closed, at least from the FBI's standpoint. There was no need to secure information for an ongoing manhunt. In fact, there was some back-slapping and hand-shaking among agents as they celebrated the conclusion of a historic mission. The FBI had tracked him for more than thirteen years, making him one of the more famous fugitives ever to be on its Identification Order list, also a leader in time spent on the run.

Knowing that Parker's involvement in the Nashville shooting had long since been considered slight, if not downright accidental, one of the agents made an interesting telephone call.

"Is this Daryl Parker, younger brother of Steve Parker?" he asked when the call was answered.

"Yes, it is."

"Well, sir, your brother has a lot of problems, obviously, and there's no need for them to be compounded," the agent said. "We're willing to let you go through his apartment in Philadelphia and remove all you want to before we have somebody up there take a look for us."

"I'm sure there's nothing there to hide," Daryl Parker replied. "But I'll take a look. And I appreciate that."

"Well, all we ask is that you turn over any weapons to us," the agent concluded.

"There won't be any there," Daryl replied. "Steve doesn't fool around with guns. He wouldn't have one."

No weapons were found in the apartment, nor was anything else that would add intrigue to the case.

As that telephone conversation was being conducted, Steve Parker was at the Baltimore Police Department Woodlawn Detention Center in the same cell in which Canady had hanged himself. Parker had heard that his friend had a broken arm when he was buried, and this had heightened his suspicion that he had been killed instead of committing suicide. So he carefully examined the surroundings.

Long after his extradition to Tennessee, where he was awaiting another murder trial, Steve Parker related in February 1988 many questions he had about that death:

When I was in that holding cell, on a Thursday night, there were six or eight other prisoners there. Ralph was in there on a Tuesday night, last seen alive at about 3:00 A.M. I'd imagine other prisoners were there with him, or else they chose to transport them out of there at a weird hour. Why would he have been left alone in there when my fellow prisoners were with me all night?

There were at least six police officers working in the precinct the night I was there, including two women. It was a long and narrow holding cell with small individual cells, more like cubicles, off from it. Every thirty minutes or so, never more than an hour, one of the police officers would stick his head in the door and take a head count. He'd holler, and we'd stick out our heads from the smaller cells. He'd make the head count, then leave. How could Ralph have killed himself if that had happened when he was there?

There was a telephone on the wall at the end of the holding cell. I know that because I was on it almost all night. All you had to do is punch zero and make a collect call. I kept it occupied because I didn't want my family to learn about my arrest from anybody except me. Now, I've never been one to talk as much as Ralph did. In fact, he was on the telephone a lot to his mother because he knew she was worried about him while we were being hunted. But there were no records of Ralph placing a single call that entire night, when I know he would have had he been in that holding cell.

So, I don't think he was in there all night. Do you suppose they took him out of there, got too rough with him during their interrogation because they were emotional after hearing he had been convicted of killing a police officer, and hurt him too much, like the broken arm, then made it look like he hung himself with his shirt?

Steve Parker was reminded that the death certificate said it was a death by hanging, a suicide, and that doubts were just conjecture. He also was reminded that Canady has specifically asked O'Hara when he would be back to get him for another interview, that he had been told about 8:30 A.M., only thirty minutes after he was discovered.

"I'm aware of that," Parker answered. "But I knew Ralph well, good enough to know he wasn't suicidal. And I'm telling you what I saw in that same holding cell, including some loud and tough police officers, makes me think there are a lot of unanswered questions that should be asked and never have been."

FBI agent O'Hara sent a teletype advising personnel in Memphis and Washington that Parker had been apprehended. Canale was relayed the information by telephone.

"John, they got Parker today in Baltimore," agent Joe Bonner told him.

"Good," Canale replied. "Then I'll have a good night's sleep."

The mood at FBI headquarters was even more stoic. A terse teletype was issued to offices nationwide: "At approximately 4:50 P.M. on June 25, Steve Parker, IO fugitive, apprehended and positively identified in Baltimore. In custody at Woodlawn Detention Center. Discontinue investigation."

The apprehension of Steve Parker brought to its close a manhunt that had lasted nineteen years and six months. Finally all five men involved in the shooting were under control.

Canady was dead.

Alexander was free after parole.

Herron was serving a soft prison sentence, in comparison with those meted in December 1968.

Bill Allen and Parker were incarcerated and awaiting another murder trial.

Parker had public sentiment on his side. It had become apparent that he was not even near a gun when the shooting took place, and a juror from the 1968 trial, Mary Hall, was shaken upon hearing he was back in prison and awaiting another trial. When told what the fugitives had done while on escape from prison and the lifestyles they had developed and maintained, she replied, "That doesn't surprise me. They seemed like nice young men."

Davidson County district attorney Tom Shriver began working out a deal with defense lawyer Robert Smith. Shriver's "deal" would not double the sentence Parker was already serving and might help him secure executive clemency.

The scenario behind closed doors as reported by Smith pointed out how determined Shriver was to keep Bill Allen in prison.

First, Smith said, the district attorney told him he would allow Parker to plead guilty to voluntary manslaughter (for Pete Johnson's death), with his sentence running concurrently with the ninety-nine years he was serving for first-degree murder in the death of Wayne Thomasson. This offer would only be good, however, if he would testify to what Shriver believed had happened: that Allen ambushed the slain men. Smith said that Shriver told him that Parker, Herron, and Alexander had run from the scene while Allen and Canady hid and waited to shoot Johnson and Thomasson.

When the deal was explained, Parker refused it. "I told you that's not how it happened," Parker told Smith and again insisted that he had been telling the truth since four days after the shooting.

"Well, Shriver said it happened the other way."

"You tell him [Shriver] I'm willing to take a polygraph test," Parker told Smith. "Will he take one?"

Smith said that when he told Shriver Parker's reaction, Shriver insisted that the officers had been ambushed and that if Parker told the truth he would testify to that fact.

Undaunted, Smith petitioned Shriver to give Parker a deal that would allow him to testify in court about the truth as he perceived it. In exchange, the district attorney was asked to let a voluntary manslaughter sentence in the death of Johnson run concurrently with the first-degree murder sentence in the death of Thomasson. Shriver would then endorse an executive clemency plea on behalf of his defendant.

"I've never done that," Shriver said, indicating that he would not take part in such a deal.

Then Shriver was appointed to a judgeship, a move that turned over the prosecution in the case to the new Davidson County district attorney, Torry Johnson.

With the appeals process going nowhere, Allen was anxious to get to court. He was impatient, in fact, when in January he was told his second first-degree murder trial might not take place until fall 1988. Defense lawyer Camp and district attorney Johnson welcomed the delay.

Then the general public had reason to get itself into another emotional upheaval.

When Herron was released from prison on January 25, 1988, a Nashville television station sent a film crew to Terre Haute, Indiana. Later, it showed the former fugitive who had been at the top of the FBI's Most Wanted list longer than anybody else boarding a bus for Cincinnati as a free man. The newscast also included the controversial tape recordings of the police department radio transmissions of Thomasson and Johnson just before and after they had been shot in 1968. Adding to the drama, three principal figures in the television newscast made interesting statements.

The news reporter heard Thomasson proclaim that he had been shot three times, then injected that in reality the police officer had been shot six times.

Nashville police chief Joe Casey was told Herron planned to write a book about his life. "That's just great," Casey said. "And he'll probably get rich from it, when the families of those two police officers haven't had them around the last twenty years to take care of them."

Shriver was asked to explain why Herron was not tried for first-degree murder, as were Allen, Parker, and Canady. He said there were not enough witnesses available to prosecute him. He added that it was apparent Herron was not a trigger man in the shooting, as had been the case with Alexander in 1971.

So with Parker seemingly near some kind of plea bargain, Bill Allen was left alone on the hotseat, but he was not unduly concerned by the heat. To the contrary, he was anxious to return to court with a new jury seated, to tell the truth about what had happened.

Allen was waiting to launch an offensive defense. Assisted by his wife, he did not wait until his trial to do it.

FORTY-ONE

"I've been on the defensive for twenty years," Bill Allen
said at the Tennessee State Penitentiary in December
1987. "It's time to become the aggressor." He was reacting to a
question about a civil lawsuit.

"My civil rights were violated in the 1960s," Allen said. "So were
those of a lot of other blacks. So I'm filing a lawsuit just to create
awareness."

The lawsuit, which listed many principal figures in Nashville history as "Metro Conspirators" in the case, therefore making them
defendants, was filed in February by Ann Allen, leader of the Coalition for the Freedom of Allen. The papers she filed with a clerk in
United States District Court, under title 42 U.S.C.S., 1988, asked
for ten million dollars in punitive damages and five dollars in com-
pensatory damages.

William G. Allen was listed as the plaintiff.

Why did Allen file the lawsuit several months before he was to go
on trial again?

"Because I want to draw attention to what happened before the
trial in 1968," Allen said. "I hope that it'll help ensure me of a fairer
trial this time. I'm hoping, really knowing, there are other individuals who also had their civil rights violated during that time frame.
Some of them might want to come forward and take part in this
lawsuit."

In his letter to U.S. district attorney Joe Brown, Allen said:

> I am requesting that the U.S. Attorney's Office conduct an
> investigation into this matter as to the violation of civil rights,
> under [color of law], by the named group attached, and that they

did so with a conspiratorial alliance against me and others accused with me as to the murder of the two police officers. Information is now available that will substantiate this conspiracy and the conspirators' action to violate my civil rights. As to its value as evidence, only your office can determine that in its legal context.

As Allen filed his civil case, Steve Parker stood beside him at the penitentiary as a scheduled co-defendant in the awaited first-degree murder trial for the death of police officer Pete Johnson. He chose not to file a lawsuit of his own but endorsed the one that was filed.

Meanwhile, Ann Allen wrote a two-page letter of explanation to supporters of the Coalition for the Freedom of Allen, which previously had been named the Coalition for the Freedom of Herron and Allen.

The letter read, in part:

Twenty years ago, because of racial strife and attitudes, many injustices occurred, and this is one we seek to right.

In final analysis, this suit is not about money. Should any ever be realized from this suit, the proof will show there are ample victims that should share it. We welcome any people that wish to step forward and join this suit as victims of the conspiracy. This suit is about brutality and deprivation of basic civil rights of black people in general and Bill Allen and those associated with him in particular. It's about ridding this growing city of this ugly "good old boy network," at least exposing it once and for all [for all the people of this city, regardless of race, religion or economic background].

Former homicide detective Mickey McDaniels, who left the department to work for the Davidson County district attorney as a chief investigator until 1985, might have had that in mind on February 9, 1988. As the man in charge of homicide detectives in 1968, he was asked for an interview. "I don't have anything to say about that case," McDaniels said by telephone. When asked why, he answered, "Because it's all out in the open now."

That ended the conversation.

It came only fifteen minutes before Shriver was met for a face-to-face conversation in his chambers at the Davidson County Courthouse. It was to be a social call only, a meeting of the eyes after several telephone conversations. A forty-minute discussion ensued.

"I don't think I should comment on the case until it's resolved,"

Judge Shriver said. "Besides, it wouldn't be smart to talk about a case in which I've got a lawsuit filed against me."

Then Judge Shriver talked in general terms about the case, leaving the impression that he was not at all as vigorous as his actions had shown, nor as ruthless as things said about him in the past had indicated. Instead, he sounded like a fair-minded man who had only done his job diligently on behalf of the state. When told the Parker case seemed to be tragic, he said, "That might be true. He might've just been there." Then he said it was a perplexing thing to him that "seemingly intelligent men got involved in such a situation." He admitted that at one time he had thought about writing a book about the case because of its social significance, "what was going on in Nashville at the time, the civil rights movement that caused so much disharmony."

Judge Shriver sounded as if he had several questions in his mind, as well as a smattering of doubt about the case he had presented in court. He also said the litigation remaining against Allen and Parker "might be settled out of court."

Judge Shriver had no way of knowing Allen was anxious to ride it out, that he wanted to tell his story about what happened on January 16, 1968, and that Parker was more than willing to stand beside his friend every step of the way.

After that meeting, as well as one the following day with police major Robert Titsworth, it was worth contemplating whether Judge Shriver had been used by some Nashville police officers in 1968 when he was a youthful and energetic district attorney.

Could it be that he had been fed faulty information, such as the belated appearances of star witnesses Johnny Brown and Larry Wade, one of whom later said he was coerced into testifying? I asked this question of Major Titsworth.

"I didn't know what was going on upstairs with the investigation," Titsworth recalled. "The detectives sort of pushed the rest of us out of the way. It was like they didn't want us around. They worked upstairs. Those of us downstairs didn't know what they were doing.

"That hurt me for a long time because I felt like I had lost two members of my family when Wayne [Thomasson] and Pete [Johnson] got killed. I didn't testify in court when some other police officers did because nobody asked me to. I've wondered why, because you'd think they would've thought I knew something about the case. You'll remember I was one of the first [police officers] on the scene after the shooting. But nobody ever asked me anything about the case. Have you asked Tom Shriver why I wasn't asked to testify?"

Since Titsworth was not asked to testify in 1968, it was doubtful he would be asked to do so in the next murder trial. "I'd imagine the next trial will be similar to the first one, if there is another trial," district attorney Torry Johnson said during the summer of 1988. "I'm not totally familiar with the case at this stage, but it's logical to assume we'll present the same proof."

So as the months of 1988 moved forward, with all appeals exhausted, the murder case floated in space without direction. It had been returned to Fifth Circuit Court for trial by the Tennessee Supreme Court, but no court date had been established.

"I'm not sure if the state plans to prosecute Steve Parker, but I'm sure it'll prosecute Bill Allen," defense lawyer Sumter Camp said in September. He had been asked if he thought the district attorney was trying to decide whether to pursue the matter after Bill Allen had filed a civil rights lawsuit in federal court. "It's about time to find out when we're going to court."

Adding to the uncertainty was a professional move by Camp, who on September 12 joined the Federal Public Defender's office in Nashville.

"I'm making the move, but I'm taking your case with me," Camp told Allen on a visit to the prison. "I've got too much time invested in this case to leave it behind at this point."

"I'm happy to hear that, Sumter," Allen said with a smile. "So when do we go to trial?"

"That's a good question," Camp answered. "I've asked about the case. I've been told that it'll be put on the docket soon, maybe as early as December or January."

"That'll be twenty-one years after that night," Allen noted.

When Ann Allen made public the claim that her husband was making in a fifteen million dollar civil rights lawsuit against many of the better known public officials in Nashville, she was armed with a collection of newspaper clippings that indicated the alleged improprieties from 1968 were still happening in 1988.

Most of the articles she carried with her were centered around the death of a twenty-year-old black man named Cedric Overton, who was killed by a police officer in February 1973.

Her husband also remembered the case. Many times since his recapture in June 1986, he had said, "You're aware of the Overton case, aren't you? Well, what happened with us in 1968 isn't much different."

There was some difference, however. A police officer shot and killed a black man in 1973, while a black man had shot and killed two police officers in 1968.

Fear had been the motive in both shootings, but the police officer was fined ten dollars, whereas Bill Allen had been sentenced to ninety-nine years in prison, as were Steve Parker and Ralph Canady. Moreover, the police officers Bill Allen shot and killed were armed, while Overton, whom police officer Jackie Pyle shot four times and killed with a service revolver, was not armed, but was erroneously thought to be.

Pyle was on patrol with his partner, police officer Michael Brown, in South Nashville when they saw Overton standing beside a parked automobile at 123 Crenshaw Street. Brown pulled the police cruiser to the side of the black man, and Pyle began asking questions.

"Is this your car?"

"No," Overton replied while standing with both of his hands in his jacket pockets.

"Whose is it?"

"It belongs to my friend."

"Where's the owner?"

"Inside his house," Overton answered, while motioning with his head toward the dwelling his friend had reentered to fetch the automobile keys.

Brown started to get out of the cruiser to take a closer look at Overton. Pyle pulled his service revolver and pointed it at the black man.

"Take your hands out of your pockets."

Overton removed one of his hands.

"Both of them," Pyle said.

When Overton removed his other hand, he turned slightly toward his left. It was then that Pyle shot the black man four times.

Pyle contended that Overton was armed. When investigating police officers arrived, they discovered the black man was unarmed, so one of them dropped a knife beside him to make it look as if Pyle had had good reason to kill him.

Four police officers were suspended in the case. Pyle was terminated, then charged with manslaughter.

A jury of eleven whites and one black convicted Pyle, but for assault and battery, not manslaughter. After he was found guilty, Davidson County criminal court judge John Draper fined him ten dollars. He could have sentenced him to almost a year in the county workhouse.

FORTY-TWO

Sumter Camp arrived at the Tennessee State Penitentiary with the intention of asking Bill Allen to think about the consequences of filing another paper in his fifteen-million-dollar civil rights lawsuit.

U.S. Attorney Joe Brown had requested specific claims from Allen after he filed the lawsuit in February. In a twenty-three-page disclosure report notarized at the prison on March 7, 1988, replete with nineteen items of evidence in support of his disclosure, the prisoner provided those claims, in the process stating his feelings about the investigation and trial. To the chagrin of Camp, Allen tipped his hand about the defense he would present during the upcoming trial.

Since the papers had not been served on the defendants in the lawsuit Camp was hoping to stop the procedure when he visited the prison on March 16.

"I'm not concerned about the spirit of the filing," Camp told Allen. "You and I know most of those things happened and can be proved. What I'm concerned about is the publicity it might prompt."

"I want it out in the open," Allen declared. "That's why I've filed it. Again, it isn't about money. It's about my civil rights and the civil rights of others."

"I don't think you see my point," Camp continued. "I'm afraid the news media will use this to paint a negative image of you, to portray you as a radical, exactly like it did before the last trial. You and I know that's not what you are. But the general public, which includes prospective jurors, might not see you for what you are. I don't think it's wise to take such a chance during the pretrial process.

"Also, it's the kind of ammunition the district attorney can use in court. He can bring it up when you get on the witness stand, hammer you about it, attempt to portray you as a militant type who's attempting to cause trouble. It's not you. It's not the image we want jurors to see in that courtroom."

Allen thought for a few seconds, then answered, "But if we put it out in the open, disclose what these people did during a conspiracy in 1968, it'll keep it from happening again. They'll be careful to make this trial fair."

Camp quickly responded, "I'm advising against it."

Allen was just as quick in response. "I'm filing it. I don't have anything to hide. They have something to cover up. If it's out in the open, the new district attorney [Torry Johnson] won't play the same type game this time."

Listening to the conversation was Steve Parker, whose plea bargain negotiations with the district attorney had been put on hold because of his unwillingness to testify against Allen. He also favored the filing of the lawsuit and the serving of the subsequent report, and he expressed a willingness to stand alongside his friend until the case was resolved, even if it meant he would have to face another trial.

"I'm hearing that [former Davidson County district attorney] Tom Shriver admits my involvement in the case might be a tragedy of sorts," Parker said. "But I don't see him telling the new district attorney that. He's holding back on me with the hope that I'll agree to testify against Bill. I'm not changing. I've told the truth since 1968. I'm not lying now. If that's what it takes, I'll go to court again. I'll stand trial. Eventually, the truth has got to win."

Allen raised several points in the "statement of facts" portion of his disclosure report:

■ That his name, which was erroneously listed as Bill Adams, was secured by police officers through coercion, specifically that he became a suspect in the case the night of the shooting after police officers forced a statement from Amelia Howard, who was declared a hostile witness by the prosecution during the trial in 1968.

■ That he did not fit the description of a suspect wanted in connection with the cashing of fraudulent money orders, specifically that he had closely cropped hair, while G. L. Lilley of the police department stated the men seen at Val-Dot Liquor Store had hair over their collars.

■ That the taped recordings of police department transmissions used during the trial in 1968 had fifty-nine minutes of unexplained gaps over an eighty-minute period, specifically that they had been "tampered with" during the time in which a "chase" was supposed to have been taking place. He said Shriver "orchestrated" this activity, also that while doing so he was supported by numerous individuals within the police department. He said the testimonies of various police department representatives during the trial did not correspond with times logged on the taped recordings.

- That the testimonies of Johnny Brown and Larry Wade, high school students, were contradictory during the trial in 1968, also that their versions of what took place on Fourteenth Avenue North were the result of police department representatives coaching them after compiling erroneous reports on what transpired.

- That police department representatives made up reports that he had frequented establishments known for their selling of drugs and sex, as well as for their bookmaking activities, so as to portray him as a shady individual, when in reality he had never gone to any of those places.

- That Judge Raymond Leathers, who presided over the trial in 1968, did not take the necessary precautions during the jury selection process, specifically that he allowed the jury to be selected from a pool that lacked many blacks, also that he coached prosecuting lawyers as they went about the tricky business of questioning prospective jurors who were scheduled to hear a capital offense case.

The disclosure report contained more arguments, plus details that supported every point, which made it obvious that Allen had spent much time in the prison law library researching case histories and many hours in his cell reflecting on the issues that surrounded his situation.

Allen was approaching two years since his apprehension in Jacksonville. He was becoming impatient.

"Don't lose sight of the fact that Steve and I are in prison when we shouldn't be," Allen told Camp.

"That's why I'm here," Camp answered.

Allen nodded and smiled, then allowed the disclosure report to be served on the defendants.

The U.S. Attorney received the report on March 29. It included references to defendants not listed in the filing of the original lawsuit. Foremost among them was W. A. McDaniel, the Mickey McDaniel who had province over the investigation in 1968 and who in 1988 refused to comment about the case.

During early August, a somewhat disappointed Allen received word that a federal magistrate had ruled that a one-year statute of limitations had long since passed, leaving his lawsuit inadmissible in court. Undaunted, the plaintiff challenged that ruling on the grounds that "the conspiracy alleged in the lawsuit is still intact, meaning there is no statute of limitations." That rebuttal led to a review of the case by a federal judge, who on August 22 ordered all the defendants in the lawsuit to file reports of their respective involvements in the case with him no later than September 11.

This ruling by the federal judge prompted action by the Metropolitan Nashville Legal office, which moved to either investigate the merits of the lawsuit or to provide the defendants with grounds for a collective defense. This action was questionable because federal law states that each defendant in such a lawsuit must stand alone in his defense. Thus, a door was opened for a serious conflict of interest provided the civil rights lawsuit advanced to courtroom review. This collective defense ran the risk of having co-defendants point fingers at each other.

On August 31, Camp received a call from a member of the Metro Legal office who asked, "What's the deal with your client, this Bill Allen?"

Then on September 1 another action raised the question whether somebody was trying to hide something. Jean Patterson, the court reporter during the murder trial in 1968, was scheduled to meet with the author of this book for a review of the case. She was told not to take part in such an interview by Judge Tom Shriver, a defendant in the lawsuit, who said, "I don't think we need a book being published with a murder case coming back to trial." Shriver had been told this book was not going to be published until after the next murder trial.

The day after he told Patterson not to discuss the case, Shriver asked Camp to approach his bench during an unrelated legal proceeding in his courtroom. He then inquired about the status of the Allen case.

About seven weeks later, on October 20, the Davidson County district attorney still did not know how to proceed with the charges lodged against Allen and Parker. This came to light when assistant district attorney Steve Dozier appeared at a hearing scheduled to set a date for the trial and announced his office was not ready to declare its intentions, the second such delay in three weeks.

So a meeting was held in chambers occupied by Judge Walter Kurtz, who was to hear the case in Davidson County Fifth Circuit Court. It was attended by Judge Kurtz, Dozier, Camp, and Robert Smith, the court-appointed lawyer representing Parker.

"I assume the defense has moved for a speedy trial in this case," Kurtz said while looking at Dozier. "So what's your intentions? It looks like it'll be early spring before we can hear it as things are now."

"I don't know," Dozier answered. "I haven't been able to discuss it in detail with [district attorney] Torry Johnson. Also, we'd like to discuss it further with Judge Shriver and the police department."

Kurtz was not pleased to hear that.

"Why weren't these men tried for the death of both police officers in 1968?" Kurtz asked while looking at Dozier. The assistant district attorney shrugged his shoulders, declaring he did not have an answer.

"We might be able to show that in court," Smith said to Kurtz, who then looked at Camp.

"I've seen some quotes attributed to Judge Shriver in a Cincinnati newspaper from 1974 that might explain that in part," Camp commented.

"Such as what?" Kurtz asked.

"Well, Officer Johnson was estranged from his wife at the time of his death, and the family didn't want to pursue the case."

"I don't see where that matters," Kurtz commented, "not when there has been a death and charges lodged."

Camp nodded in agreement, smiled, and said, "There could be some more to it."

Then Kurtz made it clear that time was important. He instructed Dozier to have a plan by November 3.

The case was becoming a political football. District Attorney Johnson was not really interested in pursuing the emotional case, since his hands were totally clean, but he understood that the Nashville police department, as well as some in the private sector, wanted action. Again, Dozier indicated the district attorney might be willing to settle the case out of court, then reiterated that his office definitely favored doing that with Parker in exchange for his testimony in Allen's first-degree murder trial.

"I'm not sure I'll go for a deal," Parker said in a jail cell of the courthouse later that day. "I'll tell the truth, and that's all. Frankly, there's no guarantee the state will deal fairly with me in regard to the previous conviction. I don't have any reason to trust them."

When Camp told Allen a deal might be forthcoming, he replied, "I won't plead guilty to anything. I've said that before. I'm still going that way."

While these conversations were taking place, Judge Shriver was conducting court on another floor of the courthouse. He was approached during a recess, in an effort to persuade him to discuss the case before it was resolved. "This is in the interest of fairness," he was told, "because it appears the police department fed you some erroneous information in 1968."

"I don't think anybody should discuss the case," Shriver replied.

The judge was told everybody had been interviewed, with the exception of former chief of detectives Mickey McDaniel and him. He was told some had been honest, and some had been dishonest. When he asked for an example of the erroneous information he had been given, he was told ballistics tests indicated Officer Thomasson had been shot far fewer times than the five, six, or seven advanced during the trial in 1968.

"There were only three empty casings found on the scene," he was told, "and there were live rounds in the rifles when they were found."

"We found more empty casings than that," Shriver insisted, "at least five, maybe more. The investigation was haphazard because a lot of people handled the empty casings."

"Court testimony and the ballistics tests stated otherwise," he was told. Then it was mentioned that the bullet hole in the police cruiser door could have sent fragments into Thomasson's body, making it appear he was shot more times than he actually was.

"That was Johnson's car, not Thomasson's," Shriver replied. When that point was countered the judge became angry.

"It's obvious you think you know more about this case than I," Shriver snapped. "So it's time for you to leave."

In late October, Allen and Parker wrote a letter to Judge Kurtz, asking him to permit them to appear in his courtroom when their cases were being discussed in pretrial hearings. They also questioned whether Shriver should be involved in the case since he was now a judge and no longer the district attorney. On November 3 Judge Kurtz granted their wish, let them in the courtroom, then announced that they would be tried for first-degree murder on April 3.

There was more legal meandering before the trial, most initiated by Allen as a "jailhouse lawyer" of sorts. With all of his other lawsuits going nowhere in the courts, he filed another to block the proposed sale of the Nashville television station that had aired excerpts from the taped recording from 1968. It had been aired on a newscast the day Charles Lee Herron was paroled.

Allen pointed out, rightfully, that the taped recording was supposed to be in the exclusive domain of the Davidson County district attorney, as ordered by a court that feared public disclosure of its contents might influence the upcoming murder trial. He stated in the lawsuit that unfair pretrail publicity was generated by the public disclosure of the taped recording. Nashville authorities, including Judge Shriver, were at a loss when asked to explain how the taped recording fell into the hands of the television station. Allen's reasoning was that the proposed sale of the station could not take place when legal action against it was pending.

"I've thought all along that there are at least two versions of that tape, maybe three or more," Allen said after filing the lawsuit. "I don't know if all of them have been altered, but I know at least one was. We've seen transcriptions that don't match what was said on the tape played in court. Also, the newspaper reports from 1968 that dealt with the contents of the tape, the ones written just after the shooting, include quotes [from the tape] that are vastly different from what was said. It's all part of an ongoing conspiracy that has lasted more than twenty-one years."

On February 21, with the trial about seven weeks away, Parker was approached again about the possibility of pleading guilty to a lesser charge in exchange for his testimony. Again, he declined to do so, much to the disappointment of Smith, who was not encouraged by the prospects of taking his client into court.

Camp, however, was preparing for a hard struggle in front of a jury. He was being assisted by Rich McGee, a former partner when he was with the Lionel Barrett law firm and a shrewd courtroom operator. He fretted that there had not been much money for the investigation, and like everybody else associated with the case, he placed a premium on the selection of a jury. He knew he had to find twelve people who were either familiar with the racial tensions that existed in 1968 or who would be agreeable to being given a history lesson.

FORTY-THREE

A month before Bill Allen and Steve Parker went to trial for the death of Officer Johnson, it became obvious that the jury hearing the unusual case would have a difficult time comprehending its elements.

First, it was determined during a pretrial hearing that some transcribed testimony from the trial in 1968 would be used in the place of six prior witnesses who had died: G. L. Lilley, Ed Beach, and Robert Goodwin from the police department; Davidson County medical examiner Dr. Michael Petrone; St. Charles Liquor Store owner Matt Willard; and North Nashville resident Austin Smith. Also, it was determined that the previous trial would be referred to as a "prior court proceeding" so as not to let jurors know that Allen and Parker had been convicted almost twenty-one years earlier of first-degree murder in the death of Officer Thomasson.

Second, it was determined by Judge Kurtz that the jury would be sequestered throughout the trial and that he would keep court in session six days per week from 8:30 A.M. until 8:00 P.M. to complete the case as quickly as possible. At the request of Camp, it was agreed that prospective jurors would be questioned individually as to their prior knowledge of the events surrounding the shooting.

"I don't know why you're so adamant about that," Judge Kurtz told Camp. "You're acting like this case is the hottest thing to come down the pike. I don't think the interest in it is as significant as you think."

Judge Kurtz would have been surprised had he followed Camp, Smith, and Dozier out of his chambers that day. They found several television reporters waiting for them. Camp and Smith refused to answer questions, citing a professional ethics code that prohibits

240

such exposure just before a trial. Dozier talked to a reporter from Channel 2 in Nashville, which proceeded to produce a newscast that featured his comments, an interview with Chief Joe Casey, footage that showed the state prison, and commentary that for the most part told only one side of the story.

"We've got to show our support for the police department," said Dozier, whose father is a police officer, when he was asked why such proceedings were taking place more than twenty-one years after the shooting.

"They even had a comment when they showed the prison that went something like, 'Don't worry, folks, they're in there and they're not going to get out,'" Allen said the next day.

"And Joe Casey said we could be paroled in twenty-one years and they weren't going to let that happen," Parker said with a shake of his head. "They aren't being fair with the publicity on this case."

"They never have been," Allen replied. "But I'll admit those newscasts were more even-handed than some I've heard lately. If they'd only try to find somebody who could express our point of view, it'd be more fair."

Hearing all of this at the prison that afternoon but saying nothing was Camp, who was more concerned about securing an impartial jury for his client and Parker. He knew an ideal panel would consist of whites and blacks and men and women between ages thirty-five to fifty-five, people who could relate to the racial climate in Nashville in 1968.

"But it's a fact that Nashville is only twenty-five percent or so black, so that's improbable," Camp said. "With the district attorney having eight strikes, four per client, and the defense having sixteen strikes, eight per client, there's a chance we'll have an all-white jury again."

"We need somebody as fair and strong as Mrs. [Mary] Hall was in 1968," Parker said. "Only we need another like her to keep the other jurors from strong-arming her like those men did during the first trial."

At that point it was suggested a fairer trial might be found in another city. "We can't do that because we've got to have people on the jury who were at least aware of the racial tensions that existed [in Nashville] in 1968," Camp said.

It was revealed to Camp that Dozier and a special investigator for the district attorney had visited Johnny Brown, the "eyewitness" from 1968 who in a signed affidavit had said he was coerced into testifying as he did by Nashville police. The prosecution was having trouble finding his friend, Larry Wade, who also testified that he saw the shooting incident.

In addition, Camp also learned that John Alexander, who was involved in the shooting in 1968 but was not captured until 1971, was afraid to return to Nashville to testify in the trial. He had been forced to travel to Tennessee to be a witness in the Charles Lee Herron interstate flight trial. "I'm sure they'll have to arrest John again to get him back down here," Allen said. "As for Lee [Herron], he's in Houston and willing to testify if asked."

"Hey, aren't you representing Bill Allen and Steve Parker?" a Department of Corrections guard said to Camp at the prison that day.

"I'm representing Allen," Camp said. "Another lawyer is representing Parker."

"Well," said the guard, "I hope you have good luck with the case. I hope they both do OK in court."

The guard was not the first to express such sentiments—about a dozen had over the two previous years—nor was he the last. Five minutes later, another guard expressed similar feelings about the case.

But they would not be jurors.

"Mr. Camp, did you have something to add?" Judge Walter Kurtz asked defense lawyer Sumter Camp about an hour into a pretrial motions hearing in Davidson County Fifth Circuit Court on March 23, less than two weeks before the start of the second first-degree murder trial for Allen and Parker.

"Yes, your honor," Camp said after Judge Kurtz ruled in favor of the prosecution on a motion. "If it pleases the court, I want to make sure the state doesn't get to have its cake and eat it, too."

"Oh, Mr. Camp," Judge Kurtz replied with a smile, "I don't think you have to worry about that. I'd say the state is going to eat this piece, though. I don't know about all the cake. I sort of doubt it."

That kind of debate went on for almost three hours, with Kurtz; Allen and his lawyer, Camp; Parker and his lawyer, Robert Smith; Davidson County assistant district attorney Steve Dozier; court clerk Barbara Wise; a court reporter; two court officers; and a few observers watching the proceedings. When it was recessed for a week, to be continued in chambers, one conclusion could be made: Judge Kurtz was going to conduct a fair trial. For many reasons— beyond the fact that the judge had nice things to say about the Student Non-Violent Coordinating Committee and its role "integrating lunch counters during the 1960s"—it was clear the defense had the best of it, especially to those who knew what Camp was planning to do during the trial.

"It was a good day in the courtroom," Camp commented after the motions hearing as he ate a bowl of chips with a soft drink. "It's hard to tell where it'll go from here, but Judge Kurtz definitely asked the right questions about the case, the same ones that I've wanted answered all along."

Judge Kurtz, who had only recently started brushing up on the case, definitely had asked some pertinent questions.

"Was there anything in the record that shows why the slain police officers [Pete Johnson and Wayne Thomasson] were following the car?" Kurtz had asked Dozier.

"No sir."

Later, Camp argued that the fraudulent money order scheme advanced by the prosecution during the trial in 1968 should not be used in the upcoming trial. There was no evidence linking it to the defendants, and another car had been under surveillance in respect to that unrelated crime. Judge Kurtz then asked two more revealing questions.

"Then there's no connection to the money orders and the men in the Plymouth that night?"

"Blank money orders were found in the car at the scene of the crime," Dozier replied in debate of the point.

"Isn't it clear in the court testimony [from 1968] that the police knew nothing about the Plymouth before that? Why did Officer Johnson follow the car?"

"It came from the same location as the other car, the red Ford under surveillance," Dozier replied.

"So why is all this other stuff about money orders [and the Plymouth] involved?" Judge Kurtz asked. "There's no proof that affirms Officer Johnson knew that, is there?"

"No sir," Dozier admitted. "But it [the lack of testimony about the money order scheme] puts the state under a heavy burden to prove why the police officers stopped the car. It looks like they are stopping people for no reason."

"So tell me why they stopped the Plymouth."

Dozier offered no reply.

Later, Dozier said, "There was testimony, your honor, by a police officer [in 1968] who said he put out a report on a light-colored car with Ohio license plates earlier that afternoon, between 1:00 P.M. and 2:00 P.M."

Then under questioning by Judge Kurtz, the assistant district attorney said he had been unable to find such reference to the Plymouth while listening to the tape.

"Is the [police department dispatch] tape available?" Judge Kurtz asked.

Camp pointed out that he had noticed differences in a copy of the tape in his possession, various transcriptions of the tape, and the tape used in court in 1968. Also, he wondered aloud how a copy of the tape landed in the possession of a local television station when it was supposed to be the sole property of the district attorney.

"How did Channel 4 get the tape?" Judge Kurtz asked. Then, with a sigh, he said, "I'm instructing the state to provide me with the tape and an accurate transcript of it by next Thursday so I can study it over the weekend [just before the start of the trial]."

So two major issues from the trial in 1968—the fraudulent money order/ambush theory and the emotional police department taped recording featuring a wounded Thomasson—were being questioned by Judge Kurtz.

Judge Kurtz was in a quandary, not just because he had cause to wonder about the proof offered in regard to the money orders and the validity of the taped recordings. The 1968 convictions had been upheld in 1970 by the Court of Criminal Appeals.

"Even if I agree with you on the money order matter, Mr. Camp, I've got a problem because I'm supposed to follow this decision," Judge Kurtz said while displaying a Court of Criminal Appeals report from 1970. Then Judge Kurtz said he wanted to study the issue in greater detail before making a final ruling. He wanted to be sure the Court of Criminal Appeals had ruled specifically in regard to the money order scheme as a related crime and had not merely upheld a theory offered by the state. He said he would announce his decision on the money orders being used by the state as evidence at a later date.

Camp scored another victory during a pretrial motions hearing that dealt with unavailable witnesses. Dozier declared eyewitness Larry Wade unavailable, after pointing out that the police department had been unable to locate him, then asked Judge Kurtz for permission to introduce his testimony in the 1968 trial as evidence in the upcoming trial. In response, Camp, who had talked to both Wade and Johnny Brown, petitioned Judge Kurtz for another ruling.

"If it pleases your honor, if there are two witnesses who saw basically the same thing, we should use the testimony of the one who is available," Camp said. "That would be Johnny Brown."

Judge Kurtz agreed. He ruled that Brown would testify, if called to the witness stand, and the state could use the transcript of the testimony offered in 1968 by Wade only if it showed a reason it was needed.

Dozier knew that Brown was telling a different story in 1989 from 1968. This put him in the position of possibly having to use a star witness for the prosecution from the first trial who could become a strong witness for the defense during the next trial.

"It'll be interesting to see if the state calls Johnny Brown," Camp said. "Then it'll be interesting to see if Brown sticks with the same account he gave in the signed affidavit."

Meanwhile Judge Kurtz wondered if there were other eyewitnesses to the shooting.

"The state might call one of the other defendants from 1968, one of the other men in the Plymouth that night," Dozier answered, meaning either John Alexander or Charles Lee Herron.

"I'm worried about what Alexander might say," Camp commented the day after the hearing. "He isn't credible because it's obvious he can't accurately recall everything that happened that night, at least he couldn't during the Herron trial for interstate flight. I've heard he's angry at Bill [Allen] because he thinks he's the one who caused trouble for the rest of them by firing a rifle that night."

That produced a motion Dozier issued and won, the use of the transcripts of testimony offered by the defendants in the first trial. Although he was waiting to tell the truth about what happened the night of the shooting, Allen knew he would be considered a liar if his account from 1968 was introduced. Likewise, he had reason to worry over the testimony Canady gave in the first trial.

"That's been a given all along," Camp said about the liar predicament. "It'll come down to whether or not the jury believes Bill now, that he was scared during the trial in 1968."

Concerning Parker, who did not seem to have strained relations with anybody as the trial approached, his attorney, Smith, made a motion that his case be severed from Allen's, pointing out that it had been clear all along that his client was not involved in any shooting that night. Judge Kurtz ruled against his motion but said he would instruct the jury to deal with each defendant individually in determining guilt or innocence, and in sentencing if found guilty.

Regardless of who would end up on the witness stand during the trial, it was obvious that Judge Kurtz had a difficult task, one compounded when he ruled that there would be no mention of the prior convictions of Allen or Parker, or mention of their escapes from prison.

"I'm considering telling the jury it's a 1968 case and they're not to question why it's being tried in 1989," Judge Kurtz commented. "Let's face it, none of us have been involved in a case like this. But I'll be prepared to handle it."

A week later, Judge Kurtz had a different attitude while visiting with Dozier, Camp, and Smith in his chambers. First, he announced he had decided to allow the money order scheme to be used as evidence by the state. He also commented, "Innocent people don't jump out of cars and start shooting people."

In addition, it was announced behind closed doors that Alexander would appear in court to testify for the prosecution, specifically that he would say Allen had been involved in the money order scheme. This revelation came less than a day after he was contacted in Cincinnati where he said by telephone, "I don't have anything to say about the case. I just want to get on with my life. I've had a problem and can't remember like I used to."

Regardless, Alexander was going to be asked to remember, which, coupled with the ruling by Judge Kurtz with regard to the money order scheme, once more put Allen and Parker at a serious disadvantage.

FORTY-FOUR

Assistant district attorney Steve Dozier, who was only eleven years old when Pete Johnson and Wayne Thomasson were fatally shot, was standing in front of twelve jurors and two alternates telling them what had happened that January 16 night. While making his opening argument in the trial, he relied on theories advanced and court testimony recorded more than two decades earlier.

Dozier told the jury that Allen and Parker, as well as Canady, Charles Lee Herron, and John Alexander, had been involved in the cashing of fraudulent money orders and that they refused to stop the white Plymouth in which they were riding when Johnson wanted to question them about their involvement in the scheme. Claiming they led the police officer down a dead-end avenue, where they shot him with a 30-30 rifle as soon as he got out of his cruiser, Dozier also asserted that they shot Thomasson as soon as he got out of his police cruiser. He also claimed they then shot him several times with a 30-30 rifle and a 22-caliber rifle.

It was a familiar story, not unlike the one former district attorney Thomas Shriver had presented in the 1968 murder trial with a few exceptions: Dozier did not attempt to paint a picture of an ambush; did not belabor the speedy chase angle; and, perhaps being logical enough to know it would be difficult for a man to live through a series of pointblank shots from a hunting rifle, chose to advance the theory that Thomasson had been hit by bullets that ricocheted off the pavement beside him.

Dozier had spent little time with Shriver when the former district attorney came to his office one afternoon as the prosecution was building its case and drew a diagram of the way the cars were positioned when the shooting took place. Dozier had noted that Judge

247

Shriver had erred when showing the seating arrangement in the Plymouth, further evidence that he did not know as much about the case as he had contended for more than two decades.

Under the direction of Davidson County district attorney Torry Johnson, who wanted to continue negotiations with Parker in exchange for testimony against Allen, Dozier continued the process. But he took the time to interview Parker at the state prison and found him "somewhat believable." He even told the defendant that he was the son of a police officer and that he understood if he did not want to cooperate.

Still, Dozier wanted to convict both defendants because he honestly considered Parker an aider and abettor. So he developed his own theory about what happened, basing it as best he could on evidence and not emotion. He concluded that Thomasson had been shot "at least three times." He vigorously asked investigators to find out how many times the police officers had fired their revolvers—"I never could get anybody to say Officer Johnson didn't fire his gun," Dozier said, "nor anybody to say he had"—and even asked, "Where in hell did that spent 38-caliber bullet come from?" He had seen the report of the interview Thomasson gave three days after the shooting: "I got off four quick rounds. . . ." Like everybody else, he had considered it hearsay evidence. He had been upset when nobody could find mention of the Plymouth on the taped radio transmission, though a police officer in 1968 had testified as to the time at which the Plymouth had been mentioned.

Dozier, a Nashville native, had every reason to be emotionally keyed up for the trial, but he tried diligently to be fair, to play by the rules, and to get at the truth.

Also presented on the first day of the trial was the taped recording of what police officers said on their radios that night, although there were additions, deletions, and other discrepancies from what had been heard in the first trial in the various copies that had floated freely around Nashville, as well as in the transcriptions that had been typed.

Nobody questioned the differences, for they had not heard other versions. Or else those who knew better did not disclose the fact.

Defense lawyer Rich McGee used his opening argument to set up Allen's strategy of self-defense, although he was hampered because Judge Kurtz had vetoed important testimony. "I don't see any problem with the admissibility of this evidence," McGee had objected earlier in the day when the judge ruled that witness stand remarks about police brutality toward blacks would result in the police department's going on trial.

"I just don't believe you believe that," Judge Kurtz replied to the defense lawyer. Since Judge Kurtz had ruled previously that the testimony offered by both defendants during the 1968 trial could be used as evidence, McGee had to rely on an old faithful—reasonable doubt—when he presented the defense.

Defense lawyer Robert Smith did not seem to have such odds stacked against him while arguing on behalf of Parker. His client had told the same story in 1968 that he was prepared to tell in 1989—that he was driving the Plymouth, that he stopped the car when Johnson turned on his emergency flashing light, that he left the car after being instructed to do so by the officer, that he was well away from the car when the shooting started, and that he ran at the first sound of gunfire. Parker and his lawyer also believed that the prosecution would push harder for Allen's conviction than for his because it had attempted to make numerous deals with him, only to fail because he was determined to let the truth clear his name.

Two important witnesses were called to the witness stand by the prosecution: Johnny Brown, a so-called eyewitness in 1968, and Alexander, who had remained free until 1971 and was therefore unavailable to testify in 1968.

Brown looked a bit strange in his prison uniform, the result of a robbery conviction. It was incredible that the prosecution was laying the foundation for its case with a man who in a sworn affadivit had said that the police department had coerced him into testifying that he had seen more than he actually had in 1968.

Brown said he "remembered it well" when asked if he had been questioned by police officers after the shooting; the coercion issue, however, was not elaborated. Then he said that he and Larry Wade, a friend and another so-called eyewitness from 1968, were walking home from a basketball game at a local recreation center when they saw two police cars—without emergency flashing lights or sirens in operation—following the Plymouth up Herman Street less than three blocks from the scene of the shooting. He said they went into his house and heard gunfire—"there was more than one shot . . . shots were fired in a series"—then walked outside to see what was happening.

In essence, Brown stuck to the story that he had seen nothing and that twenty-one years earlier he had been forced to testify to the contrary by the police department, although that was neither asked nor revealed.

Then Dozier and Camp were allowed to read parts of the testimony offered in 1968 by Wade, who was declared unavailable because the prosecution could not find him (but who was interviewed by the defense in Nashville a year earlier). As it had been in the first trial, the testimony was laced with contradictions and uncertainty.

That prompted juror Judith James to lean toward juror Sue Watkins and say, "I don't think they saw anything."

Dozier had visited with Alexander in Cincinnati the week before the trial, but on the first day evidence was presented, he was worried that Alexander was not going to testify the way he had indicated he would. Suddenly, someone who had been at the shooting was about to tell the truth.

Dozier quickly moved to have him declared a hostile witness (so that he could cross-examine him), and Judge Kurtz excused the jury so Alexander could be questioned by lawyers without his testimony becoming a matter of record. He said that he was the only one among the five men in the Plymouth that night to be engaged in the cashing of fraudulent money orders and that he "did not know for sure" if the defendants knew anything about the scheme. The judge then ruled that the prosecutors could not call Alexander as a "hostile witness" and would have to treat him as they did their other witnesses.

"You could never argue to the jury that Mr. Allen and Mr. Parker were involved in the cashing of money orders," Judge Kurtz said to Dozier and his fellow Davidson County assistant district attorney Floyd Price. "Mr. Alexander isn't as privy to as much [information] as you would like."

"But there's no reason why a shooting should take place without such testimony," Price replied to Judge Kurtz, making an excellent point.

Once on the witness stand, Alexander, who had been reluctant to talk about the case with anybody, testified that he had arrived in Nashville with Parker five days before the shooting and that there had not been any talk about anybody harming police officers. They had made a "last-minute decision to drive home to Cincinnati," and there had been no chase along Hermosa and Herman streets—"no red lights and no sirens." According to Alexander, the men in the Plymouth first became aware of Johnson following them just before they reached Fourteenth Avenue North, and Parker got out of the car when instructed to do so by Johnson. Charles Lee Herron and he got out of the car and ran and they—Herron, Parker, and he—heard numerous gunshots as they ran.

In keeping with his brief but effective approach in questioning witnesses, Smith asked if Alexander had ever seen Parker with a gun.

"No."

He asked if Alexander, Herron, or Parker—any of the three men who ran from the scene—had anything to do with the police officers being shot.

"No."

Alexander left the witness stand at 7:50 P.M., near the end of a long day for an obviously weary jury that had listened to testimony since 8:30 A.M. Judge Kurtz asked the prosecution to call its next witness, retired officer Robert White. He repeated much of his testimony from 1968, most of which dealt with what he and fellow police officer Jack Burnett saw when they were the first to arrive at the scene of the shooting.

At 10:15 A.M. on Wednesday, the murder weapons were introduced as evidence. They were the subject of extended testimony by police officer Bob Hill.

Watching in the courtroom were students from Tennessee State University and Vanderbilt University. They were there to record the events in an unusual trial that included the reading of testimony from what Judge Walter Kurtz termed "a prior court proceeding"— the trial in 1968. Many of those young men and women were not as old as the case, so some received a briefing in a nearby hallway from court officer Tom Stephens before they took their seats.

The 30-30 rifle and 22-caliber rifle were introduced as evidence after Leroy Dunn, Jr., testified he had found one of them as a six-year-old four days after the shooting. He had arrived to testify in Nashville from Seattle, Washington, where he is a law student and successful computer programmer. He and his father shared a laugh outside the courtroom as they recalled the day the son almost shot his father after discovering the 22 in bushes near their house.

"I felt the bullet come past my head," Leroy Dunn, Sr., told his son after they testified.

"I thought it was a toy gun that looked real."

Even as they spoke, inside the courtroom Hill was showing the jury how the rifles worked. He cocked them with lever action and pulled the trigger, after telling jurors he discovered the 30-30 after Leroy Dunn, Jr., showed him where he had found the 22. To take advantage of an influential opportunity, Dozier held the 30-30 in his hands as he questioned various witnesses, such as former officer W. L. Birdwell, who said he picked up a large 30-30 slug fragment "between the police cruisers, fifteen or twenty feet from the warehouse." Officer Bill Nichols testified that he gathered empty casings and filled out a ballistics report after the shooting, and former Tennessee Bureau of Investigation ballistics expert Bob Goodwin said that he tested the weapons and determined that the empty casings found on the scene had been discharged from those rifles. He said he could not determine if the 30-30 slug fragment Birdwell found was fired from the rifle.

For emotional effect, Dozier cocked the 30-30 rifle and pulled the trigger several times while standing in front of the jury box as Goodwin explained how such a weapon works.

Goodwin testified that the 30-30 rifle held five shells, one in the chamber and four in the cylinder. He said two empty casings from it had been shipped to him by Nichols and that four live rounds were in the rifle when he took possession of it. "At least one round would have had to be reloaded," he replied when asked by Dozier if the rifle had been reloaded.

Then Goodwin offered testimony that supported the story Allen planned to tell the jury.

First, he said a spent 38-caliber, copper-colored, .200-grain bullet had been sent to him, the type of ammunition used by officers Thomasson and Johnson.

Then, seemingly of more importance to the defense, he testified about the weight of the lead fragments from a 30-30 slug that were removed from Thomasson's body and sent to him, one separated from the jacket of the shell and one attached. He said an unaltered ("live") slug of that type weighs about 124 grains. He said the separated fragment weighed 52.27 grains and the fragment attached to the jacket of the shell weighed 41.81 grains. The total of the two is 94.08 grains, meaning 29.92 grains of fragments were left unaccounted for from a single shell. They could have split into numerous smaller pieces and scattered through Thomasson's body with metal fragments from the cruiser door and bone fragments from his broken hip.

No testimony was offered regarding how the larger fragment found by Birdwell ended up where it did, at some point between the two police cruisers, but it was surmised by most observers and, obviously, the jurors that it had lost momentum as it passed through Thomasson's body and had come to rest on the pavement not far behind him.

"There's no way to predict how a 30-30 slug will fragment," Goodwin said on the witness stand. "There's no way to predict what it'll do once it's in the human body."

Meanwhile, Robert Smith, the defense lawyer representing Parker, found all of the talk about the death of Thomasson unsettling when the trial was being conducted because of the death of Johnson. He was more upset when it was announced that the same autopsy report on the death of Thomasson used by the prosecution in 1968 would be introduced as evidence in 1989.

"That's prejudicial and immaterial," Smith protested.

"If they are alleging self-defense, we have a right to do that," Dozier replied, while arguing the move in front of Judge Kurtz.

Judge Kurtz cited previous cases in which such evidence had been allowed and ruled in favor of the prosecution.

Smith renewed his bid for severance, asking Judge Kurtz to separate the Parker case from the Allen case. The judge refused.

After the prosecution introduced various fraudulent money orders into evidence, although none of them linked Allen and Parker to the scheme, police officer Tom Cathey was summoned to the witness stand at 4:10 P.M. He said he had heard about the shooting and had come in on his off day to help with the investigation of the case. He said he had found blank money orders and a "stamp machine" in luggage found in the truck of the Plymouth after it had been towed to the city garage at "some point after midnight." He said he prepared an inventory report on what he found in the trunk.

On heated cross-examination by Rich McGee, a defense lawyer representing Allen, Cathey admitted that he did not prepare an inventory report on the bag containing money orders and a "stamp machine" in it. Asked why, the officer replied, "Because I was put on another assignment."

"Can you tell me which bag it was [that had the money orders and ink pad in it]?" McGee asked. He was referring to a briefcase with the initials *AKB* on it, which indicated it belonged to Amos Kenny Bridges, one of the men who had been about to be arrested for his part in the money order scheme when the shooting occurred.

"No."

"Was there anything in that bag that had the name William Allen on it?" McGee asked.

"No."

"Did you realize those money orders were the one thing that linked the men in that Plymouth to a reason for the police officers to stop them that night?"

"Later on, yes."

"Yet you failed to make a written document indicating which bag they came from?" McGee asked.

"No," Cathey replied in an irritated tone.

During his part of the cross-examination, Smith asked only one question of Cathey. "Did you find anything that linked Parker to the money order scheme?"

"No, I found nothing mentioning defendant Parker," Cathey admitted.

Adding intrigue to testimony about the discovery of the money orders and ink pad in the trunk of the Plymouth were the comments John Alexander made upon hearing what Cathey had to say about it. He had testified earlier that he was the only man in the car that night who had been involved in the cashing of fraudulent money orders.

"It was Amos Bridges's briefcase, and I know I didn't put it in the car," Alexander said. "And, like I've said, I don't think any of the other fellas [Allen, Parker, Canady, and Charles Lee Herron] knew anything about it, that it had money orders in it."

Cathey testified that the briefcase with the money orders and ink pad in it was discovered in the car in the police garage "at some point after midnight" and Hill said that he and other police officers searched the apartment Bridges and Rick Hughes lived in on Hermosa Street "at about midnight."

FORTY-FIVE

What had become a woeful Wednesday in court for Bill Allen was about to get worse. As for Steve Parker, his lawyer, Robert Smith, had almost removed doubt of his innocence through the skillful cross-examination of former Nashville officer Charlie Stoner.

While being questioned by Dozier, Stoner said he followed two sets of footprints in the snow on the night of January 16, 1968, less than an hour after the shooting. He said that he trailed them along railroad tracks, going west, the path Allen and Ralph Canady had taken while running from the scene.

Then Stoner testified that he interviewed Parker in Cincinnati nine days later, five days after the defendant turned himself in at the police department there. He said he had been in the city to take courses related to problem children and juvenile delinquency at the University of Cincinnati.

During his questioning of Stoner, Smith pointed out that the story Parker told during the "fifteen-minute interview" in Cincinnati was about the same as the one he had told ever since. That round of cross-examination came after Stoner said the statement Parker offered in Ohio was "written down pretty much verbatim" and that Parker said he "saw two rifles in the car, a 30-30 in the front and a 22 in the back," that a police car pursued the 1967 white Plymouth he was driving "with sirens on and lights flashing," and that he ran from the scene when he heard gunfire.

Parker claimed that he never told anybody he saw two guns or heard sirens and saw lights flashing.

"Aren't young people frightened in situations like that?" Smith asked while pointing out that Stoner was a juvenile officer who should know that Parker had reason to be apprehensive during the interview.

"Yes," Stoner admitted.

"Did the people who contacted you about interviewing Steve Parker tell you he had turned himself in?" Smith asked, while starting a line of questioning that included information not included in the report Stoner filed after the interview in Cincinnati.

"No sir," Stoner replied. "They didn't say that."

"Steve Parker said Alexander flew to Nashville with him?" Smith asked.

"Yes."

"Did he say he didn't know the other men in the car that night would be at the apartments on Hermosa Street?"

"I don't remember."

"Did he tell you the 30-30 rifle was placed under the front seat?"

"Yes."

"Did he tell you he was driving?"

"Yes."

"Because they were going home to Cincinnati and he was tired and wanted to drive first so he could sleep the remainder of the trip?"

"Yes."

"He said he saw red lights and heard sirens?" Smith inquired, asking something Parker denied telling Stoner.

"Yes."

"Did he say Officer Johnson motioned for him to turn down Fourteenth Avenue?"

"Yes."

"That he made the turn down Fourteenth?"

"Yes."

"That he stopped on Fourteenth?"

"Yes."

"That he put his hands on the warehouse wall, as instructed by Officer Johnson?"

"Yes."

"That he heard gunfire?"

"Yes."

"That he ran down the railroad tracks?"

"Yes."

"Steve Parker didn't have to give you a statement, did he?"

"No, because I wasn't the arresting officer," Stoner replied.

"He gave a voluntary statement, didn't he?" Smith asked.

"On the advice of his lawyer, yes, who was his father."

"He denied participation in the money order scheme and the shooting, didn't he?"

"He was never asked," Stoner replied. "I was there to get information about the others [who were not in custody]."

"So you have no knowledge that Steve Parker had anything to do with any shots being fired?" Smith asked.

"No."

It would seem that Smith got that bit of testimony on record just in the nick of time. The next witness for the prosecution was Dr. Charles Harlan, the Davidson County chief medical examiner, who brought with him a nine-page autopsy report compiled on March 17, 1968, the day Thomasson died. He was about to provide his interpretation of evidence taken from a document prepared by Dr. Michael Petrone, the former Davidson County chief medical examiner. Petrone had not been a licensed expert in forensic science, but he provided moving testimony as an expert witness during the trial in 1968.

Harlan said Johnson was struck by a 30-30 slug in the area of the right breast and that the slug exited the left side of his chest near the armpit. He said the cause of death was a "gunshot wound to the chest."

Harlan said Thomasson had wounds in his left thigh, right thigh, right wrist, and chest and/or abdomen. He said the wound to the left thigh entered on the outside and exited at the groin. He said the diagram he was looking at "does not indicate which is the entrance wound and the exit wound" on the right thigh, but "the implication is the entrance is outside and the exit is inside." He said it was difficult to determine the entrance wound and the exit wound on the right wrist. He said, "I'm not sure about entrances and exits" in regard to the chest and/or abdomen wounds. He pointed out the autopsy was done after numerous surgical procedures had been performed.

"You did not examine Officer Thomasson, correct?" asked Steve Dozier.

"Correct," Harlan replied. "But my expertise and education enable me to testify."

It was at that moment that Bubba Owen, a special investigator for the Davidson County district attorney, gave a thumbs-up sign with a smile while seated as an observer in the courtroom. After Harlan again cited his expertise because of education and experience, Owen slid a note down a bench in the observation area. It said, "Is he [Harlan] good or what?"

Under questioning from Dozier, Harlan looked at the charts in front of him and confirmed that Thomasson appeared to have sustained six wounds.

On re-cross-examination, Sumter Camp, a defense lawyer for Allen, asked Harlan if he had been present when the lead fragments taken from Thomasson had been weighed.

"You've lost me," Harlan answered after a subsequent question, adding, "The two bullet fragments would have had to have struck an intermediary object."

"Like a car door?" Camp asked.

"Yes."

Dozier quickly moved to ask another question. "Or the pavement?" Thus he advanced the theory that Thomasson had been hit by ricocheting fragments after being knocked to the ground.

"Yes," Harlan answered.

Judge Walter Kurtz, in a surprising development, chose to question Harlan. He brought into evidence stronger testimony for the prosecution.

"How many bullets struck Officer Thomasson?" Judge Kurtz asked, introducing testimony about the other police officer shot that night, not the one whose death had prompted the trial he was overseeing.

"There are a minimum of four bullets and a maximum of five bullets," Harlan answered.

So the prosecution got in the last word with the medical examiner. It was to strike an even more powerful blow before court was adjourned that night.

The letter of confession that had made him a "bird in a cage" in 1968 became a matter of record when John Walker went to the witness stand at 7:40 P.M. and recounted how he had received the letter and had given it to James Havron, a defense lawyer who represented Canady during the first trial.

As jurors looked at the letter, passing it among themselves, the minutes passed slowly and quietly. Allen scrutinized the women and men who would judge him, as many of them digested the words on the sheet of paper—"I am the only one who did any shooting in the incident with the police . . ."—and gazed at him. Two jurors smiled upon reading the letter. Judge Kurtz appeared pensive while seated on the bench, the knuckles of his left hand at his nose.

Four minutes . . . five minutes . . . six minutes.

Then Walker was excused, and former FBI agent Billy Bob Williams took his place on the witness stand to testify about how he and fellow agent Don Bullard had captured Bill Allen in New York about two months after the shooting. He had been waiting to testify for five days after arriving in Nashville from Oregon.

"It became more of a conversation than anything else, with Allen telling us about certain events in the recent past," Williams said while Dozier questioned him about his "interrogation" of Bill Allen in New York. The former FBI agent said Allen denied writing the letter the day he was apprehended, then two days later said he wrote it to protect Parker and Canady, who were in the custody of police in Nashville.

"Did he have information about a shooting?" Dozier asked Williams.

"He indicated Charles Lee Herron had done the shooting," Williams answered, planting a reason for the jurors to question whether Bill Allen could be considered truthful.

Under cross-examination from Sumter Camp, a defense lawyer representing Bill Allen, Williams said "it wasn't an interrogation" that took place in New York. Instead, it was "rather quite low-key."

"During that conversation, did somebody listening to it say, 'There's the man who made two widows out of police officers' wives in Tennessee'? And did Bill Allen then say, 'Ya'll are no different than the police in Nashville'?" Camp asked Williams.

"Something like that was said, yes."

"Did anybody in the FBI office or in New York request a typed statement?"

"We didn't type statements back then."

As Williams left the witness stand at 8:35 P.M., court officer Tom Stephens stood in the hallway just outside the courtroom and shook his head in disbelief. He had heard testimony that Allen and Canady had spent the night of the shooting in an apartment on Heiman Street in North Nashville.

"It's freaky," said Stephens, who was one of two court officers who stayed with the sequestered jury at night. "Allen and Canady stayed with William Huff in apartment 1206–D that night. Guess who slept in apartment 1206–C?

"I did. And the next morning I woke up to see police officers with guns all over the neighborhood, even on top of buildings with rifles in their hands. They rushed into my apartment later that day and searched it, even looked in the clothes hamper, as if somebody could be hiding in there. I had been a police officer in Washington, D.C., before coming to Nashville, and I stood there and thought, 'Man, these guys could use a few lessons in how to conduct a search at such an emotional, obviously tense time in the black community.' They weren't too polite.

"It's strange. That was more than twenty-one years ago. Now, here I am, and there Allen and Parker are."

A few minutes after Stephens had spoken, Allen and Parker

watched an unsettling moment in the courtroom. Jurors were wrapping up a long day in court by examining the 30-30 rifle that had been introduced into evidence. When asked if anybody wanted to look at it individually, Mark Meeker, the lone white male among them, quickly jumped to his feet and leaned forward from his seat on the back row. A self-proclaimed gun buff, he took the weapon in hand and showed that he knew how to use it, quickly cocking it with lever action and pulling the trigger.

When they turned out the lights on the fifth floor of the Davidson County Courthouse late that Wednesday evening, the momentum in the case had changed. The prosecution was again the heavy favorite.

FORTY-SIX

Word spread quickly through the Davidson County Courthouse, the Criminal Justice Center, and other parts of Nashville that Bill Allen planned to plead self-defense on the witness stand. As the time for his testimony approached, the cast of courtroom observers began to look more familiar and emotions to increase.

Because of a family death, juror Roberta Jones had been replaced by alternate Shelby Williams, leaving seven blacks and five whites on the jury. By the time the prosecution completed its case at about 2:30 P.M. on Thursday, jurors had been thoroughly confused by the reading of tiresome testimony offered by Allen, Parker, Ralph Canady, and others during the trial in 1968. At that trial, Allen and Canady had lied about much of what had happened during and after the shooting. Jurors also had seen up close the weapons used that night and had heard a taped recording and testimony that left little doubt that Allen had shot the police officer and that Parker had simply been in the wrong place at the wrong time.

The question remained: Why? Even the optimistic Allen knew that if he was to have any chance of acquittal, he needed to be persuasive and composed while telling his side of the story. His chances would have been improved had jurors been able to hear some of what was being said outside the courtroom that day.

"They should be cracking bricks," said Bill Nichols, a police officer who had been instrumental in the investigation in 1968 as he pointed toward the defendants through a window pane in the courtroom door.

"If you're writing the truth about what happened, that'd be what the prosecution witnesses said," volunteered Bubba Owen, a for-

261

mer police officer who had become a special investigator for the Davidson County district attorney. "I wouldn't put any stock in what those bastards say."

It was mentioned to the two men that they might wish to discuss a meeting held in Mickey McDaniel's office at police department headquarters the night of the shooting, when the chief homicide detective and other police officers planned their investigation. Both Nichols and Owen smiled, mischievously, before the former said, "You don't think I had time to attend meetings with everything that was going on that night? I was too busy doing other things."

One of the men made a racist remark while relating what he thought the defendants had done to Thomasson, as if it was lost on him that a black police officer had been killed that night and the trial was about his death, not that of the white police officer who had died sixty-one days later.

Jean Gourieux Patterson, the court reporter from the trial in 1968, stopped by and looked into the courtroom. It was mentioned that Debbie Howington, the court reporter now on duty, had experienced many long, tiring days. "I don't feel sorry for her," Patterson said with a smile. "As I recall, we went thirty-five days in 1968."

David Vincent, a defense lawyer who had represented Parker in 1968, then had advised John Alexander to plead guilty to voluntary manslaughter in 1971 because Parker had received his lengthy sentence, sat for a few minutes and listened to old testimony being read.

Ellariz Allen, mother of Bill Allen, arrived in the area just outside the courtroom. She was fighting influenza after riding a bus from her home in Indianapolis.

Jackie Johnson, the daughter of the slain police officer, sat on a bench across the hallway from Ellariz Allen and talked about her late father. She said he ran a restaurant near Fisk University and Tennessee State University campuses as a second job, adding that her brother, Clarence Johnson, had been with her late father at the restaurant the afternoon of the shooting. Without prompting, she said, "You know my mother and father were separated at the time, but he came around the house sometimes at night." This was particularly interesting in light of neighborhood talk about the police officer's fighting to maintain a romantic relationship with a coed and being estranged from his wife at the time of his death. When it was mentioned that her father was not the person who had shot first, she said with a smile, "You know, my father was a terrible shot. We used to joke about how he couldn't hit a rabbit."

Nashville police chief Joe Casey entered the courtroom as the Bill

Allen testimony from 1968 was being read. Shortly thereafter, he and Steve Dozier walked outside and chatted in the hallway, almost at the same time Charles Brock, a firearms instructor at the Nashville Police Academy, entered the courtroom carrying in separate white cloth bags the two Smith & Wesson 38 Specials used by Johnson and Thomasson.

Police officer Tom Cathey, another key figure in the 1968 investigation, as well as a witness for the prosecution in 1989, smiled when it was again mentioned to him that Thomasson had shot first that night. When told that Thomasson had been shot first, not after Johnson as the prosecution had always advanced, he smiled again and said, "He might very well have been."

So there was reason to wonder what else Thomasson had told police officers and others who had visited with him at the hospital a few days after the shooting, specifically how much detail he had advanced beyond the report Cathey had prepared after their somewhat high-spirited interview. However, such disclosures were protected from the jury by hearsay evidence rules, so it became obvious the people sitting in judgment of Bill Allen and Parker would have to choose between believing a defendant who had lied previously or disregarding his story.

Defense lawyer Robert Smith, who had decided not to let his client, Parker, go to the witness stand because he felt the jury had heard enough to acquit him, did not want to leave anything to chance. After the prosecution rested its case, he asked Judge Kurtz for a judgment of acquittal.

"Respectfully denied," Judge Kurtz responded. "I think the jury has heard enough to make its own decision as to the guilt or innocence of Mr. Parker."

"I'd rather not take a chance with the jury, although I agree it's clear Steve did nothing wrong," Smith said during a recess just before the defense began presenting its case.

At 3:20 P.M. Brock went to the witness stand, where he identified the revolvers the police officers used, although his testimony merely pointed out that Johnson and Thomasson had the 38 Specials in their possession that night.

Then came a surprise for observers who were pulling for the prosecution. Officer Robert Titsworth was called as a witness for the defense. The thirty-seven-year veteran, who had been totally honest about the night of the shooting and the tensions that existed in North Nashville during the 1960s, continued to tell the truth as he answered questions asked by defense lawyer Sumter Camp. His appearance in the courtroom prompted a wink from Owen as he looked toward Nichols while seated on a rear bench.

When Dozier began his cross-examination of the veteran officer, he surprised a lot of people with his testimony.

"I don't know whether a report was made or not," Titsworth answered when asked if a written document had been prepared to confirm whether or not Johnson and Thomasson had fired their guns.

"To my knowledge, I don't know if Officer Johnson fired his revolver," Titsworth said. "I do know Officer Thomasson fired his revolver."

Owen glanced toward Nichols with a shocked look on his face.

"Had you ever known Officer Johnson to discharge his revolver at a suspect?" Dozier asked.

"No sir," Titsworth answered.

Dozier then asked if he had knowledge that Johnson had fired his revolver that night, to which Titsworth said, "I didn't make a report on either revolver. I assumed the homicide division would do that, which is normal procedure. I'm not sure what took place because I wasn't involved in the follow-up investigation."

At that moment, Judge Kurtz asked the lawyers to approach the bench for a conference. In the jury box, juror Anita Buford thought to herself, "Officer Titsworth was about to tell it, let it all out. So why did they stop him?"

In subsequent testimony, Titsworth said the police officers were wearing riot gear, hard helmets, and heavier clothing, "because we'd gone through unrest the summer before." Dozier asked did he mean as long as ten months before, discounting the fact that Nashville police officer John Sorace had made appearances in Washington, D.C., for congressional hearings on race matters in Nashvillle as late as November 1967, two months before the shooting? During that appearance he advanced his belief that "these people [civil rights leaders] are communist-supported."

"There was probably some unrest the week before the shooting incident," Titsworth answered when asked if he had knowledge of anything happening in North Nashville to heighten the tensions that existed between police officers and blacks. "We received calls over there almost every night."

After Titsworth was excused, Owen leaned toward the author and said, "Off the record, he——." What he said "off the record" was not complimentary of Titsworth as a police officer.

The next two witnesses, teachers who knew Bill Allen during his high school years, testified that he was "peaceful" and of "good character." Dozier countered those opinions by bringing into evidence that Bill Allen had been arrested in September 1967 in Cincinnati and charged with disorderly conduct, resisting a police officer, and assault and battery, and that he had been convicted of those offenses in November 1967. "That's not the Bill Allen I know," answered Cecil Whitman, a math and science teacher and football and basketball coach at Haynes High School, who left the witness stand without learning that the sentence for the offenses had been suspended by an Ohio judge. "I can only tell you how I knew him."

At 4:05 P.M., Bill Allen went to the witness stand to tell the story he had wanted to tell for many years, even during the trial in 1968.

Age: 43. *Father:* A former worker at DuPont for thirty-five years. *Mother:* A former health department nurse. *Grandmother:* A retired teacher. *Grandfather:* "Basically, a father to me." *Childhood:* A worker since age six, "when I sold vegetables off of a wagon at roadside." *Education:* Three years at Tennessee State University as a biochemistry major, after compiling a 94.6 grade point average in high school. *More:* Worked for U.S. Industrial Chemicals in the research lab in Cincinnati for about nine months, as well as for the Citizens Committee on Youths, an antipoverty program. Returned to Nashville in November 1967, went to Newark, New Jersey, to visit a girlfriend and returned to Nashville the Saturday before the shooting. Knew Steve Parker better than any of the other men in the 1967 Plymouth, John Alexander the least.

"I wasn't aware of that," Bill Allen answered when asked by Camp if he knew about the money order scheme in North Nashville. "I wasn't passing any. I didn't know anybody who was passing them.

"Yes, I was at the apartment on Hermosa Street. Yes, I put two guns in the car, a 30-30 and a 22, thirty minutes before we left the apartment. I bought the guns earlier that day from Dave Daniels, a man across the street. He worked at a sporting goods store on West End Avenue. Dave was all the time coming around with something to sell. He bought stuff from salesmen and resold them, gym clothes and stuff like that. I was buying the guns for my father. He was a hunter who worked on guns. It was a hobby for him."

Camp showed Bill Allen the rifles that had been introduced into evidence.

"Yes," he said. "Those are the rifles.

"I put one in the back seat and one in the front seat because I didn't want the stock on the 22 to break the scope on the 30-30. [He said the 30-30 scope had caps on both ends of it when he placed it in the car. He said the 30-30 still had a store tag attached to it.] Also, my dad always said guns could be considered concealed weapons if they were in the trunk."

Bill Allen said he was going to his parents' house, catching a ride with the other men who were going to their homes in Cincinnati. He said Daniels had loaded both rifles for him when he delivered them to complete the transaction. "He wanted to know if I wanted to test-fire them. I told him no because they were new and appeared to be in working order."

Bill Allen repeated that he had no knowledge of the money order scheme. He said the white Plymouth was parked behind the apartment on Hermosa Street, that Canady, Alexander, and Charles Lee Herron were in it when he got in it and that Parker entered the car last and was the driver. He said they entered Hermosa Street by driving down an alley that ran beside the apartment complex. "We saw no police cars when we got on Hermosa Street. I became aware of a police car between Sixteenth Avenue and Fourteenth Avenue. Somebody in the back of the car said a police car was behind us. I became aware of the red light [on the police car] when he [Johnson] came around us. We stopped at the intersection of Herman Street and Fourteenth Avenue after Officer Johnson pulled alongside of us and then sort of in front of us."

Bill Allen said Johnson pointed for Parker to drive the car down Fourteenth Avenue. He said Parker followed orders, going down an incline, and that the car "shifted slightly to the left" on the icy pavement. He said the street leveled out and Parker stopped the car.

"A hushed silence came over the car," Allen said. "A hushed fear is what it was.

"Mr. Parker got out to see what the policeman wanted. I didn't hear what was said. Mr. Parker put his hands on top of the car, at the rear door. He leaned down and said, 'You boys get out, too.' Everybody started getting out. Mr. Parker went to the [warehouse] wall and put his hands against the wall. Then Mr. Alexander and Mr. Herron broke and ran.

"And Officer Thomasson started firing.

"The first thing that I saw, Mr. Canady went to the ground. He was at the rear corner of the car. Officer Johnson was behind the door of his car.

"At that point, everything happened so fast. I dived back into the car, into the floorboard. I was ducking for cover. I'm thinking Mr. Canady has been shot. I'm not so sure if any of the rest of my friends had been shot. I'm thinking at that point, uh . . . I'm expecting a bullet to tear through me at any second. I grabbed the rifle, cocked it and—"

Camp interrupted Bill Allen in midsentence. "Did you murder those police officers?" asked the defense lawyer, causing Dozier to object loudly and quickly.

Camp continued in a softer vein. "Did you shoot the police officers?"

"Yes sir."

"What happened?" Camp asked.

"I thought Mr. Canady had been shot. I thought some of my other friends were being shot. I raised up. I felt I had to shoot back. And that's what I did. I shot back."

Bill Allen paused just before he said, "I shot back," and his voice became muffled as he uttered those words.

"Go on," Camp encouraged.

"I shot in the direction of Officer Thomasson. Then I shot in the direction of Officer Johnson. I recall shooting twice. I heard at least six or seven other shots. There were shots coming from Officer Thomasson and Officer Johnson. I couldn't tell you how much shooting there was, not for sure. It was a compressed thing. It happened in a matter of seconds, probably less than ten seconds."

"When the shooting stopped, I went toward the rear of the car to see how bad Mr. Canady was hit. He was scrambling on all fours at that time. I said, 'How bad are you hit?' He said he wasn't hit. And I said, 'Get the other gun and let's get out of here.' He cocked the 22 as he came out of the car with it. It went off one time, straight up in the air."

Allen paused, then dropped his head a bit and said, "I'm telling you I take full responsibility for this tragedy today."

After a pause and a question from Camp, Allen said he and Canady "took off down the railroad tracks." He said they heard sirens as they ran. "To be on the scene, I knew we'd be killed. I knew we had to get away from there.

"I was nervous, confused, and scared. I knew I couldn't stay in Nashville. I would've never made it to the police station. I would've been killed."

Camp was skillfully directing his client, who was answering in straightforward, unemotional, and relatively soft tones. Both had a captive audience, and the jurors seemed all the more interested when the defense lawyer asked Allen about the letter of confession he had written in New York. Also listening, with his eyes glistening from the teardrops forming in them, was Parker, who was seated next to Smith at the defense table.

"That letter is the truth," Allen said. "I wanted to tell the truth. I wanted to spare Mr. Parker and Mr. Canady the grief I had heard they were experiencing in Nashville. My Uncle Lonnie [Pinkston] had said the police were on the rampage in North Nashville."

At that point, tears began rolling down Parker's cheeks. He pulled out a handkerchief and wiped them away.

"Why did you fire those shots?" Camp asked.

"Because I thought Mr. Canady was shot. I was afraid I'd be killed."

With that, Camp indicated that he had no further questions and returned to the defense table. Smith said he had no questions, either. Dozier got out of his chair at the prosecution table; most of his questions were designed to call into question the testimony of the defendant.

"Have you ever written a letter stating self-defense?" Dozier asked.

"No, sir," Allen replied.

"In the prior court proceeding did you say anything about self-defense?"

"In that proceeding in 1968, I was under duress and coercion and didn't always tell the truth because of it," Allen retorted. "I was an intimidated kid, intimidated by the Nashville Police Department. I was in their custody."

There was a short pause.

"Mr. Tom Cathey and Major Joe Casey made threats," Allen continued.

Dozier was a bit stunned. He quickly responded, "Are you under duress now?"

"No, sir. Fortunately, I'm not."

Dozier attempted to discredit Allen by asking questions that indicated he had told FBI agent Billy Bob Williams and others contrasting stories within the span of two days after being apprehended in New York in March 1968. "Are you saying the FBI fabricated those statements?" he asked.

"Sir, in 1968 the FBI, under the direction of Mr. [J. Edgar] Hoover, made a point of discrediting all blacks who were involved in the civil rights movement, from Dr. [Martin Luther] King on down," Bill Allen replied, for the first time raising his voice a bit.

Then he made a soap box play of sorts when he said, "Ladies and gentlemen of the jury, all of these statements attributed to me—"

Judge Kurtz interrupted. "Just answer the questions."

"Is Agent Williams mistaken when he said you initially denied writing the letter?" Dozier asked.

"Yes, sir. As sophisticated as the FBI was at that time, why didn't they record some of these statements I allegedly made?"

"Is Agent Williams mistaken when he said you initially said Charles Lee Herron was responsible for the shooting?"

"I deny that."

"But you admit writing the letter?"

"That's correct, sir."

"The letter is true?" Dozier asked.

"That's correct, sir."

Eventually, Dozier asked a question related to Bill Allen's lying under oath during the 1968 trial.

"In 1968, to further explain the duress I was under," Bill Allen replied, "the night after I was back—"

Dozier objected to the answer, then continued his assault on Bill Allen's credibility as a witness.

"In 1968, I was an intimidated kid," Allen began. "I told the investigators the whole truth in 1968. Police officers Joe Casey, Tom Cathey, and Thomas Smith—"

Dozier stopped him again. "First you said you did not know who did the shooting?"

"That's correct."

"When in fact you did the shooting?"

"That's correct."

When the interrogation turned to the money order scheme, Allen said, "They would have kept that from me. I was a serious-minded person. I was into politics. I never stole from anybody. I never robbed anybody. I never cheated anybody."

"In your sworn testimony in the prior court proceeding, you said you had never seen the 22-caliber rifle," Dozier said. "Who's causing you to make these false statements?"

"Joe Casey and Tom Cathey," Bill Allen answered. "After they cocked a pistol and put it to my head after I was returned to Nashville from New York. I tried to tell them the truth, what happened that night. They didn't want the truth to come out in 1968. They wanted to protect the image of the police department."

"How many times did you say you fired the gun?" Dozier asked.

"Two that I recall."

"So how do you account for four live rounds being in the 30-30 when it was found?" Dozier asked.

"I put two more shells in it running down the railroad tracks. It was an instantaneous reaction."

"Do you recall testimony that said one bullet was found under Officer Johnson?" Dozier asked.

"Yes, sir."

"Do you recall testimony that said a fragment with a casing attached to it was removed from Officer Thomasson?"

"Yes, sir."

"Do you recall testimony from Officer Birdwell, who said he found a bullet in the street?"

"Yes, sir, I recall that."

"Do you recall testimony that said another fragment was found in Officer Thomasson?"

"Yes, sir."

"You say you only shot twice?"

"Right," Allen answered. "I recall shooting twice—once in the direction of Officer Thomasson and once in the direction of Officer Johnson."

"Do you recall the testimony of Dr. Harlan?" Dozier asked.

"I recall Dr. Harlan, yes."

"How was Officer Thomasson hit in the left abdomen?"

"I'm not sure this is correct," Allen answered while looking at a diagram handed him. "I can't tell you how that happened."

"Then how did he get shot twice in the groin?"

"There was a bullet hole in the car door. I would assume it fragmented and went into his groin."

"Would it make better sense that you shot him under his door?" Dozier asked.

"I did not do that," Allen strongly objected.

Eventually, Dozier handed Allen the 30-30 rifle and asked him to demonstrate how it works. "You just put it up and shoot," he said, looking as if he felt awkward. But he aimed it, as requested.

"You had six shots fired at you?" Dozier asked after the rifle was returned to court clerk Barbara Wise.

"That's correct. I'd say a minimum of six were fired by the police officers."

Bill Allen was handed a picture of Johnson lying dead on the scene. He was asked by Dozier to explain how he ended up in that position.

"He [Johnson] was standing on his floorboard shooting at me, standing up over the door."

When Dozier returned to the subject of Allen's lying under oath, he recounted the night he claimed Casey threatened him in the presence of other police officers. He said that he attempted to tell the truth—"The dude started shooting and I shot back"—which prompted the officer to point a revolver at him and say, "If you say that in front of the judge, we'll have to kill you."

At that statement, people began to shift in the previously stilled courtroom. It was a surprising statement, although in retrospect it appears that Bill Allen had attempted to get around to it earlier in his testimony. More shocking was the fact Judge Kurtz chose to ask the witness a few questions before excusing him.

"How much additional ammunition did you have?" Judge Kurtz asked.

"Dave gave me a couple extra shells when he brought the guns to me," Allen replied.

"You had them in your pocket?"

"That's correct."

"Did you have more ammo in the car?"

"No, sir."

It was 7:12 P.M. when Bill Allen left the witness stand. His testimony was followed by the reading of the testimony of his deceased father during the 1968 trial, during which he had testified that his son "never messed with guns." The testimony of his uncle, Lonnie Pinkston, and of his mother was also given.

At least part of the truth had surfaced after more than twenty-one years. But the prosecution was already lining up rebuttal witnesses to make Bill Allen look like a calculating liar.

That night, Casey and Cathey were contacted by telephone and scheduled to testify as rebuttal witnesses the next morning. It was Cathey who, more than a year earlier, had said in a private conversation, "I know Joe Casey was present" when William Bostic was on an elevator the night of the shooting.

With Smith scheduled to produce only a few character witnesses on behalf of Parker (with no intentions of putting the seemingly innocent defendant on the witness stand), the prosecution was about to try the Thomasson case again in an effort to convict Bill Allen of the murder of Johnson.

So a tense Thursday ended and a fateful Friday began.

FORTY-SEVEN

Tears started flowing as the two women pulled back from an embrace. One of them, Ann Allen, was struck by such an emotional storm that she ran into a nearby restroom to regain her lost composure. The other woman, Mary Pope, who had been the wife of Pete Johnson when he was killed, stood with a heavy mist in her eyes and with lipstick stains on the shoulder of her turquoise jacket.

"I'm truly sorry this happened," Allen had said to her a few minutes earlier.

"I don't hold any malice. You didn't even know your husband then."

Allen simply nodded.

"A lot of years have passed," Pope said. "I don't hold any bitterness toward anybody, especially not you."

This show of compassion offered by women who had reason to be staunch adversaries occurred out of the view of the jury, about thirteen hours after Bill Allen had spent one hour and seven minutes on the witness stand. The two women had watched the defendant converse and shake hands with Clarence Johnson, the only son of the deceased police officer, as court was adjourned the previous night.

"I'm serious when I say I'm sorry and take full responsibility," Bill Allen had told Johnson.

"I'll accept that man-to-man," Johnson had said, knowing he still harbored the feelings he had expressed as the first witness in the trial.

After identifying himself as the son of Pete Johnson, Clarence Johnson had asked Judge Kurtz for permission to make a statement, and the judge sent jurors out of the courtroom. Then

Johnson faced the two defendants and said, "I've just got a lot of feelings I want to release. I've watched the way you people operate and how you manipulated the jury to pick the people you wanted. You two started out as petty thieves and you turned out to be cold-blooded murderers."

Before the thirty-six-year-old man on the witness stand could say anything else, all three defense lawyers had jumped to their feet to object. Observers squirmed on their seats, and reporter Jim Molpus of the *Nashville Banner* scribbled notes quickly. "I don't care if you object," Johnson said. "My father was shot with a high-powered 30-30 rifle. He was dead before he hit the ground."

Bill Allen and Steve Parker looked straight ahead, showing little reaction. They had heard Dozier, the son of a police officer, call the deaths of Pete Johnson and Wayne Thomasson "two of the most brutal and senseless murders in the history of this county" during his opening argument. They knew most of the citizens of Nashville had heard enough similar talk to agree with that description.

What they had not known was that Judge Kurtz would soon rule that the defense could not introduce evidence about the court-documented "violent reputation" of Nashville police during the 1960s, nor that it could use "hearsay evidence" related to Pete Johnson's and/or Thomasson's firing their revolvers during the shooting.

Those important decisions left Bill Allen with the undesirable task of proving he was defending himself against much more than two police officers and Parker with the burden of explaining how he ran from the scene as the shooting started because he was frightened.

The prosecution was the favorite, no doubt, which could be the reason many of the principal characters in the case stopped by the courtroom that week to check on the proceedings. They included police officers who stood in a nearby hallway almost every day and made racist remarks.

If justice was going to be served in this highly charged setting, the jury would have to provide it without hearing the entire story of what had transpired more than two decades earlier. What the jurors saw, at the very least, was some misinformed witnesses who had been *told* what happened in the minutes leading to the shooting and during the seconds in which it unfolded.

Later that morning officer Tom Cathey and police chief Joe Casey refuted Allen's claim that they had threatened him in 1968 not to tell the truth in court about what happened during the shooting.

The trial was moving toward its conclusion, with closing arguments expected that day, and the prosecution was going for the kill in the crowded courtroom.

Cathey was reminded that he was still under oath before he started answering questions delivered by assistant district attorney Steve Dozier. He was holding the uniform jacket Thomasson was wearing when he was shot, even though the trial was for the death of Johnson.

"Are there holes in the jacket?" Dozier asked.

"Yes sir. Several," Cathey answered before explaining five tears of various sizes in the jacket.

He was handed the pants Thomasson wore that night, as well as a holster, belt, and bullet container that he pointed out was full with "six live rounds in it." He pointed to a hole on the right side of the belt, then to "a smaller hole" on the left side of the waistband.

"Are there any other holes in those pants?" Dozier asked.

"There are two large holes in the crotch of the pants," answered Cathey, who said he took possession of the uniform at the hospital the night of the shooting and transported it to police headquarters.

"Have you ever spoken to the defendant Allen?" Dozier asked in an effort to refute the testimony Allen had offered the previous evening.

"I have never spoken to the defendant Allen."

Cathey was cross-examined by defense lawyer Rich McGee, who was representing Allen. His interrogation got off to a false start when he reminded the police officer that during his earlier testimony he had said he had "little to do with the investigation," that he was placed in charge of searching the trunk of the Plymouth in which the defendants had been riding. Dozier objected to that line of questioning. When Judge Kurtz sustained the objection, McGee argued the point. "It will remain sustained," the judge replied.

Officers seated in the rear of the courtroom chuckled. Ann Allen, wife of Bill Allen, quietly rose and exited the courtroom, then returned in a few minutes. The mother, sister, and brother of Parker remained in the courtroom, after having testified briefly about his background earlier that morning, as did the widow of Johnson and her four children.

After Cathey repeated that he had transported the police uniform worn by Thomasson from the emergency room to headquarters—"I did not sign for the clothes," he said—McGee asked if he had talked to the wounded police officer on January 19, three days after the shooting. "I did," Cathey said, perhaps wondering if he would be asked if Thomasson said he shot his revolver that night.

But that question was never asked because of hearsay evidence rules.

"Is it possible some of the damage to those pants could have been the result of hospital personnel's taking them off of Officer Thomasson that night?" McGee asked in reference to the tears in the crotch area.

"I can't say that's correct," Cathey answered.

"You would agree they would be more interested in treating the police officer than in protecting the condition of his clothing?"

"Yes. I would hope so."

Renewing his questioning of Cathey, Dozier asked if the police officer had been present when an autopsy was conducted sixty-one days after the shooting. "I was," Cathey replied.

"Did the wounds you observed that day correspond to the bullet holes in the uniform?"

"Yes."

Then McGee asked Cathey about the behavior of a slug that strikes a hard object, how it fragments.

"All I can say is what I saw," Cathey answered.

"Didn't you take the fragments removed from Officer Thomasson's body to police headquarters?" McGee asked.

"I placed the objects in a container and gave them to our central intelligence division."

The crowded courtroom was filled with anticipation as Nashville police chief Joe Casey, who had been a major in 1968, took the witness stand.

"After Mr. Allen was arrested, did you threaten him?" Dozier asked Casey.

"No, sir," Casey replied.

"Did you cock a weapon and point it at his head?"

"No, sir."

"Did you at any time tell him not to tell the truth under oath?"

"No, sir."

"Did he at any time ever say this was a case of self-defense?"

"No, sir. I had never seen Mr. Allen until yesterday in this courtroom."

McGee asked Casey one question, "If you didn't talk to Bill Allen, why are you being asked to testify about what was said?"

Again, the last question belonged to Judge Kurtz. "Just to make it clear, Chief Casey, you never had a conversation with him in 1968?"

"No, sir," Casey replied.

McGee was not the only suspicious person in the courtroom. Juror Anita Buford, who was seated as close to Cathey and Casey as anybody except Judge Kurtz, carefully watched their actions as they gave their answers, particularly their faces.

"Joe Casey couldn't look at that man and say he was a liar," Buford told Wilma French, who was seated in front of her in the jury box. "He kept looking the other way while he testified. He kept looking toward us." French nodded in reply.

"I believe Tom Cathey said something to him in 1968," Buford said. "He couldn't look at the man and say he hadn't talked to him. I just don't know if he or anybody else did that [questioned Bill Allen] with a gun stuck to his head. Regardless, there's something missing in his account." Again, French nodded in reply.

At that point the jury was given a break before hearing closing arguments and being charged by Judge Kurtz. It was welcome relief for all of the jurors, who at that moment had to begin reconstructing some of the things they had heard and seen.

"Why did they bring Officer Thomasson's uniform in there?" Buford asked during the recess. "Why not Officer Johnson's uniform? Aren't we here because Officer Johnson was killed?"

"We're all sort of in the dark," Anna Howell answered, indicating that at least one more juror was confused. "Evidently they've been tried before. I'm assuming from all of the talk about a previous court proceeding that they've been tried and convicted, then escaped."

"But we're not supposed to assume anything," Buford said. "Remember, Judge Kurtz told us not to think about civil rights issues, just the evidence."

So jurors returned to the courtroom for closing arguments at 10:25 A.M., obviously hoping the assistant district attorneys, Dozier and Floyd Price, and the defense lawyers, Sumter Camp and Robert Smith, could piece together the puzzle during closing arguments.

Incredibly, the final round of arguments was conducted with Cathey seated next to Ann Allen. The Johnson family shared the same bench.

Price, age thirty-five, a South Carolina native who went to high school in Birmingham and received his undergraduate and law degrees from the University of Tennessee, went first, reconstructing the events of that cold night in January 1968. He said Johnson was performing normal duties in North Nashville when he heard that a call had been out about men passing fraudulent money orders. He said he moved to an area that he and others were familiar with and located the automobile being sought. He said Johnson saw the white Plymouth and announced that he wanted to stop it because the individuals inside "might have information" about the money order scheme. He said "the chase began," then reminded jurors that Thomasson had tried to stop the automobile but "they drove around him." He said "they were trying to get away from the police officers." He said "this chase went on for almost a half mile before they could get the vehicle to halt." He said Johnson pulled his revolver and put on his helmet "because of the chase."

Pointing at Bill Allen, Price said, "The proof is clear this man got out of the car with a 30-30 rifle and shot and killed Officer Johnson." Price said it was willful, malicious, and premeditated—"murder in the first degree." He asked jurors to consider a loaded gun, the number of times he shot ["Johnson, one; Thomasson, five-to-seven; no fewer than three"] and the fact he reloaded the gun. Price said, "It's cold-blooded, first-degree murder—a design to kill, a design to murder an eleven-year veteran of the Metro Nashville Police Department."

Pointing at Parker, Price said he was an aider and an abettor who is "equally responsible." He said, "Do you believe there was no discussion of a police officer following the car? This man, Parker, wants you to believe there was no discussion of the money orders. That is totally unlikely. This man, Allen, formed a design to kill. This man, Parker, knowingly participated."

Twenty-five minutes into his closing argument, Price raised his voice and started to drive his point home: "While the chase was going on, they were plotting. [One said] 'I'll take care of this problem. I've got the remedy. I'll just blow Officer Johnson away.' So what did he do? He blew him away—deliberate, willful murder."

When Camp rose to address the jurors, it was obvious he planned to do so with a reverent, quiet, remorseful tone. He asked one question: Why did the shooting incident happen?

"We judge cases on facts, not emotions," Camp noted, after pointing out that the events had produced a tragedy. "You have to make decisions on the facts, then apply them without emotion.

"It isn't disputed that William Allen did the shooting. But the state didn't give you a reason why he did it because it couldn't find one," Camp declared. "Oh, they'll tell you these big-time money order thieves killed two police officers. But I submit to you that you don't kill people over paper [he waved two stolen money orders overhead] and that's all the state brought you. So what happened on the scene that night is purely circumstantial."

Knowing that reasonable doubt was his chief selling point, Camp told a story to jurors:

"You put a mouse in a box. You put a cat in the box with the mouse. You put the lid on the box, tie a string around it, and go away for thirty minutes. When you return, you don't see the mouse, just one happy cat. You didn't see what happened, of course, but you can surmise what took place.

"But then in the corner of the box you see a little mouse-size hole. Now there's your reasonable doubt.

"The state tells you the money orders were the motive for the killing. Well, that couldn't be a motive if Mr. Allen wasn't involved in that scheme. There's no proof he was involved. There's no proof Mr. Parker was involved. Where are the money orders with Mr. Allen's signature or Mr. Parker's signature on them? If the state had found money orders with their names on them, believe me, you would have seen them. Not even Mr. [John] Alexander says Mr. Allen or Mr. Parker was doing that. The state called him as a witness. If the state is going to rely on him, then let's consider what he said.

"*Might have* and *could have* are words of doubt. If you have to use those words, then there's doubt."

Camp said the prosecution advanced the "chase theory" only to keep Parker in the case. He pointed out the snow and ice on the roads, the hazardous driving conditions, as well as the fact it took the Plymouth more than a minute to travel a half mile. "That's less than thirty miles per hour," Camp said. "Where is the big chase? You heard Johnny Brown say there was no chase, no light flashing on the police car, and no siren blaring when he saw the cars on Herman Street. You heard police officer Raymond Black say there were no lights flashing and no siren blaring when Officer Johnson started up Hermosa Street. You heard Mr. Alexander say there was no chase. You heard previous testimony from Ralph Canady, Mr. Parker, and Mr. Allen that there was no chase.

"What is the proof of a conspiracy? The state wants you to assume things happened in that car. Mr. Alexander said there was no discussion about the police officers until they saw the flashing lights between Sixteenth Avenue North and Fourteenth Avenue North. Mr. Canady said the same thing.

"The court will instruct you that it's not illegal to carry a loaded weapon in a car.

"And look at how these men were dressed—sportcoats and Hush Puppies. Look where they stopped the car—under lights. That's a heckuva place to ambush somebody. If this was an ambush, why didn't they just jump back in the car and take off? Also, how do you surprise a man whose pistol is out of his holster and in one of his hands?"

Camp used the "put me out with him" statement Thomasson made on a taped recording of police radio transmissions to make sure jurors knew both officers arrived on Fourteenth Avenue North at about the same time. "He [Thomasson] doesn't say, 'I see people with guns' or 'Shots are being fired,'" Camp said before reminding jurors that all of the men in the car that night were college-educated and had good backgrounds.

Then the defense lawyer discussed the testimony his client offered on the witness stand.

"Bill Allen told you what happened," he said. "He didn't have to testify, but he wanted to. He could have put it off on Mr. Herron, who isn't here, Mr. Canady, who isn't here, on Mr. Alexander, who was here but left after he testified. Instead, he took the witness stand knowing it would mean he'd have to admit he lied earlier about what happened. He admitted that and then told you the truth.

"In 1968, Bill Allen smacked a hornet's nest. I can assure you the Nashville Police Department was upset about it. So ask yourself if it is reasonable for him not to have told the truth earlier about what happened."

Camp then took jurors back through the events of the shooting, pointing out that Titsworth had testified that Thomasson fired his gun. "Bill Allen fired at Officer Thomasson in self-defense," Camp said. "The dye was cast. Officer Johnson had to react to that. He fired at Bill Allen. Bill Allen fired back at him.

"Where's the evidence that Mr. Allen shot Officer Thomasson more than once? You've seen only two 30-30 casings because there aren't any more than that. Where's the evidence that he was shot four, five, or six times as the state is talking about? There are at best three shots.

"It's interesting that Tom Cathey and Bill Nichols don't seem to remember anything about the police officers' revolvers. There's a reason for that. They don't want anybody to know anything about the weapons."

Camp was holding a Smith & Wesson 38 Special in a hand, one used by either Johnson or Thomasson. He waved the revolver as he talked about "reasonable fear," pointing out the bullets used in such a weapon are more powerful than those used in a 30-30 rifle. He aimed the gun at Bill Allen and said, "Now who's going to stop at a moment like that and say, 'Oh, excuse me, were you firing at me?' For Mr. Allen, there was nowhere to go. There was nowhere to run and hide. That's reasonable doubt, and if you have any doubt, you have an obligation to find Bill Allen not guilty."

After forty minutes in front of the jury, Camp said in closing, "It's a tragedy, but it's not a murder."

Smith, who looked younger than his thirty-eight years, a Tennessee State University and Howard University Law School graduate, was a reserved man with a quick smile and pleasing demeanor. He had appeared perfect as a defense lawyer for Parker throughout the trial. Their approach was low-key, matching their personalities, and the closing argument he presented was compatible with that style.

"I hope you will hold the state responsible for proving my client guilty," Smith said after thanking jurors for their attention and praising them for serving "the best justice system in the world" because a defendant is presumed innocent until proved guilty beyond reasonable doubt.

"Everything Mr. Parker has said has been substantiated by the state's witnesses," Smith said. "I didn't call those people to testify. The state did that."

Then Smith discredited much of the same evidence Camp had attacked before him, only in different ways because it was obvious he had a most defendable defendant.

"There was no ambush," he declared, setting up a strong point in his argument. "Mr. Parker isn't going to turn his back and put his hands on a wall if he knows shots are about to be fired. I don't know of any man who's going to turn his back if he knows there's going to be a shooting.

"You've heard what could have happened, might have happened, and may have happened. You can't guess. It has to be beyond reasonable doubt.

"About these money orders, you don't have somebody flittering into town from Cincinnati to commit a crime, then getting out of town again. Besides, Mr. Parker was working in Cincinnati. Why would he be stealing money orders?"

Smith addressed those points and others in twenty-five minutes. He brought home his point by first mentioning moral certainty as a companion to reasonable doubt.

"If you make a mistake, you send an innocent man to prison for life," Smith told jurors. "So you can appreciate the difference between proof of guilt and reasonable doubt and moral certainty. Don't wake up tomorrow and say, 'I sure hope that man was guilty.' The proof, or better yet the absence of proof, says he isn't guilty.

"After this trial ends, you'll forget about this courtroom after a while. Steve Parker won't forget it. This is his day in court.

"The beauty of our form of justice is a person can't be placed in prison just because somebody thinks he ought to go there. He comes to court with a cloak of innocence wrapped around him. Mr. Parker is still clothed in that cloak of innocence. The cloak of innocence is wrapped warmly and lovingly around his shoulders.

"Ladies and gentlemen of the jury, I leave Mr. Parker with all that he has, with those he loves, and with all who love him in your hands."

It was at noon that Dozier began addressing jurors with a quick punch line: "The defense sometimes throws a lot of bugs on the floor in hopes that you'll be distracted from the facts. That has happened here. It's the burden of the state to stomp out those roaches."

With that said, Dozier wasted little time before going for the throat.

"There were two lives in 1968 that ended," he said as he wheeled and pointed toward Bill Allen. "They were ended by that man— that cold-blooded murderer.

"If you come back and say 'not guilty,' you are telling him that you believe him. Well, which Bill Allen are we to believe? You've heard page upon page of his lies. But he wants you to believe his version now. Are you going to believe that cold-blooded murderer or Police Chief Joe Casey and Police Officer Tom Cathey? If you come back and say 'not guilty,' you've got to say you believe that cold-blooded murderer and perjurer has decided to come forward and tell the truth. In order to believe his self-defense version, you've got to discount all the other versions.

"That cold-blooded murderer [Dozier pointed at Bill Allen on each such reference] says he fired two rounds. Why did he want to deny that in New York? Why did he want to deny that during the prior court proceeding?"

Dozier began talking about Thomasson, specifically how the tears in his police uniform matched the wounds testified about in court. "The only way he got those injuries was when he was on the ground," he said. The district attorney pointed out that it was his question that prompted the revelation by Titsworth that Thomasson had shot his revolver, which was obviously an effort to remove any suspicions in the minds of jurors of a police department cover-up taking place. "Until that testimony was presented, he [Bill Allen] was going to say he shot Officer Johnson first. Just think about what he's asking you to swallow."

Dozier walked to a corner of the courtroom and took the 30-30 rifle in his hands. As he went, he talked about "cold blood running through the veins of Bill Allen." Then he told how the defendant "turned toward Mr. Johnson, whom he would want you to believe was clipping his fingernails, shot him, and then shot Mr. Thomasson, who was trying to get back in his car. Then he shot again. Then he shot again, under the door. Then he shot again.

"Then he ran down the railroad tracks, reloading the rifle. Does that sound like a man trying to defend himself?"

In an effort to discount the closing argument advanced by Camp, who said people do not kill people over paper, Dozier said, "People have been killed for a lot less than that." He pointed out that trained police officers are not going to shoot as many times as Bill Allen said and "not hit a soul." He pointed out that police officers have a right to stop anybody they wish, that "people who are innocent don't run" when that happens. He called talk about an unlawful arrest and excessive force by police officers "nothing more than garbage."

Dozier began closing his argument by pointing out that Johnson would be remembered by his family and "thousands of police officers," but he could not be brought back to life. He asked jurors to use common sense to convict Bill Allen and Parker of first-degree murder.

"Please don't let an aider and abettor, that man [pointing at Parker], and the person who perpetrated this crime, that man [pointing at Bill Allen], go free," Dozier said. "Please don't do that."

The cases had been presented, so Judge Kurtz recessed court for lunch before instructing the jury. Dining together at that tense hour were the mothers of Bill Allen and Steve Parker, as well as other members of their families who gathered at a small cafe across the street from the courthouse. Not all of those people made it back to the courtroom before the judge gave his important, comprehensive instructions.

Judge Kurtz explained each option to the jurors. He told them that first-degree murder must meet the following criteria: unlawful killing, malicious killing, willful killing, deliberate killing, and premeditated killing. He told them second-degree murder must meet the following criteria: unlawful killing, killing with malice or forethought. He told them voluntary manslaughter must meet the following criteria: intentional killing and sudden passion that led to the killing. The sentence for first-degree murder, he said, was between twenty years in prison and ninety-nine years in prison. He said the sentence for second-degree murder was between ten years in prison and twenty years in prison, unless a more taxing sentence was invoked at the discretion of jurors. He said the sentence for voluntary manslaughter was between two years in prison and ten years in prison.

In the area of self-defense, Judge Kurtz said a defendant "must be justified in using force to kill an attacker whom he or she thought was going to kill him or her." He said a defendant must do "all he or she can to avoid a confrontation," that he or she can only act if "all efforts at retreat fail."

Judge Kurtz also offered some elaboration that fit the case in question.

"Reasonable doubt is not absolute," he said.

"Testimony of witnesses who have previously testified falsely under oath should be weighed with care.

"Expert testimony is often speculative and full of pitfalls.

"As for the defendant William Allen, his testimony should be given the same weight as other witnesses.

"As for the defendant Steve Parker, his failure to testify should not present an inference as to guilt or innocence.

"Prior testimony in a previous court proceeding is to be considered as testimony.

"Flight alone is not reason to consider guilt. An entirely innocent person might take flight for certain reasons.

"In the area of aiding and abetting, that person is guilty only if he or she is performing an act that helps along the crime or is prohibiting someone from stopping the crime.

"Malice is the wicked intent beforehand, the contemplation of the act.

"Premeditation occurs when the intent to kill is weighed beforehand. It can be instantaneous. But it must be free from excitement or passion."

At 2:12 P.M., Judge Kurtz sent jurors into the deliberation room, after telling each one, "Do not surrender your honest opinion about guilt or innocence."

Jurors had been instructed fairly. The question at that point was whether they had heard the entire story.

FORTY-EIGHT

"**W**hich defendant should we consider first?" said Mark Meeker, a white male who had "campaigned" successfully to become foreperson for the jury.

"Mr. Parker," came the response almost in unison.

"Does anybody think he's guilty of a crime?" asked Meeker.

At once, he saw eleven shaking heads.

"Then there's no reason to take a secret ballot. Everybody who thinks he's innocent of all charges, raise your hand."

At once, eleven raised hands accompanied his own.

Parker, who had been sentenced to ninety-nine years in the Tennessee State Prison in 1968 for first-degree murder in the death of Officer Thomasson, had been acquitted of the death of Officer Johnson in April 1989. His involvement in both cases had been the same.

"We've cleared a man of all wrongdoing in fifteen seconds," Anita Buford said as the jury deliberated. She also wondered if Parker had been convicted of a crime—and how that could have happened.

"Let's talk about Allen," Meeker said. "It's obvious to me he shot the police officers."

"That's what he said."

"I'd say it's first-degree murder," said Shelby Williams, the woman who had served as an alternate before replacing Roberta Jones on the jury.

When they looked around the room, seven jurors were nodding in agreement. Buford, Sue Watkins, and Judith James were shaking their heads. Two others were wondering, including Anna Howell.

"Maybe Allen was scared, like he said," Howell said.

284

"I certainly left the courtroom thinking he was," Buford agreed. "Didn't the judge say something about passion, that it couldn't be first-degree murder if he was scared?"

"But he also said premeditation can be quick, in a snap of the finger," Williams said.

"He knew he was going to kill those men when he reached for the gun," Meeker claimed.

"I'm not sure about premeditation," Watkins responded. "I'm a nurse. I do a lot of things in a scant second to help a patient, without thinking so much. It's a reaction. I'm wondering if that's what happened with Allen."

"Then let's read what the judge said," Meeker said.

The jury looked at the elements of first-degree murder: unlawful killing (yes, they agreed); killing with malice (yes, they agreed, after some debate); willful killing (yes, they agreed); deliberate killing (yes, they agreed, with the fact the 30-30 rifle was retrieved from the car); and premeditation (maybe, they concluded). A somewhat subdued debate continued.

"I'm wondering how many times the police officers shot their guns," Buford asked.

"Just once, I think," one of the jurors said. "That's the only used 38 Special bullet they found."

"But I'm not sure about everything police officers said on the witness stand," another juror said.

"I agree with that," Buford said. "I got mighty confused when they talked about who handled the revolvers and what they did with them. I've got mixed emotions about what [Bill] Nichols, [Tom] Cathey, and some of the others testified to. It's a mystery how so many people handled the revolvers, yet nobody knew what happened to them and how many times they were shot."

"Let's try to be logical," Howell said. "Let's go through some things that might have happened. We've all seen things like this on TV."

"Like what?" asked another juror.

"Well, like police officers firing warning shots," said Howell. "I'm thinking that's what happened, that the one bullet they found was fired into the air to get those men to stop running."

"But if they were running, maybe there was self-defense."

"It can't be self-defense," Williams said. "Allen didn't run."

"That's right," Howell said. "Right here it says a person must retreat as far as he can. He stayed near the car, ducked into the floorboard. Why didn't he just sit in the car? Police officers don't shoot people who are just sitting there."

"But can it be premeditation?" Buford asked. "I mean, this was quick."

"The law says premeditation can be instantaneous," Meeker replied. "That's it in black and white."

"I understand that," Buford responded. "That's the law. But I'm not sure it's a good law."

"It's the law," Williams answered.

By 3:30 P.M., the guilt of Allen had almost been determined. But some of the jurors wanted to take another look at photographs of the Plymouth and of Johnson on the ground, the pathology report prepared after an examination of Johnson, and diagrams of the scene of the shooting. So they requested that Judge Kurtz assemble them in court.

Telephones began ringing.

Steve Dozier and Floyd Price were called in their offices on the first floor of the courthouse.

"The jury has a question for the judge," said Rich McGee, the defense lawyer who assisted Sumter Camp with the Allen case, after he answered a telephone in his office just across the street from the courthouse.

"That's a good sign," Camp replied. "At least they're asking questions. I've seen murder cases that were decided in seven minutes."

Perhaps the most apprehensive defense lawyer, however, was Robert Smith, who was handling the Parker case. "I don't know if they're talking about Steve or Bill," he said. "If it's Steve, this could be bad."

The jury looked at the requested materials for about thirty minutes, commencing at 3:55 P.M., then returned to the deliberation room. Television cameras were already in place outside the courtroom, positioned so pictures could be taken through the small panes in the doors. The Johnson family waited on benches in the hallway.

The defense lawyers returned to the office across the street to wait. "Since they've got a dinner break coming, the jury might not have a decision tonight," Camp said. "And that'd be fine with me."

As the three of them sat in the Lionel Barrett law office and discussed the events of the week with Barrett, they spent a lot of time discussing the personalities involved.

"I got involved with this case late," said McGee, "and, frankly, I wasn't too excited about it. I had heard horror stories about Allen and Parker.

"But then I met them and began studying the elements of the case. I was surprised by what I saw and learned. Now I'm wanting to go an extra mile for them because they're damn nice guys and they've been victimized by untruths."

Camp and Smith felt the same way and expressed as much as they ate a quick dinner at a restaurant near the law office. "If that jury comes back and says what I hope it says, what it should say, I'm going to do everything in my power to get Steve [Parker] out of prison," said Smith. "Even with a not guilty verdict in this case, we've still got a ninety-nine-year sentence from 1968 hanging over his head."

Camp was asked what he expected for Allen. "You can't predict what a jury will do," he responded. "Not guilty because of self-defense is the right decision. But I don't expect it, not with the evidence we were not allowed to present. Anything less than first-degree would be a victory."

The telephones started ringing again at 7:50 P.M. "They're back with the verdict," McGee said.

"That's not good," Camp replied.

"I don't think so either," McGee agreed as the three defense lawyers started walking toward the courthouse across the street.

By 8:07 P.M., all the familiar faces were in the courtroom. Allen had changed suits, from navy to beige, and he looked as optimistic as ever. Parker appeared likewise. In fact, the defendants appeared fresher than anybody else in attendance.

The jury was seated at 8:10 P.M.

"Whatever your feelings are about these verdicts, I would appreciate very much if there is no expression when they are announced," Judge Kurtz instructed the observers.

"Will the foreperson please announce the verdict, starting with Mr. Allen," Judge Kurtz intoned.

Meeker rose to his feet.

"We find the defendant William Allen guilty of first-degree murder and set his sentence at 78 years."

Allen, with his hands folded in front of him as he stood at the defense table, dropped his head ever so slightly. He closed his eyes. McGee dropped his head more so, giving the appearance of a disgusted man staring at the table. Camp looked toward Meeker, showing little emotion, then at Judge Kurtz. Dozier and Price sat at the prosecution table without showing emotion, as if it was business as usual for them. Ann Allen, the wife of Bill Allen, leaned forward on a bench and closed her eyes.

Little emotion was shown.

"Will the foreperson please announce the verdict for Mr. Parker."

"We find the defendant Steven Parker not guilty."

Parker put an arm around Smith's shoulder and gave him a quick hug. A sparse smile appeared on his face, but it quickly faded as he looked toward Bill Allen. His mother, sister, and brother began crying, with tears of happiness and relief running down their cheeks.

"Mr. Parker, the charge against you is dismissed," Judge Kurtz announced. "We'll deal with the pending escape charge against you on May 4.

"Mr. Allen, the jury has found you guilty of first-degree murder by premeditation and has sentenced you to seventy-eight years in the Tennessee State Penitentiary. I find you to be a dangerous offender and rule that the seventy-eight-year sentence is to be served consecutively to the ninety-nine year sentence you received after your prior conviction.

"As for the escape cases against Mr. Allen and Mr. Parker, we'll set it on the docket and take it up later."

After the jury was dismissed, the courtroom began emptying. Bubba Owen, the special investigator for the district attorney, hurried to shake hands with members of the Johnson family. Price did likewise, then took the time to shake hands with members of the Parker family.

With only four people remaining in the courtroom and with her husband in a holding area adjacent to it, Ann Allen rushed toward a door, pushed it open in a huff, and hurried in the direction of Bill Allen.

Watching her run were numerous members of the news media who were waiting to interview the assistant district attorneys and the defense lawyers.

"At least we got the shooter, the one we wanted," Dozier said to a television reporter. "Mr. Allen won't even be eligible for parole for forty-five years."

"I feel OK about Mr. Parker," Price told a newspaper reporter.

"The William Allen fight isn't over," Camp declared to a television reporter. "It's a long way from that. Emotion could have clearly been the decisive factor in this case. It's impossible to understand why my client reacted the way he did or why the police officers reacted the way they did unless you understand the entire picture, all of the issues in this case. It's not over, certainly not for us."

"Tonight, Steve Parker had the weight of twenty-one years removed from his shoulders," Smith said to a television reporter. "This is certainly liberating for him and confirms that he always told the truth about his involvement in this incident. But his happiness is tempered by the verdict the jury gave Mr. Allen. He's happy in one way, obviously, but quite somber and concerned about Mr. Allen.

"The not-guilty verdict allows Steve to clear one hurdle along the way toward complete exoneration. It'll be a building block process as we attempt to secure the freedom he deserves. We'll take administrative steps, meaning we'll probably attempt to secure executive clemency for him."

As this was taking place in the large hallway just outside the courtroom, Judge Kurtz was meeting with jurors in the deliberation room. He explained the strange elements the trial had featured, such as references to the "previous court proceeding," and he told jurors about the prison escape and more than a decade on the run.

The judge was also answering numerous questions.

"Why weren't these cases tried together?"

"I've asked that question myself," Judge Kurtz answered. "I can't tell you why."

"Did anybody interview Officer Thomasson after the shooting incident to find out exactly what happened?"

"I don't know about that," Judge Kurtz answered. "It would've been hearsay evidence if they had."

"Why was the trial for Officer Thomasson's death held before the trial for Officer Johnson's death?"

"I can't tell you," Kurtz replied. "That's something else I've wondered."

"What happened to Ralph Canady?"

"I'm told he committed suicide the night he was captured in Baltimore," the judge answered.

"Where is Charles Lee Herron?"

"His case has been resolved. He served his sentence and was paroled."

"Why weren't these men tried between 1968 and 1974, when they escaped?"

"There was some question about the paperwork filed by lawyers," the judge answered. "That's part of it."

"What will happen to Mr. Parker?"

"I hope his lawyer raises serious questions about the validity of the trial in 1968," Judge Kurtz answered.

But that would take place later, perhaps 2012 if his first chance at a parole hearing was upheld.

Judge Kurtz, a forty-five-year-old upstate New York native and graduate from The Citadel who had earned four bronze stars during the Vietnam War before arriving in Nashville in 1969 to attend Vanderbilt Law School, was wrestling with a few reflections from the trial in his chambers.

There was no reason for him to question whether the trial had been fair, at least from the standpoint of the testimony offered. He had conducted it masterfully, even if a few questions he asked witnesses for the "sake of clarity" and his "curiosity" were damaging to the defense.

Judge Kurtz later said he wondered why the defense had not asked Bill Allen about his state of mind as it related to the Metropolitan Nashville Police Department in the days and months before the shooting, knowing that he had granted that opportunity in the same ruling in which he said he would not let the police department be put on trial.

Part of that ruling read:

> In a case involving an issue of self-defense, the defendant's state of mind is always relevant. . . . A case well illustrative of this principle is State v. Miller, 194 S.E. 2d 353 (N.C. 1973). In that case the defendant was convicted of murdering a police officer during a gambling raid. The court ordering the award of a new trial stated: "The Court of Appeals held, and properly so, that the defendant should have been permitted to testify with reference to what others had told him concerning recent raids of gambling games in the Charlotte area." . . . A defendant may testify as to his subjective fear of the deceased based upon the deceased being a member of an organization which the defendant perceived as dangerous. . . . As to the testimony of third parties as to the reputation of the Nashville Police Department in 1968, the court rules that this in inadmissible. No cases from any jurisdiction have been cited. This would turn this murder trial into a trial of the Nashville Police Department with witnesses from both sides testifying as to what the reputation of the police department was at the time. . . . This really is not relevant to the state of mind of the defendant at the time of the killing.

Although he had been briefed about the case by a friend, Chancellor Robert Brandt, an assistant district attorney in the first trial and an outspoken man afterwards, Judge Kurtz had been surprised by much of the testimony he had heard. Obviously, as his sentencing ruling in the case of Bill Allen indicates, he did not give much credence to the self-defense story, as parts of a memorandum he wrote on April 10 indicate:

> The jury in this case found the defendant William G. Allen guilty of first degree murder and imposed a seventy-eight (78) year sentence. This defendant has been found guilty of first degree murder and sentenced to ninety-nine (99) years in 1968. . . .
> Upon the return of the jury verdict on April 7, 1989, this court ordered that the seventy-eight (78) year sentence run con-

secutively to the previously imposed ninety-nine (99) year sentence. The reasons for this ruling are as follows:

1. The defendant killed two (2) metropolitan police officers. The facts clearly show that he had little or no regard for human life and no hesitation about committing a crime where a threat to human life is high. . . .

2. Deterrence is especially applicable in this case. It would appear that when police officers are killed in the line of duty, a defendant should be aware that he or she faces severe consequences if found guilty. Police officers serve the public in a dangerous capacity and receive inadequate pay or recognition. Anyone who assaults a police officer must be made aware that he or she faces the strictest application of the law. This is not to say that a police officer's life is worth more than any other citizen, but it does recognize that when a police officer is on duty and carrying out his or her function in a lawful manner, that that police officer is entitled to the highest protection of the law. Potential defendants who realize this will hopefully be discouraged from assaulting police officers.

In other words, the judge wanted to make an example out of Bill Allen, even as he sentenced him and sat alone for a few moments in his chambers to think about the "complex and tiring" trial he had directed.

It was interesting that the defendants and few other people were left in the courthouse as Judge Kurtz tossed those thoughts through his head.

Parker appeared from a back room at about 9:15 P.M., dressed in prison attire with handcuffs in place. A man who had been found not guilty was being escorted back to prison.

"It's one step down," Parker said without a smile. "But right now, I'm more worried about Bill."

Bill Allen appeared a minute later, dressed in prison attire with handcuffs in place. He paused for a moment, then shook his head. A slight mist appeared in his eyes.

"At least I told the truth," Bill Allen said as he walked from the courthouse.

EPILOGUE

While completing the research for this book, I paused at least a dozen times outside the Criminal Justice Center in Nashville, Tennessee, to look at the names on a monument located there. It was built in honor of police officers who have given their lives for the city they served.

There are thirty names on that monument, with the first to die coming in 1903 and the most recent in 1982. For me, none of them are more significant than Charles Wayne Thomasson and Thomas ("Pete") Johnson.

Their deaths were senseless, as were all of the others. The same holds true for every law enforcement officer killed while doing his or her duty. In the United States the number was incredible in 1988—one killed every fifty-seven hours. That figure points out how base our society can be toward the men and women who serve it and protect its citizens from danger and crime.

Every citizen should contemplate that fact. I know I consider it every time I see a uniformed police officer. For the rest of my life every time I see a police officer, I imagine I will think of Wayne Thomasson and Pete Johnson and their families they left when they died in 1968. I will always be remorseful when considering the circumstances under which they gave their lives.

They were not bad men.

They were victims of a society caught in the throes of long-needed change. All of us have had to confront the cancer called racism, and their names should be honored among those who died during that struggle.

I do not consider them racists.

I consider them victims.

292

But there are other senseless casualties emanating from that shooting and the emotionally motivated justice, or lack thereof, that grew out of it.

Let us not forget that Ralph Canady is dead. He, too, left children behind.

Let us not forget that Bill Allen and Steve Parker are in prison. They are separated from women who love them and children who need them in their lives.

Let us not forget Charles Lee Herron and John Alexander, who got a better deal than the other men involved in the shooting, but who had their lives disrupted for far too long.

It would be difficult to count all the people whose lives were hurt by this distasteful case, relatives and friends included. I think it is safe to assume there are a multitude more like them in this nation who are victims of the fallout left by the civil rights movement. As the wounds left by a war never heal completely, so it is with scars left by social change.

Mistakes should be forgiven, but not forgotten. That is the only way we can learn from them.

Still, we must be realistic.

Thomasson and Johnson were victimized. Not by Allen, but rather by the tensions that existed in North Nashville in the late 1960s. Coincidentally, other police officers added to the friction.

Only two months before the shooting, John Sorace of the Metropolitan Nashville Police Department made strong statements in the U.S. Congress about blacks who were campaigning for their civil rights. He was relating them to international Communism. This was a popular notion among far too many white people in the Deep South during the 1960s, and it would be foolish to believe his remarks were not heard and discussed by his fellow police officers and by blacks in North Nashville. Those words had to have increased suspicion among whites and blacks. Likewise, it would be ridiculous to think the action of the Tennessee House of Representatives in passing a resolution at about the same time requesting that Student Non-Violent Coordinating Committee spokesman Stokely Carmichael, an American citizen, be deported was not a subject of conversation.

No doubt, former Davidson County district attorney Tom Shriver knew about these attitudes in 1968, when he pushed hard to send Allen, Parker, and Canady to the electric chair.

I am confident Judge Walter Kurtz, who is not a native of Nashville, did not know the magnitude of these tensions when he refused to allow testimony about them during the trial in 1989.

Let us take the case of Parker as an example of how things have changed. In 1968, he was convicted of first-degree murder. In 1989, he told the same story about his involvement and was found not guilty.

"This is the end of an era for the Nashville police department," said Bubba Owen, a special investigator for the Davidson County district attorney. "You see, things have changed. Things are done differently now than they were in 1968."

But Allen's plight serves as an example of how through the years connived cases can become so tangled by lies compounded by even more lies that there is no way to unravel them, other than through the use of simple logic. Allen wrote a letter one week after the shooting in which he said he was the only person who shot the police officers; but, as juror Anna Howell said after hearing the case in 1989, he made a crucial mistake when he failed to explain why. She is correct.

With little to gain from it, Allen said the same thing on the witness stand more than two decades later. This time he did choose to tell why. Furthermore, the account he gave in court was the same he had recited to me more than a year and a half earlier, almost to the word, and it is extremely difficult for a dishonest person to do that. Although others have continued to tell lies, even changing their recollections during follow-up interviews, Allen's dialogue remained constant.

In 1968 the truth was sprinkled with lies, and the defendants were sentenced to ninety-nine years. In 1989 the truth was accented by why the shooting took place, and the defendant received seventy-eight years.

One hundred seventy-seven years. Almost a guarantee that Allen will die in prison. So what did he say four days after the second conviction? "The pendulum has swung as far as it can against me now. Things can only get better from this point on.

"I admit I was down and out for about twenty-four hours after the verdict. But one morning I started thinking about something my grandfather told me when I was about eight years old. It was raining, thundering, and lightning, and I was scared as I stood on the back porch. He put a hand on one of my shoulders and said, 'Bill, this storm is a lot like life—scary at times—but I promise you things will get better. When the rain stops, the clouds will leave, and the sun will shine again.' That renewed me."

The next day the *Nashville Banner* carried an editorial applauding the conviction of Allen. It said justice had been served. It also said Thomasson had been shot seven times, an all-time high for the number of bullets that had struck him.

Maybe a tale about old hope gone afoul would have helped Allen as he digested the contents of the editorial, but I chose not to tell him about a conversation I had the morning after the second trial with juror Anita Buford, age twenty-nine. She had been only eight years old in 1968.

After listening to her account of what jurors were saying and doing during the hours of testimony and the deliberations that followed, I explained some of the things I had discovered while researching this book.

"What if I told you that I read a document prepared by Tom Cathey that said Officer Thomasson had shot his revolver four times that night, that the man who had written it claimed that everybody in the police department knew?" I asked.

"Oh, my gosh!" Buford exclaimed. "If we jurors had known that, we would still be in there."